W9-CNB-664

# What is Political Theory?

What Is Political Theory?

# What is Political Theory?

Edited by
STEPHEN K. WHITE and J. DONALD MOON

SAGE Publications Ⓢ London · Thousand Oaks · New Delhi

Introduction © Stephen K. White 2004
Chapter 1 © J. Donald Moon 2004
Chapter 6 © Roland Bleiker 2004
Chapter 7 © Roxanne L. Euben 2004
Chapters 2, 3, 4, 5, 8 and 9 reprinted from Political Theory vol. 30 no. 4
© SAGE Publications Inc. 2002

This edition first published 2004

Apart from any fair dealing for the purposes of research or private study, or criticism or
review, as permitted under the Copyright, Designs and Patents Act, 1988, this publication
may be reproduced, stored or transmitted in any form, or by any means, only with the prior
permission in writing of the publishers, or in the case of reprographic reproduction, in
accordance with the terms of licences issued by the Copyright Licensing Agency. Inquiries
concerning reproduction outside those terms should be sent to the publishers.

 SAGE Publications Ltd
1 Oliver's Yard
55 City Road
London EC1Y 1SP

SAGE Publications Inc.
2455 Teller Road
Thousand Oaks, California 91320

SAGE Publications India Pvt Ltd
B-42, Panchsheel Enclave
Post Box 4109
New Delhi 100 017

**British Library Cataloguing in Publication data**

A catalogue record for this book is available from the British Library

ISBN 0 7619 4260 2
ISBN 0 7619 4261 0 (pbk)

**Library of Congress Control Number available**

Typeset by Kelli E. Palma
Printed in Great Britain by Athenaeum Press, Gateshead

# CONTENTS

# LIST OF CONTRIBUTORS

**Roland Bleiker** is reader in Peace and Conflict Studies at the University of Queensland, Australia.

**Wendy Brown** teaches political theory at the University of California, Berkeley.

**Adriana Cavarero** teaches political philosophy at the University of Verona, Italy.

**Roxanne L. Euben** is associate professor of Political Science at Wellesley College, Massachusetts.

**Ruth W. Grant** teaches political theory in the Department of Political Science at Duke University.

**George Kateb** teaches political theory at Princeton University.

**J. Donald Moon** teaches political theory at Wesleyan University.

**Ian Shapiro** is William R. Kenan, Jr. Professor and Chair in the Department of Political Science at Yale University.

**James Tully** holds the Jackman Chair in Philosophical Studies at the University of Toronto, Canada.

**Stephen K. White** teaches political theory at the University of Virginia and is editor of the journal *Political Theory*.

# PREFACE

This volume began its development as a special issue of the journal, *Political Theory: An International Journal of Political Philosophy*, in 2002. That year marked the thirtieth anniversary of the founding of the journal, as well as the fortieth anniversary of Isaiah Berlin's famous essay, "Does Political Theory Still Exist?"[1] It seemed an appropriate time to take stock of how scholars today assess the traditional enterprise of political theory: its character and its prospects in the new century. The present volume expands the range of such considerations by including a new section on "Political Thought in a Global Perspective," containing two additional essays taking up the question of how the tradition of Western political thought should understand itself and its tasks in light of non-Western perspectives and globalization processes. Further, there is a new essay that specifically considers the legacy of John Rawls's work.

The editors would like to thank Bonnie Honig for her perceptive insights at the planning stages of the volume. We are grateful as well to Lucy Robinson of Sage Publications for helping this project evolve into a book.

*NOTE*

1. Isaiah Berlin, "Does Political Theory Still Exist?," *Concepts and Categories: Philosophical Essays*. Edited by Henry Hardy, with an introduction by Bernard Williams (Princeton: Princeton University Press, 1999). The essay first appeared in English in Peter Laslett and W.G. Runciman, eds., *Philosophy, Politics and Society*. Second Series (Oxford: Blackwell, 1962). An earlier version of the essay appeared in French in 1961.

# PLURALISM, PLATITUDES, AND PARADOXES
## Western Political Thought at the Beginning of a New Century

*STEPHEN K. WHITE*

*I.*

The early 1970s saw a broad revival of political theory in the English-speaking world. One indicator of this phenomenon is that *Political Theory* and *Philosophy and Public Affairs* were both founded then.[1] Before this period, there was no journal in English that focused specifically on political theory or political philosophy. The term "revival" is especially appropriate, because the field had been famously pronounced "dead" by Peter Laslett in the 1950s. With that declaration, he wanted to call attention to the apparent breakdown of a Western tradition of reflection on "political and social relationships at the widest possible level of generality" that applied "the methods and conclusions of contemporary thought to the evidence of the contemporary social and political situation."[2] Laslett speculated briefly upon the causes of this demise. Our "situation" in the 1950s was one of trying to comprehend fully the horrors of Nazism, while pondering with growing terror a future of potential global nuclear destruction. In such a world, Laslett suggested, the previously perennial motivation to construct neat images of political order had perhaps just lost its footing. Further, the conjuncture of "contemporary thought" provided little support for the normal pretensions of political theory. Marxism, in its orthodox forms, declared political theory to be nothing more than class ideology. Similarly, logical positivism and the emerging empirical social sciences, operating in tandem, promised a future in which parts of the traditional real estate of political theory were declared to be, alternatively, either so bog-like as to be incapable of supporting any solid intellectual constructions or so inappropriately managed as to require wholesale expropriation by the new, more systematic sciences of society.

Although Laslett was ostensibly filling out a death certificate, one cannot read his essay today without suspecting that, as in the case of Marc Anthony's speech, incitement was what was really on his mind.[3] Isaiah Berlin's classic essay of 1962, "Does Political Theory Still Exist?", is best comprehended as a response to this incitement. While the essay is cast in the form of a question as to whether political theory still has life, Berlin actually had no doubt whatsoever that the answer was positive. In fact, he even suggested that political theory, in its most robust form, "can be pursued consistently only in a pluralist, or potentially pluralist, society." "Pluralist" here refers to societies in which "ends collide," and there is some embodiment of this insight in moral and political practices.[4] Now Berlin knew that his proclamation involved more than a little hyperbole; but he clearly wanted to highlight how ironic it was to be talking about the death of political philosophy precisely at that moment in Western history when the soil for its flourishing was richer than ever.

Such funerary talk was encouraged, Berlin admitted, by the absence of any grand political theory in the twentieth century. As of the 1960s, one could not point to a work of political reflection comparable to that of Hobbes, Locke, or Rousseau in earlier centuries. Such "commanding" works had the power to convert "paradoxes into platitudes or vice versa."[5] Locke, for example, might be seen as taking the seemingly irreconcilable seventeenth century values of absolute sovereignty, on the one hand, and individual freedom and popular consent, on the other, and transfiguring them into the platitudes of liberal, constitutional government. Interestingly, Berlin did not waste much time trying to explain why such works of grand theory had not appeared in the twentieth century; he merely noted that their absence was in no way conclusive evidence for the death of political philosophy. Berlin's inattention to this topic was certainly wise, given the fact that less than a decade later John Rawls's *A Theory of Justice* (1971) appeared, a work that, for many scholars, certainly deserves to stand in the tradition of grand theory.[6] Using Berlin's categories, one might describe it as an attempt to take the tensions and paradoxes revolving around liberalism and the twentieth century welfare state and transfigure them into a set of platitudes about justice in contemporary societies.

Even if one accepts this elevation of Rawls into the pantheon of greats, it must be admitted that the platitudes promised in 1971—substantive, universally applicable, liberal principles of justice—had a comparatively transient quality. As is well known, Rawls himself later became skeptical of his own framework, admitting that it did not recognize deeply enough the "pluralism of comprehensive religious, philosophical, and moral doctrines."[7] He shifted his stance as a result, trying to re-craft universal principles grounded only upon what could be the object of an agreement between "incompatible yet reasonable comprehensive doctrines."[8] For present purposes, I am less concerned with the specifics of this effort and more with the general drift it displays, both in Rawls's work and within the tradition of Western political thought as a whole.

As we approached and crossed the millennium mark, the realization increasingly deepened that we indeed live in a world in which "ends collide"— both across "comprehensive conceptions" and within them—and we see no clear evidence that there will be an end to this any time soon. The implication of this realization is, of course, not that all ends collide all the time, but rather that we no longer have the comfort of any secure, grand narratives that guarantee reconciliation. Certainly, there are events in the twentieth century—the defeat of Nazism and fascism, and the collapse of the Soviet Union—that seem to give us comforting distance from some of the worst horrors of the past century. But the edifying platitudes that have sometimes appeared in the immediate aftermath of seemingly decisive and irreversible steps forward tend to have an ephemeral character. When Berlin, at the end of his essay, spoke of "new and unpredictable developments" in political theory, perhaps part of what he was intimating was that our future would be one of an ever deeper confrontation with pluralism; and that political theory in such a world would produce paradoxes out of platitudes far more than the reverse.[9] From the 1960s to the present, it is the production of paradoxes that stands out as Western moral and political thought have confronted the challenges of feminism, multiculturalism, environmentalism, critical race theory, and novel claims on the part of both nationalism and cosmopolitanism.

Rawls, like many others, is trying to come to terms with what he calls the "fact" of pluralism.[10] It is immensely important, however, to be sensitive as to what exactly is implied in the reference to such a "fact." Rawls wants to emphasize that pluralism is a brute historical reality that we cannot deny except at the cost of dangerous self-deception.[11] He is, of course, correct. And yet there are facts and there are facts. It is an important fact that Bill Clinton received more votes than Bob Dole in the 1996 U.S. presidential election. It is also an important fact that each of us is mortal. If the reality of pluralism is understood more as the former sort of fact, it will drift toward the status of a platitude. If it is understood more as the latter sort, it may become instead a continual source of ferment in our lives, since engagement with this "fact" involves richer, more complex experiences that entangle us in ways that are both cognitive and affective, ways that have constitutive effects upon our identities. Although liberals, including Rawls, have historically been defenders of many moral-political values closely associated with pluralism, like freedom and toleration, critics in recent years have asserted that their engagement with pluralism has sometimes had a too comfortable, platitudinous quality about it.[12] Liberals, unsurprisingly, have denied this charge. Regardless of who is right here, the overall point seems to be that we are constrained to an ever more extensive engagement with pluralism. And we must become, accordingly, increasingly involved with exploring the ethos and strategies that should animate and guide this adventure. One might describe what is at stake here as a commitment not to let the fact of pluralism become a platitude.

In addition to this challenge, there are two others that seem likely to be especially pressing for political theorists in the years ahead. Both emerge with the unwieldy phenomenon of what has come to be called globalization. First, there is the turbo-charged, worldwide penetration of capitalism. The growing antiglobalization protests of recent years highlight the need for political theorists to do a better job of conceptualizing the force and effects of capital on cultural and political life. No doubt Foucault's analysis of "disciplinary" power will continue to be useful in this undertaking, as will the emerging insights of what has come to be called "cultural studies."[13] But my guess is that there is a lot of room for "new and unpredictable" reconceptualization across this terrain.

A similar sense of urgency and uncertainty accompany another challenge. The difficulties for democracy that are created by the scale and power of globalized capital are paralleled by the anomalies that emerge with the increasing flow of ideas and peoples across national borders. Obviously, these flows constitute part of the general challenge of pluralism for the ideals of liberal democracy. But they also constitute an overlapping challenge to the nation-state as the traditional unit within which these ideals have had their home. In short, political theory faces the daunting task of radically rethinking the spaces of democratic life. Here again we are awash in perplexing questions. One of the most prominent is: Will a multitude of new, mobile, decentralized, transnational, democratic spaces become available at the very same time as the growing power of globalized capital and heavily bureaucratized, international political organizations deprive them of much of their potential significance?

As one speculates today about such possible future directions of political reflection, there is perhaps at least one currently extant platitude: there is at present no dearth of political theory, at least in the English-speaking world. Complaints now center not on its demise, but rather upon such things as where exactly our energies are best expended (see, for example, Chapter 9 by Ian Shapiro); or whether we have become too domesticated and professionalized—and thus too unpolitical (as Wendy Brown and Don Moon suggest); or whether there is something generally wrong with theory today (as Adriana Cavarero urges).[14]

*II.*

The following essays are grouped into three sections. Those in the first, "Traditional Resources, Novel Challenges," consider which—if any—of the traditional resources and canonical authors of Western political thought aid us in negotiating our way through the challenges of contemporary political life. Of course, as one confronts this question, it quickly spawns another: Who and what should be *added* to the cache of perennially valued resources in order to better confront novel problems? If, as Hegel said, the owl of Minerva flies only at dusk, then perhaps we are at an appropriate point from which to look back upon the past century with this second question in mind. The contributors to the first section recommend that we answer it with the names of John Rawls, Hannah Arendt, Martin Heidegger, and Michel Foucault. Others who might have been named (and were, by Quentin Skinner) include Hans-Georg Gadamer, Jacques Derrida, and Jürgen Habermas.[15]

J. Donald Moon's Chapter 1, "The Current State of Political Theory: Pluralism and Reconciliation," argues that Rawls's work offers an improvement upon Berlin's in regard to understanding the problem of pluralism, and how it relates to political theory's practical task of productively engaging political conflict. For Berlin, pluralism is the notion that basic values are incommensurable; for Rawls, pluralism means only that there is "reasonable disagreement" about values. The point Moon wants to draw attention to is that, if we know there is literal incommensurability between two contending positions, political theory cannot have much to offer the parties; however, if the problem is "reasonable disagreement," there is at least some possible space for further theoretical reflection and criticism, with the aim of possibly diminishing the scope of disagreement. Moon wants to affirm this space for theory to address our conflicts in a possibly productive way by appealing continually to what is "reasonable." Recent critics of Rawls have, of course, attacked this constructive image of theory for being too unconcerned with the exclusions that remain embodied in any such project. Moon admits that Rawls sometimes fails to acknowledge sufficiently the inevitable dangers associated with his ideal of bringing reconciliation to a world of conflict and suggests a further dampening of that traditional expectation of Western philosophy. Political theory in the future will have to find ways of articulating the affirmative moment in Rawls's vision, while at the same time keeping vivid the "tragic" character of all such affirmations (p. 25).

George Kateb's "The Adequacy of the Western Canon," asks whether the familiar texts of political theory before the twentieth century contain sufficient resources for us to grapple adequately with the horrors of the last one hundred years. Although he would agree that the canon continues to throw light on many problems today, it fails to offer enough guidance when it comes to such prominent phenomena of the past century as

> World War I, World War II, the use twice of atomic weapons, their repeated threatened use by the United States, the theories of nuclear deterrence, the gulags, the Holocaust, induced famines, such American wars as the Korean War and the Vietnam War, and numerous massive massacres. (p. 31)

The scale of such humanly inflicted suffering is unprecedented, and we need to better grasp the mentalities that inspired and sustained it. Now the canon certainly throws light upon moral psychology; but, for Kateb, we need to look to more recent philosophers to better understand the workings of the imagination in both its "hyperactive" and "inactive" perversions. The former characterizes those who initiate political horrors; the latter, those who acquiesce in their implementation. Kateb urges us to look to Heidegger, and even more to Arendt, as the preeminent "theorists of the imagination . . . in its political relevance." (p. 36)

Adriana Cavarero also draws inspiration from Arendt in her contribution, "Politicizing Theory." But this inspiration tends in a more radical direction. If Kateb looks to Arendt for augmentation of the cannon, then Cavarero looks to her as a resource for a deep skepticism about the tradition. The traditional meaning of theory, etymologically tied to "seeing" (*theoria*), has modeled the activity of the theorist on the solitary act of grasping an object within a field of vision. Within such an image, politics becomes "subsumed by the central problem of *order* . . . a harmonic order . . . that corresponds to justice." But the "*proprium* of politics," Cavarero asserts, is just "the unpredictability of plural interaction." This means, in effect, that at the core of the enterprise of theory since Plato there has been "a mortification of the genuine sense of politics" (pp. 55, 59-60).

Cavarero thus confronts us with something of a paradox. The late twentieth century's quickening of theory becomes in reality the revival of a deadening gesture. An authentic renewal of political reflection, on the contrary, would have to proceed in such a way as not to let the "visual features of *theoria* . . . perform the meaning of politics" (p. 67). Cavarero looks to Arendt's "ontology of plural uniqueness" as the best orientation for resisting this temptation. She contends, moreover, that such an orientation can inform a conception of political life that is adequate to the contemporary challenge of globalization. In short, it can help vivify a sense of political action that is centered around neither territorial states nor cultural identities, but rather around "*locality without territory*" and "the unrepeatable uniqueness of every human being." (pp. 73, 74)

Although James Tully does not follow Cavarero fully in her radical skepticism about the canon, he nevertheless also aims to decenter certain preoccupations of traditional reflection on politics. For Tully, the preeminent question today is: "How do we attend to the strange multiplicity of political voices and activities without distorting or disqualifying them in the very way we approach them?" (p. 89) Theory that puts this question at the center of its concerns will have to distance itself to some degree from reflection oriented primarily around clarifying the character of our existing political practices and elaborating normative guidelines with universal reach. Perhaps the most prominent contemporary representatives of the latter, Kant-inspired tradition of theory are Habermas and Rawls. The alternative to this tradition is not a complete rejection of Enlightenment ideas or the tradition of Western political thought in general, but rather an emphasis on different strands of the Enlightenment legacy and the careful cultivation of a "subaltern" tradition. Here the focus is more on "practices of freedom" than on "settled forms of justice"; more on a permanent critical attitude or "ethos" oriented toward uncovering particular modes of oppression than upon the articulation of rules of right governance (pp. 97-98). Intellectual sustenance for this ethos comes more from figures like Mary Wollstonecraft and Foucault than from Kant and Rawls.

If Tully thus wants the initial moment of systematic political reflection to be animated by what has been called a "hermeneutics of suspicion" of power, that moment does not exhaust the energies of theory. It must patiently and affirmatively contribute, as well, to the particular struggles and experiments of citizens attempting to negotiate their always "imperfect practices" (p. 98). This doubling back of reflection from a 'deconstructive' to a 'constructive' or affirmative moment also forms a central feature of Wendy Brown's vision of political theory.

Brown looks to renew the idea of political theory in a way that both creatively engages late modern challenges to its traditional identity and yet does not surrender its constitutive orientation to "the problem of how we do and ought to order collective life" (p. 117). The security of the identity of theory's object—"the political"—is endangered today by diluting, disseminating, and hybridizing forces (economic, cultural, natural, the bodily, the domestic, the sexual, the social, the civic, the local, and so on) through which power operates in myriad ways. Brown urges us to turn more attentively to these forces, and that means schooling ourselves carefully in those bodies of thought that have become more actively entangled with them, such as anthropology, cultural studies, political economy, geography, media studies. But at the same time that we open our disciplinary identity to such hybridization, we should also remember that the "theoretical politicization of any activity or relation is not the same as theorizing the political" (p. 117). This means that political theory today must continually "tack" between these two poles,

> retaining the emphasis on collectivity while expanding our sense of the reach and opera-
> tions of power that collectivities harbor and through which collective life can be stud-
> ied—the complex subjects and subjectivities, the rich range of discursive practices com-
> prising them. (p. 116)

The foregoing chapters already begin to take up several challenges associ-ated with non-Western perspectives and with the processes of globalization. The second section, "Political Thought in a Global Perspective," turns more directly to this terrain of questions. Scholars of international relations have traditionally seen global phenomena as their turf; and political theorists have, respectively, taken their task to be engaging the problem of political legiti-macy within the settled boundaries of sovereign states. But processes of globalization, with their tendency to blur such boundaries, upset this tradi-tional division of labor. In this new situation, political theorists may have something to offer. This potential contribution, Roland Bleiker argues in his essay, is best grasped as one that begins to craft a better political imaginary within which to engage the myriad phenomena that travel under the rubric of globalization. The deepest challenges involve, first, learning to live with the cultural, ethnic, religious differences that today confront us more directly and persistently, as the flows of people, products and ideas move ever more rapidly through boundaries that before offered protected spaces of identity; and second, articulating re-figured ethical-political foundations that can pro-vide a basis for negotiating the uncertainties of globalization in a fashion that resists the dangerous seduction of

> religious fundamentalism, liberal triumphalism or the good-versus-evil rhetoric that
> characterized the US response to the terrorist attacks of September 2001." (p. 125)

As I noted a moment ago, Cavarero's essay discusses the classical associa-tion of *theoria* with seeing. Roxanne Euben's contribution further probes the etymology and history of that Greek word and highlights the fact that the "seeing" of theory was in fact originally associated with traveling, with doing what we would call today comparative political and cultural analysis. Accordingly, we should understand that the obligation to explore non-West-ern insights is not a novel burden imposed by our changed circumstances in the twenty-first century, but rather something that was, and should remain, intrinsically a part of the very nature of healthy political reflection. This truth has sometimes been overshadowed in modern Western political thinking, as Euben's example of James Mill shows. He proudly announced in *The History of British India* in 1817, that too much first-hand knowledge of India might cloud his ability to recommend policy for that British colony in a fashion that was appropriately detached and impartial.

When confronted with such shortcomings in Western thought, we have sometimes tended to comfort ourselves with the platitude that at least we do far better in such matters than non-Western intellectual traditions. Today, Euben says, this assumption is especially prevalent in regard to the Muslim world. Her essay aims to upset this complacency. If we are willing to "travel" a bit beyond current stereotypes, she contends, we find that within Islamic thought there is a developed tradition of *talab al-'ilm*— travel in search of knowledge. For Euben, "travel" occasions those inescapable practices of translation between the familiar and unfamiliar that are part of the realm of ordinary experience, and are not confined to any one culture or historical epoch. Taking travel as a practice of translation thus pluralizes the locations, genres and cultures in which theorizing may be said to occur.

As my earlier discussion of Laslett and Berlin illustrated, a persistent challenge to the activity of political theory since the end of World War II has come from social science in general, and political science in particular. This challenge has taken many forms as the social sciences themselves have undergone a series of transformations of self-understanding under the successive impacts of the Kuhnian revolution, hermeneutics, pragmatism, poststructuralism, and so on. Despite these transformations, some scholars in social science departments still harbor disciplinary ideals that, at best, denigrate political philosophy or, at worst, leave no room whatsoever for it. This means that a perennial task for political theorists is to delineate the differences between theory and science, as well as show why the systematic study of politics requires both types of insight. In Section III, "Political Theory and Political Science," Ruth Grant and Ian Shapiro turn their attention to this task.

Grant's chapter, "Political Theory, Political Science, and Politics," contends that while it is the business of the sciences to investigate cause and effect, it is the business of political theory to be concerned with the "understanding of meaning and judgment of significance" (p. 178-179). These activities are characterized—intrinsically—by "uncertainty, disagreement, and lack of closure" (p. 178). There is always something discomforting about these qualities, particularly when arrayed against the claims of science to produce clear and reliable knowledge. And this is especially true in the United States today, when universities are under increasing pressure to rationalize their existence in terms of quantifiable production measured according to the standards of science and business: the accumulation of knowledge that has immediately useful applications. In such a world, political philosophers must illuminate the fact that there is such a thing as better or more poorly educated judgment, the former being guided by interpretive understandings of political life that are "simultaneously conservative, critical, and constructive" (p. 182).

Although the humanistic and the scientific can be thus differentiated, Grant reminds us as well that, at least in regard to politics, this division is marked by a "permeable line": meaning and judgment that ignore causal relations are impoverished; similarly, causal relations cannot be adequately comprehended without some consideration of meaning and significance (p. 186). The task of political theory today is to reaffirm its historical and philosophical dimensions, and yet do this in a way that attends closely to the changing portraits of politics that scientific research produces.

At the same time, political science must recognize the importance of the political questions that cannot be resolved through the methods of scientific research alone and of the distinctive contribution of interpretive theory to our understanding of them.

Ian Shapiro's chapter steps precisely into this issue of the necessary but uneasy relation between political theory and political science. One of the most important roles for theorists today, he urges, is to function "as roving ombudsmen for the truth and right by stepping back from political science as practiced, to see what is wrong with what is currently being done and say something about how it might be improved." The difficulty that Shapiro detects today in the scientific study of politics is that it is too often "method driven" or "theory driven" rather than "problem driven" (pp. 194-195). What he means by this is that proponents of a particular research program, such as rational choice, have a tendency to let the presuppositions basic to that program play a tendentious role in the selection and characterization of the problems they investigate; in effect, the way the problem gets characterized is biased toward the vindication of the research program itself.

In response to critics who retort that all empirical research is necessarily theory driven (as Kuhn and the later Wittgenstein showed), Shapiro claims that there is a difference between research that is "theory laden" and "theory driven" (p. 198). The former recognizes that there is no raw data about political reality that can be described in a theory-neutral fashion; the latter uses this hermeneutical fact to cloak its drive to justify a "pet approach" (p. 200). The work of the political theorist lies in carefully exposing this error. The critical leverage here comes from Shapiro's broadly pragmatist philosophical approach. His essay works through a variety of examples of theory-driven research, in each case articulating redescriptions of the same chunk of political reality and arguing that the redescription is more adequate. "Adequacy" here is cashed out in two senses. Theory-driven research is sometimes inadequate because its characterization of a problem neglects from the start the prior efforts at characterization by a wider public of scholars and journalists. In *social* science, one is simply unlikely to enhance the empirical validity of one's claims by ignoring this pluralized public of investigators. Theory-driven research may also be judged faulty when it inconspicuously lends support to hegemonic normative perspectives implicit in its problem definitions. Political theorists here must speak in the name of a potential, broader democratic public in "scrutinizing" or unmasking such accounts and "proposing alternatives." (p. 213)

## NOTES

*I would like to thank Joshua Dienstag, George Kateb, and Don Moon for their thoughtful comments on earlier drafts of this essay.*

1. The first issue of *Philosophy and Public Affairs* appeared in 1972.
2. Peter Laslett, "Introduction," in *Philosophy, Politics and Society*, 1st series, ed. Peter Laslett (Oxford, UK: Blackwell, 1956), p. vii.
3. Shakespeare, *Julius Caesar*, Act II.
4. Isaiah Berlin, "Does Political Theory Still Exist?" in *Concepts and Categories: Philosophical Essays*, ed. Henry Hardy (Princeton, NJ: Princeton University Press, 1999), 149-50.
5. Ibid., 143.
6. John Rawls, *A Theory of Justice* (Cambridge, MA: Harvard University Press, 1971).
7. John Rawls, *Political Liberalism* (New York: Columbia University Press, 1993), xvi. Although this book was published in 1993, key shifts in Rawls's ideas appeared in essays published in the 1980s; see pp. xiii-xiv.
8. Rawls, *Political Liberalism*, xvi-xvii.
9. Berlin, "Does Political Theory Still Exist?" 172.
10. Rawls, *Political Liberalism*, xvi-xvii.
11. Curiously, the growing awareness of pluralism may go hand in hand with an actual decrease in the amount of cultural pluralism in the world; cf. Pratap Mehta, "Cosmopolitanism and the Circle of Reason," *Political Theory* 28 (2000): 636.
12. See, for example, William Connolly, *The Ethos of Pluralization* (Minneapolis: University of Minnesota Press, 1995), idem, *Why I Am Not a Secularist* (Minneapolis: University of Minnesota Press, 1999).
13. Michel Foucault, *Discipline and Punish*, trans. A. Sheridan (New York: Vintage, 1977).
14. Perhaps the most famous, recent skeptic regarding political theory is Richard Rorty, *Contingency, Irony and Solidarity* (Cambridge, UK: Cambridge University Press, 1989).
15. Quentin Skinner, "Introduction," in *The Return of Grand Theory in the Human Sciences* ed. Quentin Skinner (Cambridge, UK: Cambridge University Press, 1985).

1        THE CURRENT STATE
         OF POLITICAL THEORY
         Pluralism and Reconciliation

*J. DONALD MOON*

**D**uring the past 30 years there has been a proliferation of work in political theory. On the surface, at least, the field has never been so vigorous, with a growing number of journals, professional associations, and panels at meetings of learned societies. Viewed from the perspective of the 1950s and 1960s, this flourishing could only be seen as unlikely. For example, in 1962 Berlin published his well known essay, "Does Political Theory Still Exist?".[1] It was in part a response to Laslett's "Introduction" to the first volume of a series, *Philosophy, Politics, and Society*, in which he had declared that, "For the moment, anyway, political philosophy is dead".[2] But 15 years later it had been reborn.

Here I will not survey the entire field of political theory. What I will do is to explore the prospects and roles of theory today, taking Berlin's discussion of pluralism as my point of departure. I will first argue that Berlin's account of pluralism has rather ambivalent implications for political theory. As he suggests, social pluralism may occasion theoretical reflection and criticism, but his account of value pluralism seems to deprive theory of at least part of its point, what Rawls calls its "practical" task of addressing political conflicts. I will then argue that Rawls offers a more adequate account of pluralism, and of the practical role or task of theory—its role in addressing the conflicts that arise in a pluralist society. Rawls also charges theory with the task of reconciling us to the political and social world, or at least the world as it could be in a realistic utopia. In doing so he places himself in a long line of theorizing going back at least to Plato. I will then consider the charge that, in holding onto the ideal of reconciliation, Rawls fails to acknowledge the limitations of any theorizing, which are suggested by the work of Foucault and some of those he has inspired. For them, the aim of reconciliation necessarily gives rise to forms of exclusion and violence because it blinds us to the ways in which the protean character of human life necessarily exceeds any categories. In that view, any form of society will necessarily carry with it its own patterns of exclusion and our task is to be sensitive to them. I will argue that this fear is real, but overstated, and that theory can help us appreciate the losses we necessarily face while at the same time giving us the possibility of reconciliation to a social world that realizes a realistic utopia, in which some of the divisive political conflicts can be narrowed or even overcome. I will close with some scattered comments about the ability of theory as it exists in the academy to realize the complex tasks of theorizing today.

## I. BERLIN ON PLURALISM

Like much of the discussion at the time, Berlin's paper focused on the centrality of normative issues to political philosophy, arguing that political philosophy's existence was assured because we—at least the "we" of the liberal democracies in the postwar period—face the need to choose the direction of our common life, and so are necessarily drawn to systematic and critical reflections on the values governing those choices. Berlin thus identified pluralism as a condition for the existence of political theory as an intellectual enterprise, but he used that term in two different senses.

In the first sense, a plural society, unlike a totalitarian society, or at least the idealized model of totalitarianism so popular at the time, is a society where political choice is open, and where the adherents of different ideals contest over the direction their society should take. When there is social pluralism, that is, when politically active and influential groups within the society hold conflicting ethical and political values and principles, normative disagreement can give rise to systematic reflection and criticism, and so to political (and I might add moral) philosophy.

Implicit in Berlin's account, somewhat ironically, is a vision of positive freedom. More specifically, it is a vision of politics as a sphere of human freedom, within which a collectivity can self-consciously shape or determine itself. In this respect, the "political," or the sphere of politics, may be distinguished from the "social." To a great extent, what happens in social life is, as Machiavelli suggested, a result of fortuna. It does not reflect what "we" *do*, but rather what happens to us. Or to put the point more precisely, social phenomena are often composed of what each of us does, but their aggregate shape and the outcomes we experience are not chosen, but reflect the causal

or quasi-causal laws operative in our society. They are the unintended consequences of intentional behavior. For example, a huge but certainly unplanned
rise in the birth rate after 1945 in the U.S. was succeeded by an equally
remarkable and equally unplanned drop two decades later, and are likely to
generate fiscal and social policy crises of an aging society in this century. Or,
to offer another example, the introduction of the automobile together with
rapid productivity growth led to the suburbanization of our cities and new
patterns of economic and racial segregation, and to deepening social conflict,
all of it again unintended and unplanned. By contrast with the social, then, the
political can be a sphere of freedom in which we seek to master the forces that
otherwise control us, directing our destiny.

Machiavelli tells us that, at best, maybe 50% of the time we can master
fortuna and shape our own destinies; perhaps he is optimistic, for political
life is often as opaque as the rest of social life, and is the sources of its own
share of unintended outcomes. Consider, for example, the outbreak of World
War I. None of the participants sought to start a general war, let alone a war of
such great scale and destructiveness. More generally, even if they are over-
statements, there is surely some truth in reductionist accounts of political life,
which view political movements and parties as reflections of social interests,
and political outcomes as themselves the concatenation of these same social
forces. To the extent that politics can be summed up, in Lasswell's memora-
ble phrase, as "who gets what, when, and how," it is at best an "intervening
variable."

Still, that view of politics cannot be the whole story. To the extent that
there is room for deliberation about our collective future, and conflict about
the values that can and should guide it, we—or some "we"—may be drawn to
political theory, to systematically reflecting on and criticizing those values.

Berlin also invoked the idea of pluralism in a second, and more distinctive
sense, proposing that value is inherently plural, which is to say that there are
many different things that are in some sense "good" or "desirable" or "worthy," and these goods are incommensurable in the sense that they cannot be
rationally ordered.[3] Not only are they not reducible to a single dimension of
value in the way, say, that utilitarianism seeks to measure everything in terms
of utility, but they cannot be ordered so that we can determine what should
have priority in any particular context.

That is not to say that we can never make such judgments; sometimes a situation or choice might be worse on every dimension of value than an alternative. But Berlin claims that over a vast range of human experience we face
incommensurable choices. Not only must we give up some good in order to
attain another, but we are denied the consolation to have chosen the greater or

the worthier good, or even that we have aimed for the appropriate balancing of the goods in question.

Berlin famously argues in much of his writing that the plurality of value has important political implications. Since there is no final solution, no way of determining the right ordering of all the important goods of human life, no attempt to realize a particular order for a society can be rationally justified, and so in the end can only be imposed by force. In the face of the real plurality of value, Berlin argues, we must opt for a liberal and at least ideally a democratic society that allows space for its members to make different choices, to pursue different ways of life expressive of different moral views, and so accommodates the incommensurability of value.

But there is at least a tension, perhaps even a contradiction, between these two notions of pluralism in terms of their implications for political theory. For if the existence of social pluralism as conflict about the values that should guide social policy provides the occasion for critical reflection and analysis of those values, the fact—if it is a fact—of the plurality of value means that political theory is limited in what it can offer in the face of such conflict. Perhaps we can help identify those cases where choices can be clearly ordered—when there's nothing to be said on one side, because no matter what the dimension, the other is superior. But obviously those situations are not the most problematic we face. To the extent that values are simply incommensurate, what is there to say? As Wittgenstein famously put it, of that which we cannot speak, of that we must remain silent. And political theory, whatever else it is, doesn't flourish in silence.

## II. RAWLS ON PLURALISM AND THE
## PRACTICAL TASK OF POLITICAL THEORY

In his paper Berlin noted the absence of large scale, systematic or what may be called canonical works of political philosophy in the twentieth century up to that time. Brian Barry has remarked that, in this period, the prevailing attitude towards political philosophy was something like that of the Church of England towards miracles: it was something that had happened in the past, but was not to be expected any more.[4]

It is often said that Rawls's work showed that miracles could still happen, or, in this case, systematic or canonical forms of political philosophy could still be done. And no doubt, as many have said, much of the revival and current energy of political theory is due in part to Rawls's work. Further, his masterful *Theory of Justice*[5] confirms Berlin's view in an important way. In the first place, his theory speaks to a deep conflict in the political life of capitalist democracies over the priority and meaning of liberty and equality, thus confirming Berlin's point about social pluralism, and the resulting conflicts, providing the occasion for political theory. And Rawls takes moral pluralism to be inevitable, at least in a modern society in which basic freedoms are realized.

But in another sense Rawls's account breaks sharply with Berlin. Where Berlin locates moral pluralism in a theory of value, one that appears to be a version of realism, according to which value judgments are to accord with the structure that the world of value actually has, Rawls seeks to build a political theory that is agnostic about such questions. What is crucial for pluralism in Rawls's view is not the fact, if it is a fact, that value is plural, but that there is reasonable disagreement about values, and moral and political issues generally—including the question of whether value is plural.

Of course, in setting out Rawls's position in this way, I am drawing on a later formulation of it, particularly *Political Liberalism*, where Rawls explains the possibility of reasonable disagreement by invoking what he calls the "burdens of judgment." Reasonable disagreement, he writes, "is disagreement among reasonable persons," who "share a common human reason, similar powers of thought and judgment: they can draw inferences, weigh evidence, and balance competing considerations".[6] Disagreement among reasonable persons is possible, he argues, because the grounds on which we make judgments (both theoretical and practical) are often inadequate in various ways. The evidence may be conflicting and so hard to assess, or people may disagree about the weight to be assigned to different considerations, or different normative considerations may be found on both sides of an issue. Although it is possible to resolve many issues, others cannot be settled, and reasonable people will continue to hold different views in spite of their having sincerely considered the arguments and evidence that others have offered.

I would suggest that the grounds for reasonable disagreement must be deeper than Rawls's account suggests. He focuses on rather narrow differences, particularly regarding the adequacy of the evidence and the relative weight of different moral or evaluative considerations. It would be hard to disagree with this line of argument; specific judgments of the sort Rawls mentions are almost always understood to be defeasible. The more profound difficulties involve the frameworks of description and explanation we use in arriving at the kinds of judgments Rawls seems to have in mind. They often involve deep philosophical issues about the nature of being and what kinds of knowledge are possible. Such disagreements are particularly intractable, and often underlie the more specific issues Rawls mentions.

This idea of pluralism as reasonable disagreement, unlike Berlin's account of the plurality of value, opens up space for political theory. It is precisely because we disagree, and because these disagreements are tractable, that we are led to theoretical reflection and criticism. In particular, disagreements about the directions in which we should take our common affairs does not, or at least not necessarily, reflect acts of commitment, in which we opt for different priorities among the incommensurable values we hold. Rather, our disagreements may involve all kinds of different reasons: we may disagree about the facts, about what has happened in the past, and what the consequences of different courses of action would be. We might disagree about the explanatory and interpretative frameworks we use to analyze the facts and imagine the future. We might disagree about the ontology of social and political life, about the basic concepts of human nature or the self, about the reality of collective entities such as the nation or a culture. We might disagree about values, and for that matter whether values are plural, or whether they are or can best be regarded as in some sense commensurable. And these disagreements give occasion to theorizing, as well as other forms of discourse and expression. We can offer reasons to one another for conceiving of the political world in one way rather than another, we can counter those reasons and modify our conceptions in response to what we learn and what we come to experience. And we can put forward our accounts in public settings, from academic conferences to classrooms to newspapers and journals of opinion to parliamentary commissions and congressional hearings. And we can modify our theories in response to the ways in which they are taken up in the political arena. Consider, for example, how the discourse about work and welfare has changed in both the academy and in politics in the past two decades.

So Rawls's view of pluralism is more hospitable to political theorizing than Berlin's, and like Berlin's appears to provide a grounding for a liberal and democratic society, which in turn reinforces the very pluralism which occasions theorizing. But one may wonder what the point of theorizing is, if it involves endless arguments, however rational and responsive to those of others. If the conflicts of pluralist society occasion theoretical reflection, can theory contribute to the practical task of resolving those conflicts? Can it help us "see whether, despite appearances, some underlying basis of philosophical and moral agreement can be uncovered" so as to resolve or at least narrow "divisive political differences" that confront a particular society—such as the conflict between liberty and equality in western democracies?[7] And how could it do so, if the conflicting perspectives are all "reasonable," in the sense that none can be definitively dismissed as irrational, or as "rooted solely in ignorance and perversity, or else in the rivalries for power, status, or economic gain"?[8]

### III. POLITICAL CONSTRUCTIVISM

As long as we conceive of the task of theory as providing the correct answers to the questions we face as a collectivity—answers rooted in some true account of human nature, reason, history, the structure of value, God's will, or some other touchstone of reality—political theory will seem both impotent and imperialist. Impotent, because the quarrels among political theorists demonstrate their failure to find the truth. Imperialist, because this conception of the task of theory seems to set theorists above the world, dictating answers to it. Needless to say, this is not a happy picture.

And it is precisely this picture that Rawls's conception of theorizing enables us to avoid. The existence of reasonable disagreement about fundamental questions of morality and ethics, including questions of justice, means that the appeal to truth cannot be an adequate basis for political order. As Rousseau put it,

> All justice comes from God, he alone is its source; but if we were capable of receiving it from so high, we would need neither government nor laws. No doubt there is a universal justice emanating from reason alone; but this justice, to be admitted among us, must be reciprocal.[9]

No doubt, it could happen that our conflicting views about justice could, over time, converge on a true account of justice (and other moral values), as criticism leads to the detection and correction of errors, just as (at least in some accounts) our conflicting views about the subject matter of the natural sciences tend to converge. But as long as this convergence has not occurred, and—even more significantly—as long as any convergence may be subverted by new criticisms and new disagreements, truth as a basis for political order must remain elusive. Theorizing that is reflexive, that is conscious of its own limitations, and that is motivated (at least in part) by the practical task of resolving conflicts, begins with an acknowledgment of reasonable disagreement. Rather than delivering correct answers, it aims to provide framework inclusive enough to encompass plurality and conflict, but which can narrow those differences so that justice can be admitted among us.

Much of Rawls's work is devoted to spelling out a conception of justice that is "reciprocal." I will not review that conception in any detail here, but it is important to observe that this conception of justice might be thought of as "justice as social cooperation." Central to this conception is the "idea of a well ordered society—a society effectively regulated by a public conception of justice".[10] A well-ordered society "is a fair system of social cooperation over time from one generation to the next",[11] in which the "role of the principles of justice . . . is to specify the fair terms of social cooperation".[12] Crucial to this conception is the distinction between social cooperation and "socially coordinated activity—for example, activity coordinated by orders issued by an absolute central authority".[13] All social life requires coordination; cooperation is coordination realized through rules or procedures that participants accept as "appropriate to regulate their conduct," in part because the rules enable them to realize their own good in ways they regard as fair. As Rawls puts it, "Fair terms of cooperation specify an idea of reciprocity, or mutuality: all who do their part as the recognized rules require are to benefit as specified by a public and agreed-upon standard."[14] Reciprocity or mutuality does not necessarily mean that people benefit equally; whether equality is required depends upon the publicly accepted standards, the standards or principles of justice accepted in that society.

The obvious question this gives rise to is "Where do those standards come from?" For traditional forms of theorizing, standards of justice are drawn from a general or, as Rawls puts it, a comprehensive moral, religious or philosophical doctrine. In this view, a theory of justice is a branch of moral philosophy, one that explains how the advantages of socially coordinated activity should be distributed, and in general what principles should govern the political and other key institutions of society. Comprehensive doctrines offer a vision of human life and well-being, which grounds an account of how society should be structured in order to realize human flourishing and to cultivate forms of human excellence. Such doctrines give rise to what Rawls calls "common good conceptions of justice," for the claims of justice are rooted in some view of the proper ends or goods of human life.[15]

For a well-ordered society to be based upon a common good conception of justice, there must be widespread (though perhaps not universal) acceptance of the comprehensive doctrine that defines its "common good." Otherwise, participants could not accept the rules or procedures that govern the society as "appropriate to regulate their conduct." That is why this way of thinking about justice is inadequate in societies characterized by a diversity of comprehensive moral, philosophical, and religious doctrines, each of which enjoys the support of a significant number of adherents. In pluralist societies, different visions of human life will lead to conflicting moral claims. As long as the requirements of justice are rooted in comprehensive moral doctrines, this conflict will continue, and the likely outcome will be a structure of domination, in which the adherents of some particular account (or a coalition of groups) gain enough power to impose their views on the rest, or some uneasy compromise reflecting a balance of power among factions. Such a society cannot be well ordered, in the sense that it is based upon a common understanding and acceptance of the principles of justice, which is effectively realized in its practices and institutions, and which can serve as a framework to settle the major disputes about the division of social advantages that arise within it. And when people have good reasons to persist in their own particular beliefs, and must suffer the imposition of others' values upon them, there is an obvious sense in which such a society can be said to be unjust, for it is based upon domination and held together by force.

"Political liberalism" can be thought of as spelling out this requirement of reciprocity. It does so in part by conceiving of its task as one of political construction. Rather than conceiving of its task as setting out principles of justice that correspond to the structure of moral facts, political liberalism specifies a procedure to determine principles of justice that all members of a society can find acceptable, in spite of their subscribing to different comprehensive moral and philosophical views. It does not affirm or deny that these principles might be, in some sense "true," but brackets the question of truth in order to advance the practical task of addressing divisive political issues.

In political liberalism, reciprocity is expressed first of all in the commitment to living cooperatively with others, which requires that one be "ready to propose principles and standards as fair terms of cooperation and to abide by them willingly, given the assurance that others will likewise do so,"[16] and second, in their acknowledgment of reasonable disagreement itself. Political liberalism conceives of the principles of justice as the object of reasonable agreement among citizens who seek to live cooperatively with one another while acknowledging reasonable disagreement on comprehensive moral, religious, and philosophical doctrines. They therefore seek principles that all have reason to accept as a basis for governing the basic institutions of their society, and adjudicating their claims to the distribution of the advantages of social cooperation. Political liberalism, then, embodies what we might call the fundamental principle of democratic legitimacy. In Rawls's words:

> since political power is the coercive power of free and equal citizens [acting] as a corporate body, this power should be exercised, when constitutional essentials and basic questions of justice are at stake, only in ways that all citizens can reasonably be expected to endorse in the light of their common human reason.[17]

Rawls puts forward his substantive theory of justice as one that all could accept, provided they are committed to living cooperatively with others and that they accept the existence of reasonable disagreement about ultimate moral and philosophical issues.

In passing, Rawls remarks that a liberal society also has a common good conception of justice in that its members share "the common good of achieving political justice for all its citizens over time and preserving the free culture that justice allows".[18] Although his comment appears to be somewhat ironic, the point is important. The common good of political liberalism is, above all, the commitment to living cooperatively with others in the special sense defined above. This means that the principles on which society is organized will be based upon a subset of one's fundamental commitments, and thus may on occasion come into conflict with other values or norms one holds, but that one is in general willing to have the more narrow, political or shared values prevail in the face of such conflicts. To value social cooperation in this way is no trivial thing. Nor does it offer a picture of perfect harmony, for sometimes the conflict between the aspirations a citizen holds and the requirements of justice may be very deep, and may not always be resolved in favor of justice.

A political (or constructed) conception of justice specifies the content of what Rawls calls the "idea of public reason" for a democratic society.[19] In his account, "public reason specifies at the deepest level the basic moral and political values that are to determine a constitutional democratic government's relation to its citizens and their relation to one another".[20] Public reason, then, is substantive, comprising the principles and values that citizens and public officials should employ in determining the basic principles of justice and the constitutional essentials of a particular society. However, its content is not invariant, but depends upon the context, upon the specific set of divisive political issues the theory addresses.

This can be seen most clearly in Rawls's reflections on the problem of international justice, where he (notoriously) puts forward a conception of "public reason" for international society that takes the basic units of international society to be "peoples" rather than individuals, and allows for nonliberal, nondemocratic societies to be full members of an international society of peoples. He has been roundly, even abusively, criticized for this approach by those who defend a strong form of moral cosmopolitanism, which holds that all people should have equal rights, and that global inequalities should be limited by some kind of egalitarian principle (such as Rawls's own difference principle). But if we acknowledge that even such basic ideals as human freedom and equality could be the subject of reasonable disagreement, a global order based on such ideals could be coercive in a way that undercuts the ideals themselves, at least if there were societies which shared to a high degree a "common good" conception of justice. The commitment to human freedom and equality requires that political arrangements accord with the fundamental principle of democratic legitimacy, but peoples who hold common good conceptions of justice would have reason to reject the norms of democracy themselves, and so the imposition of these norms would be self-contradictory. Of course, if moral cosmopolitanism were true, if humans were entitled to equal rights and if justice required global equality, the objections of other peoples could be dismissed. But political theorizing that takes seriously the possibility of reasonable disagreement must take a different tack. Thus, Rawls seeks a conception of international justice that supports principles of public reason for a global society that addresses the divisive political conflicts we face, without presuppositions that silence some of the voices that are parties to those conflicts.

## IV. POLITICAL THEORY AND RECONCILIATION

In addition to the practical task of resolving conflicts, Rawls suggests that theorizing has three other objectives: orienting us and reconciling us to our political lives, and projecting a realistic utopia.[21] I have been focusing on the practical concern of political philosophy, which "is to see whether, despite appearances, some underlying basis of philosophical and moral agreement can be uncovered" so as to resolve or at least narrow "divisive political differences" that confront a particular society—such as the conflict between liberty and equality in western democracies.[22]

I want to turn now to the way in which political theory today might orient and reconcile us to our way of life, beginning with Rawls's account. The tasks of reconciliation and orientation are closely related. Political philosophy gives us orientation by providing a unified account of how we may think about our political and social institutions as a whole, and how we collectively share "basic aims and purposes as a society with a history," so that we may see how our various "ends can cohere within a well-articulated conception of a just and reasonable society".[23] And in doing so it contributes to reconciling us to our way of life, calming "our frustration and rage against our society and its history by showing us the way which [our] institutions, when properly understood from a philosophical point of view, are rational, and developed over time as they did to attain their present, rational form".[24]

Rawls's comments on this issue are sketchy, but we must wonder to what extent this Hegelian turn to reconciliation is really possible for him, given the account he offers us of modern society and the burdens of judgment. Hegel could see the task of political philosophy as reconciliation in part because he had an account of history as the realization of human freedom and reason. As he puts it so memorably:

> To comprehend what is, this is the task of philosophy, because what is, is reason. Whatever happens, every individual is a child of his time; so philosophy too is its own time apprehended in thoughts. . . . To recognize reason as the rose in the cross of the present and thereby to enjoy the present, this is the rational insight which reconciles us to the

actual, the reconciliation which philosophy affords to those in whom there has once arisen an inner voice bidding them to comprehend . . ..[25]

But Rawls does not posit that our society is in fact rational. Rather, he insists that the fourth task of political theory is to project a rational utopia. For, he argues, we can be reconciled to our world only if it is rational, and though we must act on the "belief that the social world allows at least a decent political order," we must probe "the limits of practicable possibility" to project an image of a just order that can be attained "under reasonably favorable but still possible historical conditions, conditions allowed by the laws and tendencies of the social world".[26] Reconciliation is possible, then, but only in the context of a realistic utopia: only when political theory offers us a critical perspective on our own practices. Rawls himself rejects modern capitalist democracy, even in the form of the social democratic welfare state we find in Europe. For him, the ideal is a property-owning democracy which, like the universal welfare state, minimizes class inequality but which, unlike the welfare state in any form, reduces the vast inequalities of wealth and so of political power that corrupt democratic life.

## V. THE LIMITS OF RECONCILIATION

Although Rawls continues to seek reconciliation, it is essential to see—and to learn to live with—a certain tension at the heart of the ideal of reconciliation. For Hegel, reason could still give us access to truth, and reason works itself out in and through history. Thus, by coming to have understanding we can find ourselves at home in the world.[27] But one of Rawls's crucial moves is to abandon that strong sense of reason, substituting "reasonableness" for truth as the basis of political order. And while he sometimes writes as if "reasonableness" was something that could be expected of just about anyone who didn't suffer some obvious cognitive or moral deficiency, in fact people can reject political liberalism's idea of "reasonableness" without committing any cognitive error, particularly in the case of "reasonableness" understood as the commitment to live cooperatively with others, even when that involves subordinating some of the values or ideals one holds. In general, whether something is reasonable depends upon how it fits in with a larger system of beliefs and ideas, and one can reject political liberalism without being unreasonable in the ordinary sense of the term.

Rawls's invocation of "reasonableness" is an effort to hang on to as much as possible of an older faith in the possibility of a political order that is fully adequate, because it both expresses and provides scope for human needs and capacities, and so an order we can all accept as rational beings. But, one might wonder, do the burdens of reason that forced Rawls to abandon that hope also push against the version of a consensual political order he now affirms?

Today many critics charge that we must question this drive for theoretical closure which has inspired so much political theory, including Rawls's.[28] This questioning has occupied political theorists inspired by Foucault, who has taught us much about the dangers in taking consensus, even or particularly rational consensus, as our ideal. "The farthest I would go," Foucault has said, "is to say that perhaps one must not be for consensuality, but one must be against nonconsensuality." To be for consensuality would be to "grant that it is indeed under its governance that the phenomenon has to be organized".[29] Foucault, at least at this point, does not tell us what is problematic about taking consensus as a regulatory ideal, nor how we can be against nonconsensuality without being for consensuality, but these issues have been taken up by others, who argue that taking consensuality as a regulative principle may prestructure political and social life in ways that can seriously disadvantage, and in extreme cases can even silence, certain voices.

Peter Euben, in a wonderful exploration of the significance of Greek tragedy for political theory, suggests that the tragedians, like Foucault, are "suspicious of any theoretical impulse," and "warn about the tyranny of mind with its passion to transform enigmas into problems with solutions, dissolve mystery, and impose one voice on debate." [30] The tragedians teach us to live with otherness, and not to see it "as a disease to be cured," but to leave "the other as other," for the effort to cure, to gain closure or reconciliation, can only be realized by denying what cannot be overcome, and so comes at the cost of a certain blindness.

In a similar vein, William Connolly insists that there is no predesign of human material to fit a particular order, and so he concludes that "every form of social completion and enablement also contains subjugations and cruelties within it".[31] He also recognizes that the "human animal is essentially incomplete without social form; and a common language, institutional setting, traditions, and political forum for enunciating public purposes provide the indispensable means through which human beings acquire the identity and commonalities essential to life".[32] We thus face a genuine *paradox* of difference: social order is absolutely necessary for us, but any social order is also repressive.

But where does that leave the idea that the political can be a realm of human freedom, a place where we can actively shape rather than passively endure our collective conditions? How can we talk about "shaping" the conditions of our collective lives if collective decisions necessarily involve impositions? Far from being a sphere of freedom, this picture depicts politics as domination.

And that picture is compounded when we consider how the scope of political decision is limited by powerful social forces operating in an increasingly globalized economy and in systems of cultural reproduction. In her contribution to the special issue of political theory, Wendy Brown offers a diagnosis of our predicament that sees the scope of collective action as vanishingly small, describing a "political world that is largely immune to augmentation by human action".[33] But on the other hand, she sees "the singular value of political theory" as its "constitutive orientation to the problem of how collectivities are conceived and ordered in the contemporary world".[34] But what scope is there for addressing the "political" if the possibilities of the political world are as shrunken as they appear to be in visions inspired by Foucault?

No doubt, the promise of politics as a sphere of human freedom is one that we can embrace today only in a chastened form. But that does not mean that we must altogether abandon the project of reconciliation, where reconciliation is tied to the idea of a realistic utopia. For that project does not require that we blind ourselves to the ways in which the realization of our ideals may involve new and unexpected forms of exclusion or domination. A political theory that acknowledges the burdens of reason, and that aims instead to construct principles that serve to narrow "divisive political differences" can itself help us to see and appreciate the limits of theory, just because it begins with the need to listen and respond to the plurality of voices we actually confront in a concrete setting, and not transcending them in a projection of its own account of what is right or true. Such a political theory can exhibit the range of disagreement, of contestation in political life, and so keep alive the possibilities that are excluded when we work and think only within a particular framework as, to a large extent, we must. Rawls may be faulted, perhaps, for not always acknowledging, or acknowledging as clearly, a fifth task of political theory: to appreciate the limits of theory itself, and the ways in which any set of political arrangements necessarily embodies their own potentially unjust or harmful exclusions and forms of repression.[35] We cannot escape the tragic dimension of our lives, individually or collectively, and political theory can help us see that the effort to do so invites a greater tragedy, and so to avoid it.

But the facts of pluralism and conflict do not mean that politics is simply domination. The differences between conflicting positions can be narrowed, and people can come to see the point of their opponents' views, even if they do not share them. And common interests can be realized, so that losses can be endured. To appreciate the ways in which visions of harmony and consensus fail does mean that in political life we can only go "from domination to domination",[36] any more than the realization that our scientific knowledge is fallible, and that even cherished truths may be overthrown by future research means that we never know anything. Narrowing differences, discovering common interests and values, and elucidating the sources of disagreements are among the "practical" tasks of theory. The pluralism of reasonable disagreement that a pluralist society presupposes can be both the occasion for theorizing, and a check on theory's totalizing tendencies.

## VI. THE TASKS OF THEORY TODAY

I would like to close with a few words about the professional organization of political theory in light of the argument I have been making about the tasks of theory. I have stressed the practical task of theory in addressing conflicts about the best or appropriate ends to which we should collectively direct our common life, and how that task gives rise to a certain kind of reconciliation to our social world, one that rests upon the ability of theory to project a rational utopia. And I have stressed the limits of theorizing: the conflicts that give rise to theory limit what it can accomplish. In particular, it cannot replace conflict with harmony, it can only project a rational utopia, but not one in which our different ends and aspirations can be finally resolved, a utopia which can console us for our losses.

Unfortunately, the way theory is professionally organized today makes it less able to realize these aspirations. For the realization of these aspirations depends upon a live engagement with the conditions of political life, addressing an audience that is not narrowly self-contained. To a large extent, however, political theorists have come to speak only to themselves, and even more narrowly, to those who share their own particular discourse. To some extent, political theorists may be less insular than they were 30 or 40 years ago, as political theory, like the humanities generally, has seen a blurring of its genres and boundaries. Always an interdisciplinary venture, it is now practiced in literature and anthropology departments, in cultural and gender studies, in theaters and any number of other settings.

On the other hand, it is even more exclusively an academic pursuit, reflecting the tendency for the university to monopolize the setting of intellectual life over the past two centuries. And the exigencies of academic life—living off of political theory as distinct if not opposed to living for political theory— carry its own imperatives. The proliferation of conferences and workshops and specialized journals I referred to above may be a sign of political theory's vitality, but also of its weaknesses, to the extent that we have come to speak not only among ourselves, but even within political theory only to those who share our predilections and footnotes.

To the extent that political theory becomes increasingly self-referential, it loses touch not only with the social sciences and history (a tendency partially offset by the blurring of disciplinary boundaries I mentioned above), but also the capacity to speak to the issues that face us as citizens. Reinforced by the tendencies towards self-enclosure within the field, criticism is blunted and we allow ourselves to speak at increasingly high levels of abstraction, employing an increasingly jargonized vocabulary that marks insiders and outsiders, sometimes within very narrow circles indeed. Terms that might once have been shorthand lose whatever empirical referents they might once have had, and reification becomes the order of the day. Think of terms like "globalization," "capitalism," "late modernity," "technology," "markets," "power," "nature," and, for that matter, "reasonable."

Among the social sciences from which political theory becomes alienated is political science itself. There may be less overt tension between political science and political theory than there was 40 years ago, when the death (or was it the execution?) of political theory was actively debated in a discipline undergoing a behavioral revolution that was to establish it finally and forever as one of the true sciences. But the mutual indifference and incomprehension between political theory and the rest of political science hardly represents an improvement. Failing to engage empirical studies and findings makes political theory remote and irrelevant, and the indifference of political science to political theory undoubtedly contributes to the sterility and myopia of much political research.

Berlin saw political theory as necessarily arising in, and necessary to, a pluralist society in which the political sphere can be a sphere of freedom. But whether academic political theory can play that role is an open question, and represents a major challenge facing us today.

## NOTES

1.  Isaiah Berlin, "Does Political Theory Still Exist?" In Peter Laslett and W.G. Runciman, eds. *Philosophy, Politics and Society*, 2nd Series (Oxford, UK: Basil Blackwell, 1962).
2.  Peter Laslett, ed. *Philosophy, Politics and Society*, 1st Series (Oxford, UK: Basil Blackwell, 1956).
3.  Berlin's most famous statement of this thesis is probably in "Two Concepts of Liberty," in his *Four Essays on Liberty* (New York: Oxford University Press), especially 167-72.
4.  Brian Barry, *Sociologists, Economists and Democracy* (London: Collier-Macmillan, 1970), 1.
5.  John Rawls, *A Theory of Justice* (Cambridge, MA: Harvard University Press, 1971).

6.  John Rawls, *Political Liberalism*, 2nd ed. (New York: Columbia University Press, 1996), 55.

7.  John Rawls, *Justice as Fairness: A Restatement* (Cambridge, MA: Harvard University Press, 2001), 2.

8.  Rawls, *Political Liberalism*, 58.

9.  J. J. Rousseau, *Of the Social Contract*, trans. V. Gourevitch, ed. (New York: Cambridge University Press, 1997 [1762]), 66.

10.  Rawls, *Justice as Fairness: A Restatement*, 8.

11.  Ibid., 5.

12.  Ibid., 7.

13.  Ibid., 6.

14.  Ibid., 6.

15.  The idea of a common good conception of justice is developed principally in John Rawls's *The Law of Peoples* (Cambridge, MA: Harvard University Press, 1999). But it is also mentioned elsewhere, e.g., *Lectures on the History of Moral Philosophy*, Barbara Herman, ed. (Cambridge, MA: Harvard University Press, 2000), 355, in reference to Hegel's political philosophy.

16.  Rawls, *Political Liberalism*, 49.

17.  Rawls, *Political Liberalism*, 140-41.

18.  Rawls, *The Law of Peoples*, 71, fn. 10.

19.  John Rawls, "The Idea of Public Reason Revisited" in *The Law of Peoples* (Cambridge, MA: Harvard University Press, 1999), 132-33.

20.  Ibid., p.132.

21.  Rawls, *Justice as Fairness: A Restatement*, 1-5.

22.  Ibid., 2.

23.  Ibid., 2-3.

24.  Ibid., 3.

25.  G. W. F. Hegel, *Philosophy of Right*. trans. T.M. Knox, ed. (Oxford, UK: Oxford University Press, 1952 [1821]), 11-12.

26.  Rawls, *Justice as Fairness: A Restatement*, 4.

27.  Rawls himself interprets Hegel as a defender of a constitutional, liberal state, and so in the context of his time offering reconciliation only in the context of a rational utopia, of the state as it could be, not as it actually was. See Rawls, *Lectures on the History of Moral Philosophy*, 252-53.

28.  These points are developed further in my *Constructing Community* (Princeton, NJ: Princeton University Press, 1993), 211-21, on which I have drawn here.

29.  Michel Foucault, *The Foucault Reader*, Paul Rabinow, ed. (New York: Pantheon, 1984), 379.

30.  J. Peter Euben, *The Tragedy of Political Theory* (Princeton, NJ: Princeton University Press, 1990), 30-31.

31.  William E. Connolly, *Identity/Difference* (Ithaca, NY and London: Cornell University Press, 1991), 94.

32.  Ibid., this volume, 114.

33.  Wendy Brown, "At the Edge," *Political Theory* 30, no. 4 (2002), 567.

34.  Ibid., 117-118.

35.  In his *Theory of Justice* he spoke of looking at the social world from the "perspective of eternity," and envisioned his principles of justice as holding for all times and places. But in his reformulated, political liberalism, he acknowledges that there may be a family of political conceptions of justice, and rejects the idea that one can "fix public reason once

and for all in the form of one favored political conception of justice", see Rawls's "The Idea of Public Reason Revisited", in *The Laws of People*, 142.

36. Foucault, *The Foucault Reader*, 85.

*GEORGE KATEB*

T he impetus of this essay is the question, Is the canon of political theory adequate to the task of enabling readers in our time to take in and comprehend the awful events of the twentieth century? This question can be broken down into two questions. First, Does the canon up to the end of the nineteenth century make, or help significantly to make, these events intelligible, if not expectable or predictable? Second, Are there any political thinkers in the twentieth century, plausibly eligible for canonization, who offer this kind of help? I incline to the view that the canon up to the nineteenth century does something to help, but probably not enough. The awful events of the twentieth century seem, if only in their scale, to break out of the conceptual net found in the sequence of canonical texts written up to 1900 or so. On the second question, I believe that two prominent Nietzscheans did what Nietzsche himself did not quite do: they made a substantial contribution to our ability to encompass the awful events of the twentieth century. I refer to Heidegger and Arendt. And I refer to Arendt not as one influenced by Heidegger but as a thinker in her own right, inspired by Nietzsche as Heidegger was, but doing her own political thinking to our inestimable benefit. These two thinkers are not alone in offering assistance, but they stand out.

Naturally, I do not say that the only value of the canon up to the nineteenth century or of the plausibly canonical writers of the twentieth century is found in helping readers in our time to make sense of the awful events of the twentieth century. Nor do I want to suggest that the only aspect of the twentieth century that is of interest to the student of political theory is the series of atrocious events. For example, the continuing phenomenon of unlimited government parasitically or culpably sheltered by constitutional democracy is of compelling interest. I confine my interest to awful events—actually, deliberate policies, some of them carried out quickly and some over a longer period of time—because facing the worst is surely one of the purposes of reading the canon, just as it is, of course, of reading anything worthwhile in the whole field of the humanities. It may be a matter of temperament only, but I think that facing the worst is actually the most important purpose that could be served by the canon and by a good deal of the politically relevant humanities as well. But it is not the only purpose.

I should say right away that facing the worst, trying to comprehend awful events, whether or not those of the twentieth century, consists to a great extent, even though not exclusively, of making some sense of the motivation of leaders who initiate these events and of the motivation of followers who sustain the leaders. In other words, I look to the canon for enlightenment in *moral psychology*—to use an old but not worn-out term—and I also look to the canon for some assistance in the supplementary endeavor of *moral phenomenology*. Moral psychology is the nonscience that looks externally at initiators and their followers; moral phenomenology is more detailed and often consists in self-characterization by agents, real or fictional, and for this latter enterprise, nothing comes close to equaling imaginative literature. But moral psychology is my basic concern in this essay. I should add that an interest in moral psychology is not exhausted by the wish to explain the motivations behind initiating and sustaining terrible deeds. The effort to know the springs of human conduct as broadly as possible—and from the useful vantage point of political life, its necessities and opportunities, disciplines and psychic enlargements and distortions—is intrinsically bound up with studying the canon.

Now, by awful or atrocious events in the twentieth century, I mean, primarily, but not only, World War I, World War II, the use twice of atomic weapons, their repeated threatened use by the United States, the theories of nuclear deterrence, the gulags, the Holocaust, induced famines, such American wars as the Korean War and the Vietnam War, and numerous massive massacres. My stress is not only on initiation but also on maintenance and much less so on neglect and indifference. The theme is the scale of humanly inflicted suffering on human beings and the mentalities that permit the initiation and implementation of such deeds. I grant that the distinction in responsibility between causing something awful and letting it happen or continue is often slight or nonexistent and also that the amount of suffering that is neglected when it could be mitigated or ended can be enormous or even unprecedented. Indeed, neglect can be deliberate, a pragmatic substitute for infliction. Blameworthy indifference and malevolent abstention are phenomena in their own right. Some of what I say in this essay will, I hope, be relevant to these phenomena. But my main emphasis is on deliberate infliction.

Let me just mention that besides instruction in moral psychology, three other uses of the canon are, in my judgment, especially important. They may be put in the form of questions that the canon strives to answer: Why, if at all, is government necessary? What are the claims of morality when governments and citizens act? What, for good and ill, is distinctively political? But the compound question before us is, Does the canon before the twentieth century prepare us for the awful events of the twentieth century and make them at least partly intelligible? And if, in the twentieth century, Heidegger and Arendt—especially Arendt—help, how do they help?

\* \* \* \* \*

My principal interest has been for as long as I can remember the wish to find instruction in moral psychology from the canon. Then, trying to see what light it throws on the awful events of the twentieth century, I find myself somewhat disappointed, though I am willing to grant that I may be anachronistic and therefore expect the wrong kind of instruction from the canon that runs from Plato through the nineteenth century. Alternatively, I may fail to see that this canon actually does offer adequate instruction for my purpose; I may not read carefully enough. My halting conclusion is that whether or not the canon up to 1900 could have been adequate, it is not completely so, and should not be thought to be so, despite the fact that it remains invaluable for instruction in moral psychology.

In the twentieth century, there is no break in human nature. Unchanged human nature, however, produces discontinuity in the scale of atrocious effects of deliberate state or movement policy, and could produce yet greater atrocities in the future, and even culminate in the extinction of humanity and much of nature. These are the new facts that have to be pondered. Yet writers in the canon did not contemplate such a scale because they gave scant attention to certain human capacities that have always existed and always been in play. Nor were the atrocities with which they were familiar usually traced to these capacities. But when the scale of destructive wrongdoing is as immense as it was in the twentieth century and could possibly encompass massive human and natural retrogression or decay, or inconceivable ruin, then we must pay attention to overlooked or barely noticed causes, if only we can get hold of them.

Yet if the twentieth century is discontinuous in scale of atrocities, is it not anachronistic to expect the canon up to 1900 to enable readers to face the worst in the century that followed? With few exceptions, political theory, even at its canonical best, does not aspire to predict the course of the future. But it is not prediction that is wanted. What, then, is? We can reasonably want the moral psychology that is so variously, intricately, and subtly on display in the canon to prepare readers for anything awful, whatever the scale. Are we not entitled to expect that the major politically relevant elements of human nature will be assembled in the great and good texts that are available for our instruction? The texts usually presume to speak timelessly: the human psyche is laid bare. The common root of all diverse cultures is allegedly exposed. This is the overt or tacit premise in the canon.

What is more, I think that the preponderant tendency in the canon is pessimism concerning human nature. Such pessimism is not monochromatic; it is not always deep dyed; it may be softened by a guarded hopefulness; it is certainly put forth in substantially different hues. But Plato, Aristotle, Augustine, Aquinas, Machiavelli, Hobbes, Locke, Rousseau (in spite of himself), Kant, probably Hegel, Mill in his stoical moods, Nietzsche in his way—all of them and others, too—paint a composite, even heterogeneous, but unmistakably sad or dark or tragic picture of humanity, a humanity corrupted more by privilege than by adversity, though sometimes more by humiliation or weakness than by privilege. They all say the worst they know about humanity. They think that only in exceptional or almost miraculously contrived circumstances can the worst passions of humanity be restrained or diminished and some of the best capacities brought out. The unreformed normality is, however, very grim. In such grimness, the canon retains a power to instruct that I wish to affirm. I only want that power enhanced, especially for the task of facing the awful events of the twentieth century, but also for casting a long backward look at the experience of the centuries before that. We could say that the canon up to 1900 either is not pessimistic enough or that the very nature of its pessimism concerning human nature needs some alteration or enlargement or redirection.

The twentieth century is discontinuous with previous history in the scale of its atrocious effects, yet I would have wanted the canon up to 1900 to be more nearly adequate to these awful events. My view is that the discontinuity of the twentieth century is caused by capacities or tendencies in human beings that of course long predate the twentieth century. Is it possible that these tendencies could not have been noticed sufficiently? Or, perhaps there seemed to be no need to notice them when awful events through time were thought to derive wholly from yet other tendencies that make up the composite pessimism in the canon? But I think that there has always been need to notice them. They help to account for many of the awful events all through time. Only, in the twentieth century, these immemorial tendencies in all human beings cannot any longer be overlooked; without them, that century is not intelligible.

I find that three factors work to make these tendencies to pursue atrocious policies metastatic in their effects. First, the numbers of people alive, from the late nineteenth century onward, has drastically altered the scale of effects of concerted human action, whether aggressive or defensive; whether masses are mobilized or passive; whether they are instruments or victims, or both (as they usually are). One way into the story of atrocities in the twentieth century is to highlight the culpable availability of those who have suffered as much or more than their victims: masses who become politically usable when they are populist, usually resentful, and always undemocratic in spirit if not in their nominal citizenship. An egalitarian passion serves to make them yet more usable. Second, technological advances have armed immemorial tendencies in human nature with gigantic powers. Third, religion no longer satisfies religious craving to the same extent or on the same terms, at least not where technological prowess is most advanced. In sum, the same old human nature, but radically potent and swimming or drowning in enormous numbers of people, many of whom are spiritually greedy or can be persuaded to become so, produces effects that are unprecedented in scale. I return to these aggravating factors below.

Not all three factors are always present; in the case of some massacres, for example, technology can be rudimentary, or the population not shockingly larger than it had been, or religious beliefs not very different from what they had been. In these cases, however, the adequacy of the canon is still impeachable because of its comparative neglect, above all, of the part played by one tendency in human beings, the proclivity to be prey to imagination and the intertwined proclivity to fail to exercise imagination. The vicissitudes of imagination are, I think, a key element. To be sure, from the eighteenth century on, benign imagination has been discussed as one key to right conduct. But that discussion does not range as far as we need, despite its continued usefulness. In this essay, I do not presume to offer anything like a full account of imagination, or an inventory of its uses (especially its good uses), or of the consequences of its failure to be used. I submit only preliminary considerations. What I say is tentative, with many loose ends. But the scale of horror makes it urgent to try again to understand the causes of horror.

*  *  *  *  *

Human beings have always been creatures who live in their imagination and who also refuse, when it suits them, to exercise their imagination. We have the inborn mental capacity to make the absent present (on one hand) and (on the other) the present absent. (Memory, too, makes the absent present, but what is absent and then recalled—if only imperfectly—actually happened; in contrast, imagination makes the absent event or condition that has never existed present to the mind.) I am especially interested in what I will call "hyperactive imagination"; the contrasting term is "inactive imagination" (or moral blindness). The canon does not do justice to this theme of imagination in its vicissitudes. But when hyperactive imagination and inactive imagination are seen in combination as causally efficacious in the production of awful events on an unprecedented scale, then we may have to say that the

canon up through the nineteenth century must be challenged in its very pessimism. I do not mean especially that the canon at its most pessimistic is not
pessimistic enough, but rather that we must put forth against the canon,
where necessary, a pessimism that is ever mindful of the imagination both in
its aggressive exercise and in the human disinclination to exercise it benignly.
In a vague way, one can hold that this revision adds up to a greater pessimism,
from one point of view, but to a lesser pessimism, from another.

Say that the pessimism of the canon stands on the prevalence of numerous
vices and that the especially salient political ones are pride (or arrogance),
mere vanity (emptiness never to be filled), envy, jealousy, anger, resentment,
vengeance, greed, indecent curiosity, and an apparently unmotivated malice.
They have always yielded appalling effects in everyday life and in political
life. Nonetheless, in thinking about adequacy of the political canon, we highlight the relationship between these vices and the vicissitudes of the
imagination.

It is possible to hold that without imagination there would be no vices, that
there would be only appetites or instincts or reflexes or comparatively unme-
diated impulses (a condition somewhat like Socrates' city of pigs); that vices
are emotions and hence are always woven with or even out of active or pur-
posively inactive imagination, out of a passionate sense of possibility or a
false sense of impossibility, or a will to redesign or obscure reality. That may
be so, but now the subject becomes intractably difficult for me.

So let me summarize the relationship in this unsatisfactory, schematic,
and temporary way: the vices are the irritants that set the imagination in
motion and concurrently keep it selectively inactive; reciprocally, both
hyperactive and inactive imagination sustain and increase the hold and feroc-
ity of the vices and give direction and method to them. The horror is that
hyperactive and inactive imagination (or moral blindness) in combination
make it easy, or easier, to commit atrocities on a large scale and not feel regret
or remorse, whether after victory or defeat. On every level, the participants
have little or no conviction of vice. Indeed, as I indicate later on, hyperactive
imagination, when it produces effects on the scale of twentieth-century atrocities, seems to be distant from or even to lose connection with any of the vices
and does its worst work unprompted by any of the vices, including indecent
curiosity and gratuitous malice. The sense of possibility develops its own
momentum; if it is abstract or fanatical enough, it can eventually supply its
own motivation. The momentum is experienced as destiny or mission, that is,
as a necessary pattern that must be taken to completion. Aestheticism
becomes dominant. Either a solitary gesture or a protracted atrocious policy
can be felt as a single leap into or out of the void. An alternative (also aesthetic) formulation is that the initiators and leaders tend to conceive of them-

selves as the most visible actors in a drama of which nothing merely human is the author. They must be submissive to their prominent roles. Ordinary pessimism, ordinary realism, do not appear to me to go far enough in making sense of what possesses those who initiate atrocious effects on an unprecedented scale. On the other hand, when imagination remains inactive, one can feel innocent because one feels insulated, even liberated, from one's own motives. In this context, who but the blind can feel innocent?

The assistance provided by Heidegger and Arendt and some others should be seen as making a contribution to moral psychology that helps illuminate the awful events of the twentieth century and that also casts light back on the course of human history. I propose to see Heidegger and Arendt—perhaps Arendt a good deal more than Heidegger—as theorists of the imagination, especially in its political relevance. I do not say that these two great philosophers do all the work, or that all the work that should be done has been done cumulatively with them or after them. What I hope to do in this essay is to highlight what they say about imagination and offer a few further suggestions. It does not matter that neither thinker offers a lengthy exposition of the very nature of imagination. They offer instead an indispensable stimulus.

When confronted by such humanly inflicted and humanly endured catastrophes as the two world wars, the use and threatened use of atomic weapons, and the exterminationist policies of Nazism and Stalinism and other so-called Marxist-Leninist dictatorships, we have to try to understand how such policies could have been initiated and carried out in a burst or over some years. Hannah Arendt insisted that we could not make sense of Nazism or Stalinism if we relied only on the inherited theories of tyranny or cruelty or on the standard pessimism that attributes to human beings a limitless zeal for power or wealth or self-aggrandizement. Even the Greek concepts of hubris and pleonexia—intoxicated or unconscious insolence and intoxicated or compulsive overreaching—do not take us far enough or even, perhaps, always in the right direction, though their power to incite reflection is great. Even Augustine's self-lacerating and self-perplexed analysis of stealing pears as a sixteen-year-old (in the second book of the *Confessions*) or his profound speculation on the mentality that led to the fall of Adam and Eve (in Book 14 of *The City of God*) still, in their inexhaustible suggestiveness, do not, I think, take us all the way.

These theories and concepts together with the standard pessimism must retain a place in any analysis of the twentieth century, but they must make much more room for both the aggressive exercise and the self-protective refusal of imagination. I would add that the canon's grimness is not adequate for the two world wars, not even the first one, which was the source, inspiration, and model of most of the humanly inflicted catastrophes of the twentieth century. So, I would now like to offer a view that presumes to interpret the humanly inflicted catastrophes of the twentieth century in a manner that I believe the canon up to 1900 does not fully engender. Naturally I make no claim for any originality on my part. In what I am about to say, I rely to a very great extent on Arendt and Heidegger and also of course to some lesser extent on other thinkers during the twentieth century. Undeniably, the canon up to 1900 aids us, but maybe not always on its own terms.

\* \* \* \* \*

I begin, to say it again, with the scale of humanly inflicted suffering in the twentieth century. Some human beings are responsible for the deliberate murder, torture, mutilation, derangement, and dispossession of millions and millions of other human beings, and over comparatively short periods of time. The absolute numbers of victims in the twentieth century is unprecedented, despite large-scale slaughters and traumas in the past. If I am told that although the absolute numbers were larger than ever, the percentage of human beings evilly treated, out of the total human population, was not larger and may even be smaller than in the past, my answer is that such a concern for percentages rather than for absolute numbers is, in fact, part of the mentality that makes large-scale atrocities possible. The failure to take seriously nothing but percentages shows a callousness that is part, though a familiar part, of the story of humanly inflicted suffering all through time. Every person counts immeasurably: that is one point. The other point is that an immense accumulation of murdered or savagely treated persons still matters, despite the immeasurability of each person; the scale of atrocious effects still matters, even when we say such things as the following. First, each person dies only one death; a group of persons does not literally endure a group-death in addition to the death of every person in the group. One person does not die the death of one other or many others. Furthermore, the most intense sensations or experience of pain and suffering can register directly only on that person. No sympathizer can feel directly the accumulated pain and sufferings of a group of people. Yet the suffering of multitudinous others can register on the imaginative observer (or fellow sufferer). Although the losses sustained by great numbers of people cannot be summed and experienced by any single person, the observer should try to come to terms with the scale of suffering. The observer can strain to imagine the victims, one by one, as a succession of universes passing into extinction. Benign imagination, recognizing present reality in spite of everything that obstructs such recognition—all the passions or the hard shell of indifference or inadvertence—is crucial.

Now, the scale of atrocities was immense that was perpetrated by, say, imperial Rome, imperial Spain, European and American expansion in North

America, and societies holding African slaves. In each example, inflicted deaths numbered in the millions. All the examples preceded the twentieth century. Do not these atrocious policies discredit the contention that the twentieth century was discontinuous by the scale of awful effects? I still think not, because the numbers of dead or degraded in earlier atrocities accumulated over many decades or centuries and, in each case, under successive leaderships. But the awful events of the twentieth century that I have singled out all occurred in roughly sixty years (1915 to 1975) and came from many sources. (Stalinism and Maoism had the longest run.) The combination of concentration in time and dispersal over the world seems to me unprecedented. Even in regard to earlier violent and atrocious policies, notice how rarely any canonical (or other political) text tallies the numbers or even gestures toward the scale of suffering. Does Machiavelli—even worse, do his commentators—ever mention the hundreds of thousands or even millions slaughtered by imperial Rome? In rare canonical moments, Hobbes estimates that "near 100,000 persons" died in the English civil war,[1] and Hegel says that in the New World, "nearly seven million people have been wiped out" by Europeans.[2]

If an unprecedented scale of deliberately inflicted pain and suffering in the twentieth century is granted, at least provisionally and even skeptically, I now return to the three factors—obvious except to the unimaginative—that facilitated the commission of awful events (and will facilitate it in the twenty-first century and beyond). Begin with the recent large growth of total human population in the societies that inflicted or endured the suffering. The sheer fact of numerousness inflames the imagination of power that initiates atrocious policies. Here, imagination, making the absent present, means wanting to alter reality on the basis of a new design for it. In the hyperactive imagination of power, human beings are conceived as instruments or impediments, as raw material or dirt or disease. With so much human raw material at one's own disposal to use in realizing the new design, and from another perspective, with so much humanity piled up and imagined as imperfections in or obstacles to that design, why not use or degrade and destroy human beings? There are, after all, so many of them. New instruments and impediments can always be found. When masses of people are lost, they are figured as either necessary sacrifices or disposable waste. In either case, they exist to be processed for the sake of the design. The designers scarcely if at all feel the cost of the design as a cost; it is imagined as part of the fabrication of the design, when the cost is not itself the design.

The scale of atrocious effects in the twentieth century is, furthermore, unthinkable without the magical technological prowess that culminates in, but is hardly confined to, the development of atomic weapons. Indeed, atomic weapons were actually used only in World War II (although especially the United States expressly threatened their use on quite a few occasions afterward) and not in the other atrocities of the twentieth century. But the other atrocities did rely on—perhaps we should say, were intrinsic to, or not readily conceivable without, or entailed by, or were the preponderant motive behind—enhanced technological prowess. The growth in human capacities is first of all, even if not always chronologically first, a growth in the power to dominate and destroy. The growth in the capacity to monitor, detect, organize, mobilize, enchant, debase, coerce, and kill is an integral feature of the development of modern technology, just as previous technology served, *mutatis mutandis*, the same purposes all through time. Technology is power, and power will always be abused; it exists to be abused, to perfect intimidation, coercion, humiliation, mobilization, and violence.

Abundant populations and technological prowess are two of the necessary conditions for large-scale atrocious effects in the twentieth century; they help to account for the enormously greater destructiveness of hyperactive imagination joined to moral blindness. It is tempting to say that given these two conditions, the past human record, by itself, would indicate—strongly suggest—that large-scale atrocious effects would inevitably appear. The pessimism of the canon up to 1900 should have flowed smoothly into the twentieth century. But does it do so? It might be safer to say that the canon would have taught this lesson quite without intending to do so. I mean that the succession of political theories—or, at least, most of the texts in the succession—exemplify or are symptomatic of the imagination of power, the *will* to redesign reality, if circumstances are favorable. Few of these texts are a call to arms; few hold that it is desirable that political actors strive, by violence if need be, to realize the theorists' design or some other design that the actors themselves have drawn up. But the canonical writers should have known from their own inner workings how attractive the prospect of shaping reality is, how attractive it is to imagine that what is lamentably absent is gloriously present. (Not that the reality that any particular theorist ever wanted to replace was really good or met even a judiciously minimal level of justice.) But the explicit theme of political imagination is not prominently on display in the canon, though Plato, Hobbes, Burke, and Nietzsche and a few others are self-consciously and indubitably instructive on it. Without consideration of this theme, the human record becomes even harder to decipher.

If the canonical writers up to 1900 could not have been expected to deal with the numerousness and technological prowess that we have known for the past century and a half, they could have been a good deal more explicit and revelatory about hyperactive imagination, the passion to design or redesign reality. Numerousness and technological prowess greatly favor this sort of political aestheticism and magnify, many times over, its atrocious effects. But the strength of the inveterate aesthetic political passion has always been great and too often unnoticed. It invisibly accompanies high-minded projects of reform, renovation, restoration, or redemption.

I now take up again the death of god, the third factor that favors the imagination and helps make it hyperactive in the twentieth century and even earlier. The exacerbated will to redesign reality we ordinarily call "fanaticism." I believe that none of the atrocious policies with their stupendous scale of effects could have occurred without fanaticism. No doubt, Hobbes and Burke are canonical critics of modern revolutionary fanaticism, and both theorists throw a harsh and only a partly distorting light on its nature. But they both rashly exemplify their own fanaticism, which is an obsessive adherence to order. Many in the canon certainly address the ruthless pursuit of ends by those in control and those who try to struggle free of that control. Some in the canon are painfully aware of the effects of religious fanaticism. But what of the fanaticism shown by both sides in the two world wars, in Nazism and Stalinism, and in other protracted atrocious policies in the twentieth century? They are all cases of secular fanaticism. Their irrationality is not nominally religious (in the usual sense) in nature. Perhaps it is a paradox, but it may be the case that secular fanaticism will tend to be worse, more limitless, than religious fanaticism. Even before god died, were not slavery, imperialism, torture, and massacre mostly unreligious activities? At the same time, it may also be the case that in a more secular age, it is easier to call religious fanaticism by its right name. Putting these last points together, one could say that the death of god makes room for a more limitless fanaticism, while making it easier to brand as fanatical the ruthless religious politics and its atrocious effects, in the past. (Who can ignore the way in which religious fanaticism laid Europe waste in the sixteenth and seventeenth centuries?) And should religious fanaticism inspire societies or movements in the twenty-first century to commit atrocities on the scale of those in the twentieth century that impelled the analysis in this essay, then it will be time to reexamine the political centrality of the death of god as a factor. There is in any case never any reason for much shock or surprise if some expressions of murderous fanaticism are religious. There are parts of the world where a jealous god is still going. But then the subject would no longer be the colossal evils of the twentieth century.

Let me take up the second point first, namely, that we now can speak easily of politicized religious fervor as fanaticism. The canon up to 1900, for the most part, is pious toward religious piety. The canonical theorists are all themselves heterodox in belief or unbelievers, but few until the Enlightenment admitted as much. Give Leo Strauss his due: political philosophy is characteristically politic, all too politic. Out of self-concern or mistrust of the people, canonical writers do not think that they can call the (steady if sometimes suspended) devotion shared by all classes to one or another politically and socially active orthodoxy by its right name, that is, fanaticism—what the Enlightenment at last loudly calls enthusiasm. Only incalcitrant devotion to heterodoxy is branded as fanaticism. But the canonical theorists knew better.

I want to say that belief, orthodox or heterodox, is built out of aesthetically compelling falsehoods and unwarranted beliefs. The process by which believers sustain their belief is not cynical, but it is surely not driven by a quest for truth. It is driven by something typically opposed to truth, namely, a quest for meaning, for an overall meaningfulness in the world. The quest for meaning is satisfied by comprehensive and aesthetically compelling fictions or stories. Armed and inflamed, belief can be merciless because the meaningfulness of the world is at stake. Unconscious aestheticism becomes licentious. The canonical theorists more or less know that common opinions about the nature of the world are false, but most of them guard their scepticism—until the Enlightenment. In that caution, the canon for us must show some inadequacy. The death of god is, in part, the growth in the ability of observers to call religious beliefs false and condemn them as fanatical, when they are ruthless. Of course, I introduce the word "aesthetic" in full awareness that not all the canonical theorists would have appreciated the word or even quite made sense of it. But the idea that human beings are driven by cravings that demand that social and natural reality have coherence, purpose, and meaning is hardly foreign to many in the canon up to 1900. What are such cravings, if not aesthetic?

Fanaticism, secular and religious, and by whatever name, has always existed. I now return to the first of the two points: secular fanaticism can be worse than religious fanaticism. That is part of what modernity signifies. I mean that the death of god achieves two cultural results—certainly in the West. First, inherited religion becomes less and less able to confer meaningfulness on the world. Second, and more important, the very ability to devise comprehensive and aesthetically compelling fictions and stories about a transcendental or supersensible realm and get people to believe them with sufficient strength to build a whole culture around them nearly evaporates. Let it be allowed that there is a strong possibility that thinkers—but also half-thinkers, would-be thinkers, and pseudo-thinkers—need comprehensive meaningfulness more than ordinary people do, even if great and good thinkers struggle to discipline their need more than ordinary people do. The fact remains that ordinary people are susceptible to a kind of enchantment that lies over the bedrock of their intellectual indifference. They can be aroused for a while and enlisted in causes. Their imagination can be gratified and captured. They can have, if only briefly, satisfactions they did not dream they could have. A few can acquire an addiction to comprehensive meaning-fulness. On the whole, however, new doctrines eventually fade; their hold over ordinary minds fades. In any case, meaningfulness is now mainly secu-lar: its vehicles are nation, class, race, ethnicity, or civilization (way of life). (Some parts of the Islamic world are currently an exception to the secular rule but not guilty, or not yet guilty, by their independent force, of atrocities com-parable to those of the twentieth century in scale. Perhaps when technologi-cal prowess, or ingenuity that compensates for the lack of prowess, comes to fanatical Islam, it will enroll itself in the annals of colossal evils in modern times.) But whatever the case with Islam, all secular doctrines that insist, without appeal, on categorizing people along group-identity lines can be made or forced to yield a comprehensive or overriding meaningfulness. All are seductions of the susceptible.

Devout leaders, not cynical ones, inspired fanaticism in the twentieth cen-tury, in which almost every fanaticism was secular. They were more suscepti-ble than their followers. There have been no protracted policies with enor-mous atrocious effects without an initiating secular fanaticism that devoured leaders, who then managed to spread their contagion among their indispens-able following. None of the secular fanaticisms have any built-in limits. Although religion can inspire an utterly merciless fanaticism, it usually holds within itself some respect for moral limits to which appeal can be made. And religion's fanatically atrocious policies stem in significant part from the worldly motives of those who act in its name. What I say is naturally not meant to exculpate religion. It is only to suggest that when we try to face the worst in the twentieth century—understand that "worst" as worse than almost anything else in previous centuries, because of the scale—we cannot begin to understand the various atrocious phenomena without the category of fanaticism. In turn, we cannot understand fanaticism without the category of aestheticism. Leaders want to make the world meaningful by design. They are prepared to act without moral limits. Their aestheticism overrides every other consideration and does so, at least for a time, guiltlessly. The scale of results of such fanaticism, such secular aestheticism, given numerousness of population and technological prowess, must be and has been enormous. Indeed, so great is the scale of effects that it is impossible to assign to any of the vices—the four deadly sins (that are not weaknesses of the flesh) and their variants—sufficient power even to will it. Even the worst psychopathology cannot lead directly to such a scale. Given the scale of effects, every leader is a midget in comparison to the powers unleashed; there is some horrible dis-continuity between even the most obsessive purpose and the scale of ensuing atrocities. The policy makers amaze themselves with their own power. There is no proportion between potency and mere vice or between potency and mere goal. At the end of its journey, the initial hyperactive imagination arrives at the unimagined, which is, to the victims and the observers, unimaginable.

The leaders of atrocities are merely human beings at their worst; what makes them the worst is that they are the most deluded by their own imagination. They live in another world. They are detached from reality, except strategically and tactically. They are realistic in everything but their aims. Of course, the pessimistic moral psychology of the canon—to the extent that it does not reckon with the imagination—must be inadequate. Only an imagination grown hyperactive by aesthetic cravings that are not recognized as what they are, can, in the work of persisting in policy despite the unprecedented scale of awful effects, function as a fatal substitute for vices or personal pathology. In scanting the theme of the active imagination, the canon's adequacy to the twentieth century is abridged, and so also, perhaps, its adequacy throughout time. Its pessimism can mislead us.

* * * * *

I have suggested that the theme of imagination's vicissitudes is not confined to the fanatical and ruthlessly hyperactive force of imagination. There is another side to the story. If aggressive imagination is the rabid capacity to make the absent present, to imagine a different reality, to have designs on reality, the complementary phenomenon is to fail to see the reality that is present and thus to treat it as if it were absent, and instead to define all reality as one's own little piece of it. The theme of imagination's vicissitudes and their role in political life must include the failure of benign imagination, in the particular sense of moral blindness. Such failure is humanly congenital and incurable, but it must be understood, if policies with atrocious effects of unprecedented scale are to be faced. Hyperactive imagination cannot do its work without the accompaniment of moral blindness.

The initiators introduce the aesthetically compelling fictions and stories, redefinitions of the world through new or rearranged categories, that seduce the susceptible, including themselves. But the fanatical drive to realize what has been hyperactively imagined, to make actually present what has hitherto been absent, could not proceed unless the initiators and leaders used their capacity, all the while, to make absent what is present. The present is not allowed to be present. The people they lead and the people they destroy must cease being people in their eyes, must lose their humanity and become unreal or less real or caricatures of reality. On the other hand, it helps that the followers, to be suitable instruments, must have an added incentive to stay, in their own way, blind to what they do. This blindness, which is always at one's disposal, is guaranteed to turn lethal when the fanatically aesthetic contagion has been spread by the initiators. As far as politics is concerned, hyperactive imagination, within souls who possess it, is indissociable from inactive imagination in leaders and followers alike. Those who design a new reality must be selectively blind to existing reality. Then when they are able to pursue their imaginative design without limitations on their conduct, they must absolutely refuse to see what is present before them because they want to see only what they imagine. When followers are seduced, they are fortified in the disposition not to see what they are doing. Failure of imagination is also in part a phenomenon of aestheticism because the as it were unseeing violence done to reality is done for the sake of realizing or defending the design, its shape and meaning. My emphasis will be on the moral blindness of followers.

Perhaps an alternative formulation is that blindness is not inactive imagination or a failure to use imagination, but rather another kind of active use of the imagination. It replaces what is there by what is not, as if by a process of illusion or hallucination, or by what Orwell called "doublethink." In any case, what goes on is more than ordinary self-deception. I will not explore this conceptual issue here.

William James titled one of his most trenchant essays "On a Certain Blindness in Human Beings" (1899). His subject is expansive, but one of his meanings is that almost no one grants equal reality to others. It is necessarily the case that each person must be more real to himself than anyone else can be: he is conscious to himself in a way that no one else can be conscious to him. But with the exercise of imagination, another person can at least be understood as real to herself as he is to himself. One cannot inhabit another while remaining oneself; one cannot inhabit another at all. The inwardness of another is absent, that is, invisible, but it can be made present with a little bit of benign imagination. One can take thought and say to oneself, I am not the only reality. Whether other people are like me or different, with me or against me, more foolish or less, I cannot deny their reality as fellow human beings. They matter to themselves as I matter to myself. They are almost certainly as well intentioned or sincere or as conformist as I am. To entertain such sentiments is not necessarily to feel compassion or even empathy. It is not to imagine yourself in the place of another and thus show sympathy, or to imagine another person inside yourself and thus show restraint. These familiar moral operations of the imagination, highlighted by Rousseau and Adam Smith, do indeed show that a large part of the cure for the pathologies of hyperactive and inactive imagination is the cultivation of the moral imagination. These operations certainly work against blindness. But the feeling for the human reality of others is a distinct use of the benign imagination, and lack of such a feeling is a distinct and awful deficiency. When one is morally blind, one refuses to allow the present to be present; one keeps it out of sight of the mind's eye, even though it is there.

And when, by yet another semipathological process of both using the imagination and refusing to use it, the I incorporates itself into a We, one can still make the very difficult effort to say to oneself, in a momentary suspension of the group feeling, that these outsiders are as real to themselves as we are to ourselves. This moral use of the imagination, in which blindness lifts for a moment, does not automatically lead to the affirmation that they are as good or as morally right as we are; just that they are as inwardly innocent as we are, as devoted to themselves as we are to ourselves. (Of course, the moral claims of content must reassert themselves. The final judge of the merits of the case, however, must be a third party, except of course when there are atrocious effects. In such a case, anyone at all should be able to judge the obvious, but most people will not choose to; they will substitute partisanship for judgment). Every side is likely to contain only a few persons who are capable of at least this momentary or episodic use of the moral imagination and thereby redeem not their side but the honor of humanity.

I call the self-incorporation of oneself into a We a double process of using the imagination and refusing to use it. My reason is that by identifying with a group to the point of merger and self-loss, one sees oneself as everywhere present in others and everywhere absent as oneself. One therefore claims to be what one is not (dissolved helplessly in solidarity or camaraderie with others) and also claims not to be what one is (an individual). In miniature, strong group adherents show the symbiosis of hyperactive and inactive imagination.

The negative power of the inactive imagination to produce enormous atrocious effects manifests itself in another way, in another kind of blindness than the denial that others are as real to themselves as I am to myself, but a kind that does not preoccupy William James. The phenomenon is familiar enough, but perhaps has not been considered sufficiently by the canon up to 1900. I refer to blindness to the overall policy that enfolds one's own small contribution to it. One wills not to see with the mind's eye what one cannot see with the body's eyes. The literally invisible is made to remain altogether invisible and regarded as absent or nonexistent. Here too, the present is not allowed to be present. Such blindness is the normality of followers on every level. Being seduced by a fanatical (fantastic) doctrine makes it even easier to remain in blindness, which is the normal condition of the heart. One loses sight of—if one ever had in sight—the policy or system in which one plays one's small part. One does one's job, one goes through the motions, and comes to the end of the day. Some may even find fulfillment in their work. People are routinely able to compartmentalize their lives in another way: nice at home, they are beasts at work. Or, followers can shield themselves or be abstracted from the preconditions of what they do and the effects they help to produce. This latter tendency is especially pronounced in bureaucratic management of atrocities. But the former tendency, compartmentalization, shows itself in war and in direct superintendence or direct commission of other atrocities. From a political perspective, the most important meaning of the examined life—certainly, if Socrates is the model—is inquiry into the larger system or policy in which one is asked or told to play one's part. Even where the effects of fanatical doctrine have worn off, such inquiry is so difficult as to seem unnatural or suicidal.

The phenomenon of inactive imagination is the heart of the story of atrocities on an unprecedented scale in the twentieth century. I mean that though we may want to single out the initiators and (perhaps also their sadistic underlings) for special censure and call persons of these two sorts monsters, the hard truth is found elsewhere. It is found in blindness, the blindness of those who, though seducible by doctrine, lack hyperactive imagination but also characteristically lack the ability to grant that others are as real as they are, that everyone is as real to himself and herself as one is to oneself, and who also lack the ability to examine themselves sufficiently to notice the larger pattern that enfolds their everyday contribution to that pattern. The inertial force of blindness, in its two aspects, is the key to atrocious policies. Without followers, hyperactive imagination is powerless. To be sure, without initiators, ordinary people would content themselves with vices and pathologies and their confined effects, which are appalling enough. But they (we) are susceptible—seducible to some extent and for a while by what is aesthetically compelling, by the narratives, stories, myths, and pseudo-explanations, by the ideologies, that misrepresent reality to reshape it and make it more gratifying. There is a universal if shallow yearning to be taken in.

Seduction is more the fault of the seduced than of the seducer. To be seduced is to be given a mostly aesthetic inducement to stay blind, to forget altogether that one is blind. But even untouched by fanatical doctrine, one has too many reasons to stay blind. Then, too, we must not leave out the pleasures of collegiality and the pleasures that inhere in the web of organizational relations. These kinds of pleasure can be so absorbing that one's job, at whatever level, becomes utterly detached from its content; it becomes part of a whole self-enclosed world. Thus, followers lend their numbers to victimize people like themselves, they cooperate in their own victimization, and after a while, their leaders victimize them as if they were the enemy.

\* \* \* \* \*

I have no rigorous way of accounting for any particular design created by a hyperactive imagination. I also cannot find plausible any account that presumes to explain why at any given time seducers are successful or why their designs are lethal. But I believe that the pessimism of the canon does not treat sufficiently the ferocious power of the creative, hyperactive imagination. On the other hand, the pessimism of vices, present in the canon and of course present in the politically relevant humanities, does, however, make a substantial contribution to understanding some part of the energy behind blindness. But blindness is not a comprehensive term for the vices; blindness is a motivated failure to see reality, a readiness to treat the present as absent, a refusal to allow the present to be present. Does the canon up to 1900 address this matter sufficiently? Or is the canon very helpful about the aestheticism of our seducibility?

Now, contingency has a lot to do with the successful initiation of protracted policies that pile up an immense human cost, whether the purpose precisely is to pile up that cost or whether the purpose is pursued regardless of any cost. There is no necessity of occurrence in any given time or place, but we should expect atrocious policies to appear—we do not know where or when. To repeat my suggestion: the pessimism of the canon up to 1900 does not adequately prepare us to expect the atrocious scale of the two world wars, the use or threatened use of atomic weapons, the Holocaust, the gulags, the induced famines, the wars waged by the United States in Korea and Vietnam, the massacres all over the world. A lot of the canon teaches that we should always expect the worst from people in actual, unideal societies. Nevertheless, the scale of wrongdoing in the twentieth century is discontinuous with that which the pessimism of the canon presumes. Paul's idea of original sin (and Augustine's elaboration of it) and Kant's idea of radical evil are profound contributions to moral psychology but were not framed with this scale of wrongdoing in mind. (Only some of the biblical god's acts are on this scale, but what is his moral psychology?) Nietzsche really did not envisage the scale. Perhaps not even Dostoyevsky in *The Possessed* envisaged it, though I think he came pretty close.

What I would have expected is that the canon should prepare us to see that the scale of effects does not increase because of increased vice. To be sure, new developments in a combination that favored the unbridled play of imagination's vicissitudes—unreligious and boundless fanaticism, numerousness, and magical technological prowess—could not be foreseen. To expect that they could have been is foolish. But the real issue is not the favoring conditions that change with time but the steadiness of human nature, the unchangeable hold of imagination's vicissitudes, the transformative power wielded by those vicissitudes over the vices. Ideally, the canon would have taught that at any given time human beings will be destructive up to the limit of their technological capacity. To the imagination in its vicissitudes, the size of the moral costs—the scale of atrocities—does not matter. A large part of the reason is that the aesthetic significance of the policy (its logic, pattern, or design) will overpower the sense of costs. Indeed, the aesthetic significance may well increase as the costs increase. Reality is kept at bay by aggressive or passive aestheticism. Such steadiness, not merely in the nameable vices but in hyper-active imagination and moral blindness, and perhaps to the point of infinite destruction and self-destruction, is missed by the canon up to 1900.

*  *  *  *  *

The atrocious policies in the twentieth century that I have singled out cannot be poured into one mold. It is possible, however, to adapt Aristotle's view of the dynamism of superiority and inferiority as found in Book 5 of the *Politics*. Speaking very abstractly, we could say that putative equals, like the great powers in World War I, may become fanatical in struggling to claim superiority or resist inferiority. Next, as a result of defeat, a prior arrogant superiority turns into a humiliation that seeks vengeance. Nazism answers, in part, to that description. Or, exalted by victory, a prior humiliated inferiority seeks to revenge itself on the past. This last point may help to account in part for Stalin, Mao, Pol Pot, and their kindred.

The twentieth century is the century of mass slaughter, mass murder. The conduct of both world wars demonstrates the readiness, sustained by blindness, to pay the cost of mass murder in the fanatical pursuit of aesthetically compelling ends, especially an aesthetically gratifying picture of the world in which one side or the other is master. I am not saying that all sides are morally on a level. No, only that the pursuit of victory was so ferocious, by even the better side, that the moral cost of its victory subtracts an appreciable quantity from its moral advantage. In both wars, the good side perpetrated atrocious policies in the name of not surrendering or winning. On the other hand, the Holocaust and gulags, the massacres, the induced famines and cultural revolutions, and the use and threatened use of atomic weapons demonstrate that mass slaughter may as well be the purpose itself of policy. The number of deaths (actual or threatened) in these latter policies is so large that one cannot simply say that the infliction of death is a reluctantly employed tactic on behalf of some further end. When means are terrible on a large scale, they are not only means but are signs and displays of superhuman power. And if following Aristotle, we say that an element of vengeance figures in the use of such so-called means, as is likely, the vengeance is abstract, personalized (the target group of countless persons is figured as one monstrous person), yet impersonal (one's own group is imagined as a superperson through which one has being and identity). I say "abstract" vengeance because face-to-face bloodthirstiness or bloodlust—a staple of the canon's pessimism—is not nearly as important an ingredient as the aesthetically compelling thought of boundless vengeance. And only as abstractly aesthetic, as sublime, can vengeance be boundless. Mass slaughter is needed for the story or narrative of the destiny of abstract personages to come out right, to have the right shape. The motivation is therefore not sadism, even though the personal sadism of a minority (in aggregation) can be accommodated by the protracted policy.

The long and short of it is that the canon up to 1900 has scanted the interconnected themes of hyperactive imagination and inactive imagination: on one hand, fanatical and aesthetically compelling designs on reality, and on the other hand, blindness in the double sense of refusing to accord full reality to everyone but oneself or one's group and refusing to examine oneself in relation to the enfolding policy in which one finds oneself doing one's particular and often little but necessary job as well as one can. The complex interplay of making the absent present and the present absent is scanted. In facing large-scale policies of destruction, we should therefore hesitate before rushing directly to human wickedness as the undiscriminating explanation, as canonical writers often do. I gladly admit, however, that the canon can improve moral sensitivity and thus assist us—despite its politic reticence (before the Enlightenment) about fanatical commitments that groups make to unwarranted beliefs—in the often shunned task of calling a spade a spade.

I also realize that the canon's pessimism can profitably disabuse its readers of optimism concerning human beings. Where would moral indictment be without Socrates, or moral disappointment without Jesus? The canon revolves around these two characters. Their nearly impossible ideals are haunting, impossible to exorcise completely. (We should pay special attention to the way in which canonical writers fearing for the safety of the political realm, even when some of these writers despise it, make strained and often overly ingenious efforts to neutralize the radicalism of both of them.) Then, too, there are many particular passages in the canon that insidiously insert themselves in one's sensibility, the manner by which one characteristically looks at the political and cultural realms, and affect one's perception to an extent that one is scarcely aware of. Even for the task of being adequate to the unprecedented scale of atrocities in the twentieth century, the canon up to 1900 cannot be dispensed with. I myself have sought assistance from Aristotle, among others. Still and all, the canon up to 1900 is not sufficient in its net sense. It may not take us close enough to the plausible belief that when hyperactive imagination and inactive imagination work jointly, the scale of awful effects, no matter how vast, has no moral significance but is likely to have an overriding aesthetic significance. In this respect, human nature has been and will remain pretty constant. That means that we can expect future atrocities on as large a scale as those of the twentieth century, or even larger, or at least we need not be surprised if they occur. Who knows but that human extinction and extinction of many other species lie at the end of the journey of technologically conditioned imagination in its vicissitudes.

\* \* \* \* \*

In closing, I want to mention, without exploring, the several contributions that Heidegger and Arendt made in the twentieth century to our understanding of the scale of atrocities. I do not mean that these two are the only political or politically relevant thinkers who help us understand the atrocious twentieth century. Simone Weil on group self-love as the cause of much oppression, Sartre on the imagination and on the pathos and terror of unsponsored freedom, and Foucault on the mentality of technicians and on the biopolitics of the twentieth century are invaluable. I have relied on them all in my composite analysis of these atrocities. But I have obviously relied most on Heidegger and Arendt. I have tried to bring together the following elements from their writing.

In the case of Heidegger, the essays intelligently collected in *The Question Concerning Technology* by William Lovitt, give instruction on the nature and effects of Nietzsche's teaching that god is dead and on the human effort to replace god that was mounted for centuries before Nietzsche's teaching. To replace god is to receive the world, as it presents itself, with infuriated alienation and resentment and consequently to respond to it with a fanatical spiral of self-aroused will to treat the world as material to be known comprehensively as material and thus as ready to be remade, reshaped, and stamped with the human image, at any cost to human beings or to the human essence. The task is rationalistic and technological; technology drives the rationalism, drives the science; a fundamental irrationality underlies the rationalism and the fanatical and unbounded quest for ever more potent technology. In the process, human beings themselves become material in the hands of leaders and directors and technicians, the raw material or "standing reserve" for unprecedented projects made possible by technological prowess. There seems little resistance, on anyone's part, to using or being used. All this is lodged in Heidegger's remark that "the essence of technology is nothing technological."[3]

In an undeservedly notorious but actually profound remark, Heidegger says in his Bremen lectures of 1949, "Agriculture is now a motorized food-industry—in essence the same as the manufacturing of corpses in gas chambers and extermination camps, the same as the starving of nations, the same as the manufacture of hydrogen bombs."[4] The repetition of "the same as" makes the point that content does not matter to technicians because they can convert any purposive activity into an activity that has no purpose but the

activity itself. The difference between production and destruction is insignif-
icant because either activity to them is above all a glimpsed and taken (if not
always forced) opportunity to show their skills in feats of virtuosity. Any
society intent on ruthless production will find a seamless continuity in turn-
ing to mass destruction. Human beings, like human wants, are merely problems to be solved. Brilliantly inventive technicians and scientists consum-
mate what I have been calling moral blindness. And from a sufficient
physical distance, the hyperactive imagination of the leaders and initiators
converts their purpose into something as if it were seen from a height: a pattern to be imposed and completed, as if human beings and everything human
were only material that awaited its aesthetically (dramatically or categori-
cally) compelling shape and representation.

The canon of political theory can never be wholly adequate, even when
supplemented by the politically relevant literary humanities. Humanly
inflicted suffering is a bottomless subject, while the larger subject of moral
psychology is an unending, undying subject: it is what Socrates is eager to
think about in Hades indefinitely, if there be a Hades. Nonetheless, the canon
can be made more adequate to the subject of human suffering on an unprecedented scale in the twentieth century. The most important political theorist in
this endeavor is Hannah Arendt. On the matter of hyperactive imagination,
her analysis (in *The Origins of Totalitarianism*, 1951, and subsequent editions) of the craving that reality conform to the expectant aesthetic sense and
of the zeal with which initiators and leaders strive to reshape the world in
accordance with their imperious fictions is indispensable. (All I do is add the
word "aesthetic.") The highest totalitarian aims are not practical or pursued
by a utilitarian calculus. Utility concerns only the efficiency of methods.
Although she does not extend this idea theoretically back to World War I—
she does refer to the "insane nationalism" responsible for "the catastrophic
decline of Europe"[5]—it deserves a larger place. We can see the fanaticism of
nationhood working to produce an unprecedented scale of atrocious death
and suffering. This is not quite the same as "the catastrophic decline of
Europe." As it is, her discussion of both anti-Semitism (racism, more generally) and of imperialism in *The Origins of Totalitarianism* introduces the
theme of the rage to remake social life as an embodied and enacted fiction,
the rage to bring to perfection the lethal drama of charged categories (that is,
of ascribed identities hardened to stone).

Her posthumously published *Thinking* (1978) is marvelously suggestive
of the way in which the quest for meaning dominates philosophical thinking
and is independent of the quest for the truth of cognition. Totalitarian ideologies, but really all ideologies, are merely parodies of philosophical thinking.
The main difference—and it is huge—is that totalitarian and other fanatical

ideologies are murderous. She shows how human numerousness—what she calls, perhaps following Nietzsche in *Thus Spoke Zarathustra* (First Part, "On the New Idol"), superfluous populations—favors the large scale of murderous activity, whether the targets and victims are the initiators' own populations or their declared enemies. Then, too, both aspects of blindness (denying full reality as human beings to other human beings and having no interest in the protracted policy that enfolds one's everyday contribution to it) are memorably captured in her concept of the banality of evil in *Eichmann in Jerusalem* (1963) and in adjacent ideas in other writings.

Altogether, Arendt breaks new ground, even though her ideas of course need revision. In the background is her interest in what she sees as the radical break with the past in the nineteenth century, the dissolution of the trinity of religion, authority, and tradition. She says, "Kierkegaard, Marx, and Nietzsche are for us like guideposts to a past which has lost its authority. They were the first who dared to think without the guidance of any authority whatsoever."[6] That break is Arendt's version of the death of god, and we can connect it to the atmosphere in which fanaticism becomes mostly secular and achieves its boundlessness. There are symptomatic affinities and causal relations between the dissolution of the trinity of inherited social bonds and the unprecedented scale of atrocious effects in the twentieth century. But the three philosophers whom she singles out do not prepare us for the simple thought that the same human traits and passions can effortlessly remain themselves in the face of an unprecedented scale of atrocious effects. Undeniably, Kierkegaard and Nietzsche offer insights on hyperactive imagination and Marx on blindness (especially in his fertile and extendable notion of commodity fetishism). (By the way, does Freud help? Most of all, perhaps, in his theory of the dream work in *The Interpretation of Dreams*, 1900. Lacan's reworked Freudian view of the psyche as thrown incurably off-center at an early age and as therefore ever afterward falsely appeased also helps.) Yet Arendt's notion of living by and for fiction casts a tragic light on the whole human record, and she, more than anyone else, in the range of her interconnected ideas on the human condition, takes the canon into the twentieth century and, I am sure, beyond.

*NOTES*

1.   Thomas Hobbes, *Behemoth* (Chicago: University of Chicago Press, 1990), 95.
2.    G.W.F. Hegel, *Lectures on the Philosophy of World History. Introduction: Reason in History*, trans. H. B. Nisbet (Cambridge, UK: Cambridge University Press, 1975), 163.

3.  Martin Heidegger, *The Question Concerning Technology*, trans. William Lovitt (New York: Harper, 1977), 35.

4.   Berel Lang, "Heidegger's Silence and the Jewish Question," in *Martin Heidegger and the Holocaust*, ed. Alan Milchman and Alan Rosenberg (Atlantic Highlands, NJ: Humanities Press, 1996), 7-11, 17.

5.  "Rosa Luxemburg," in Hannah Arendt, *Men in Dark Times* (New York: Harcourt, Brace & World, 1968), 43.

6.  "Tradition and the Modern Age," in Hannah Arendt, *Between Past and Future*, 2nd ed. (New York: Viking, 1968), 28.

# 3     POLITICIZING THEORY

*ADRIANA CAVARERO*

*1.*

**T**he expression "political theory" is something of an oxymoron. Etymologically, both terms are derived from ancient Greek. "Political" is an adjective that comes from *polis*, which, according to Hannah Arendt, "is the organization of the people as it arises out of acting and speaking together."[1] It corresponds to the human condition of plurality inasmuch as "plurality is specifically *the* condition . . . of all political life."[2] "Theory" is derived from the noun *theoria*, which signifies contemplation and pertains to the human experience of seeing, to the field of vision. In its Platonic declension, which was subsequently passed on to the entire Western tradition, *theoria* is a vision of true and universal objects or ideas ("idea" literally signifies "the visible") with the eyes of the mind (*nous*). As Arendt points out, this noetic type of vision is considered by Greek philosophy to be the attitude that characterizes the only truly free way of life: the *bios theoretikos*, translated into Latin as the *vita contemplativa*. It is distinguished from the *bios politikos*, in Latin the *vita activa*, which "denoted explicitly only the realm of human affairs, stressing the action, *praxis*, needed to establish and sustain it."[3] The traits of theory and politics are therefore opposed to one another. Consisting in contemplative thought, the first entails a solitary thinker who withdraws from the world of human plurality to enjoy the noetic vision of desensitized and therefore abstract and universal objects. The second is a shared and relational space generated by the words and deeds of a plurality of human beings. Given that "only action is dependent on the constant presence of others,"[4] politics belongs to the worldly sphere, always particular and contingent, where plural interaction produces a series of unpredictable and uncontrollable events. Theory deals instead with the solitary vision of an otherworldly, abstract, universal, and, most of all, stable order of objects. Because of these opposing characteristics, theory and politics are incompatible. The fact that they appear together in the expression "political theory," the label of a scientific discipline practiced in our universities, depends, as Arendt suggests, on a formidable metaphysical lie that owes its existence symptomatically to Plato.

The history of political theory and the mortification of the genuine sense of politics begin with the myth of the cave, which is at the center of Plato's *Republic* (514a-516e). There is a twofold itinerary in the scene of the myth: one route ascends and the other descends. With the ascent, the philosopher leaves the cave of human affairs to contemplate ideas, or rather he abandons the uncontrollable world of action to take refuge in the reassuring world of theory. With the descent, the philosopher returns to the sphere of the *polis* to impose the principles he has derived from the objects of theory: "the ideas become the unwavering, 'absolute' standards for political and moral behaviour."[5] The just *polis* of the *Republic* consists in a political order *built upon* and governed by the order of ideas. Plato is explicit in this regard: the philosopher is a painter of constitutions (*polition zographos*) who, once he has cleared his canvas of any effectively existing feature of the *polis* (in this case, contemporary Athens), designs the just city taking as his model the idea of justice he contemplated in his mind (500e-501c). Since it was designed by the philosopher, who alone contemplates (*theorein*) ideas, the just city has philosophers for its rulers. Philosophers are in a position to order: both in the sense that they construct the political order and in the sense that they give orders to others, they command. Fortunately, the Western tradition does not inherit this Platonic conviction that bestows on philosophers the scepter of command, but it does inherit from Plato the canons of political theory as a specific discipline that applies the principles of *theoria* to politics.

One could also call it political philosophy, but the issue does not change. Philosophy, for the Western tradition that begins with Plato, is theoresis *par excellence*. *Theoria* and *philosophia* coincide. Political philosophy and political theory, from both an etymological and a conceptual standpoint, raise the same oxymoronic problem, the crux of which is always the following: the characteristics of theory, derived from experience pertaining to realm of sight, are transferred, as foundational criteria, to the register of politics. Although its principle is action, politics becomes a sphere that is constructed and regulated by principles of vision.

In "The Nobility of Sight," an essay of phenomenological derivation greatly admired by Hannah Arendt, Hans Jonas demonstrates how the characteristics of *theoria* depend on the typically Greek privileging of the sense of sight.[6] Sight perceives objects that are in front of the one who sees and are, for the most part, characterized by a permanence in space and time. They are stable, enduring, present. Moreover, sight perceives several objects simultaneously, and it sees them as distinct from one another in their discrete difference. Sight pertains to the dimension of space, and "real space is a principle of co-temporaneous, discrete plurality irrespective of qualitative differences."[7] Sight implies, furthermore, an active position of the subject, who not only can open and close her eyes when she wants to but is not affected by the objects of her vision. Objects do not look at the subject and, most of all, they do not constrain the subject to look. The object that I see "is present to me without drawing me into its presence."[8] Sight secures, in other words, a position that is detached and uninvolved. The world is there, it is visible, but it is up to us whether we look at it or not. Seen from a distance with detachment, things acquire an objective status of stability and permanence, guaranteeing the reality of *being* as *presence*.

The entire philosophical lexicon, which since Plato conceives *theoria* as the contemplation of real, lasting, immobile, and true entities, insofar as they are visible or inasmuch as they are ideas, is founded on the effect of objectivity and presence produced by this detached gaze. The decisive element is *presence*; a presence that belongs both to the spatial dimension concerning the object that stands before the contemplator and to the temporal dimension of an instantaneous *now* that he eternalizes. Transferring the experience of the bodily eye to that of the mind, *theoria* absolutizes the self-contained circuit between this permanence of the object and the *now* of the gaze. Frozen in an immobile presence, mental images come, in this fashion, to constitute the specific spectacle of *theoria*. Contrary to Derrida's claim, Western metaphysics is videocentric, not phonocentric.[9]

Along these lines, Hannah Arendt reminds us that, according to Pythagorean doctrine, life is a festival to which the best people come as spectators (*theatai*).[10] *Theoria* and passion for viewing spectacles share the same lexical root. Even the Olympic gods love the spectacle of the world. In Homer, they watch what happens from above and, at times, go down to earth to offer themselves as a portentous spectacle for the mortals, who repay them with an astonished stare. The life of the philosopher, for the Pythagoreans as for Plato, is the best life precisely because, as *bios theoretikos*, it falls within the category of spectacles. The objects of the philosophical spectacle are not, however, tangible things, persons, events, or even portentous apparitions. They are instead ideas contemplated by the mind that, eternalized in the *now* of their presence, return the divine privilege of this eternity to the contemplator. Envied by mortal creatures, the gods who enjoy the spectacle of the world are immortal. The philosopher imitates them and surpasses them by conquering an expanded present, the fruit of immaterial visions, which suggests that the sphere of thought is eternal. Eternity, understood as a dimension immune to the movement of temporality, thus becomes the mark of truth.

The spectacular mark of truth finds its definitive foundation in the Platonic doctrine of ideas, but it originates in the attitude of the Ionic philosophers. Struck by the totality of things appearing to their gaze, or rather by a *physis* that presents itself as an *all*, they inaugurate the spectacular and prelogocentric phase of philosophy. Before Heraclitus and Parmenides, philosophers are not concerned with *logos*. Astonished, they admire the multiform totality of nature, and they attempt to give a *single* name to its principle: water, *apeiron*, air, atoms. This astonishment still leaves traces in the work of Plato and the young Aristotle; they refer to wondering (*thaumazein*) as the experience that gives birth to philosophy.[11] For those who know how to view it, the spectacle of the world is a beautiful order, a *kosmos*, that captures the onlooker's attention and provokes wonder. In the philosophy of the classical period, which transforms this wonder into the contemplation of noetic objects, the question of order is shifted from the world of *physis* to the register of *theoria*. *Theoria*, in fact, regards objects that are characterized by an order (*kosmos, taxis, harmonia*); an order, specifically, that binds objects together in a totality and thus proposes itself as a system. "To bind" is *legein* in Greek, a verb that also means "to speak" precisely because discourse is a connection of words that binds them, one to the other, in a certain objective order, that is, in accordance with the rules of the system of signification we call language. Thus, one can understand why *logos*—as the modern translations of Greek texts attest—can mean both discourse and reason, both language and thought. However, the significance of *logos* for the philosophers of the classical period lies not in the phonic aspect of spoken words nor in the register of signifiers but in the objective order of mental signifieds (the *ideai* of Plato and the *noemata* of Aristotle) contemplated by *theoria*. As the entire history of philosophy proclaims, despite the variety of its authors and the conflicts of its factions, these signifieds and, obviously, the order that organizes them must be *clear* and *distinct*. Even science, understood in the modern sense of the word, is convinced of this. The lexicon of vision relates to theory whether we intend theory as metaphysics or we intend it as science. Consequently, in spite of our scrupulous efforts to distinguish disciplinary specificities that have as their object politics, the oxymoronic problem that concerns political theory regards not only political philosophy but also political science.

Certainly, in contemporary debates, this distinction has precise methodological explanations, and it goes back to the modern separation of science and philosophy. The dispute over the regime of truth, which characterized the twentieth century and which continues today, adopts *science* as a true and incontrovertible model of knowledge. The canons of science thus become the criteria of measurement for verifying the scientific character of the discursive tradition that Western culture has handed down under the name of *philosophy*. The result of this operation is that a large portion of this discursive tradition, or rather, the part that is not included within the canons of science, is negatively branded as *metaphysics*: a sort of literary production lacking in scientific rigor and, for this reason, untrustworthy. The problem is far more complex than this brief treatment suggests, and it leads to the well-known distinction between analytic philosophy and continental philosophy, among other things. As complex as the matter is, however, it still does not eliminate the constitutive adherence of science—and philosophy broadly intended—to the sphere of noetic vision. To put it another way, even though science characterizes itself, particularly in modernity, as a rigorous form of knowledge that is distinct from certain "metaphysical" styles of philosophy, its roots are in *theoria*. Significantly enough, in the classical period of ancient Greece, this problem does not exist (and not simply because the term "metaphysics" is a posthumous label given to what Aristotle calls "first philosophy").

For the Greeks, there is only one form of objective knowledge—certain and rigorous, true and incontrovertible—whose stability is guaranteed by the features of *theoria*: its name, *episteme*, signifies precisely "that which stays still, stable and is always the same." *Episteme* includes philosophy, mathematics, geometry, astronomy, and physics insofar as they are forms of knowledge founded on the noetic vision of universal, stable, incontrovertible, and true principles. This does not imply that, already with the Greeks, within the sphere of some of these disciplines, empirical verification is excluded or the processes of induction, deduction, or even of falsification are devalued. But it does entail that, notwithstanding the specificity of these fields of investigation, the regime of truth always belongs to the noetic sphere of *theoria*. To think, to reason, to argue, to classify, to verify is always a noetic activity that implies *theorein*. The adherence of theory to "seeing" is not a metaphoric accident due to the Greek etymology of the term, it is the original mark of its conceptual substance and its historical inheritance. As the Enlightenment taught us, to reason is to clarify, to make clear, to illuminate obscure points, to see better, to bring to light, to free the investigation from the darkness of ignorance and error.

2.

From Plato onward, notes Hannah Arendt, "the dichotomy between seeing the truth in solitude and remoteness and being caught in the relationships and relativities of human affairs became authoritative for the tradition of political thought."[12] This dichotomy also established a hierarchy, or rather, a firm belief in the superiority of the principles of theory, insofar as they are true, evident, stable, and certain with respect to the unpredictable and uncertain, mobile and contingent, world of human affairs. Consequently, as the

Platonic myth of the cave well illustrates, to "save" politics from the unpre-dictability and contingency of action, the task of discovering universal prin-ciples capable of regulating politics was entrusted to *theoria*. The principles of theory were then applied to politics. Stripped of its own characteristics, that is, of plurality, action, and the direct involvement of agents, politics was conceived in accordance with characteristics pertaining to the solitary expe-rience of contemplation instead of the relational and plural one of action. One of the most noteworthy results is that politics is subsumed by the central problem of *order*, or rather, it becomes "any form of action necessary to keep men together in an orderly fashion."[13] This is evident in the political doctrine of Plato's *Republic*. Contemplating ideas, the philosopher sees how they *bind themselves* to one another in accordance with a harmonic order—in which each thing plays its part—that corresponds to justice (*dikaiosyne*) (443c-d, 500c). Symptomatically, therefore, within the Platonic horizon, justice is not simply an element of order, a value among others, it is order itself. This explains why the just *polis*, constructed on the idea of justice, reflects the order of ideas. The celebrated role of analogy in the philosophy of Plato, according to which the harmony of the cosmos corresponds to that of the polis and the individual soul, is no more than an homage to the order of ideas taken from *theoria* and applied to every other realm of inquiry.

This inherence of order to *theoria*, which is the crux of the political pro-posal of Plato's *Republic*, constitutes a lasting inheritance that went on to characterize the disciplinary status of political theory. As the tradition attests, political theory identifies the question of politics with the question of order. Authors and epochs set forth the problem and resolve it in different ways, but the problem itself continues to center on the essence of politics as order. Hobbes and Locke, for instance, constructing the State on the theoretical fic-tion of natural individuals and the social contract, do nothing but return, the specificity of politics, once again, to the question of order. They confirm that political theory recognizes its specific object in an order—governable and predictable, convenient and reassuring, just and legitimate—that neutralizes the potentially conflictive disorder inscribed in the natural or prepolitical condition of human beings. The "state of nature," insofar as it is an image of disorder on which political *theory* imposes a remedy, in fact corresponds to the sphere of human affairs that Plato placed at the back of the cave. No dif-ferently than the Greek philosopher, modern political thought continues to think of justice as order. A book like John Rawls's *A Theory of Justice* offers proof of this as, for Rawls, justice always refers to the formal dimension of rules and procedures.[14] Order, the genuine object of *theoria*—of philosophy and science—is affirmed by the entire tradition as the fundamental issue of politics. Ignoring the oxymoron at its core, political theory thus cancels the unpredictability of plural interaction that constitutes the *proprium* of politics and replaces it with the predictability of order.

### 3.

Thus, according to tradition, political theory consists in theorizing politics, or rather in the reduction of politics to the principles of *theoria*. It seems necessary, therefore, to overturn this assumption and to finally think political theory in terms of *politicizing theory*. It is not easy for political theory to break away from the constitutive characteristics of *theoria*. There is, in fact, something of a paradox in expecting that theory would repudiate *theoria*. The present political crisis—for the most part, a conceptual crisis that demonstrates the obsolescence of the categories of the nation-State with respect to the phenomenon of globalization—can, however, encourage us to radically rethink political theory. We do not need to find an alternative expression that names, in a less compromising fashion, the legitimacy of a discipline that, against its own tradition, finally decides to think the *proprium* of politics. We need instead to dedicate the work of thinking, or if one prefers, the work of theory, to understanding this *proprium*. To use a formula that is reminiscent of Spinoza, politics asks to be studied according to its own principles insofar as politics is a field of plural interaction and hence of contingency. These principles, exemplarily illustrated by Hannah Arendt, have to do with the plurality of human beings insofar as they are unique beings rather than fictitious entities like the individual of modern political doctrine, and they have most of all to do with a relational dimension of reciprocal dependency, which exposes as false the autonomy and self-sufficiency on which individualism insists. A political theory that freed itself from the prejudicial characteristics of *theoria* would therefore have to renounce the primacy of order and, consequently, the disposition to conceive universal, homogenous, and orderable subjects.

In the history of political philosophy, political order and the political subject appear as coherent aspects of the same construction. Each construction of political order as a given form is also a construction of its subject, or better, of the one whom this form constructs and subjects to itself: a subject that is, notoriously, male and phallologocentric. For the just *polis* of Plato, this subject is substantially the philosopher; for the *polis* of Aristotle, as we read in his *Politics*, it is, more democratically, man (*anthropos*) who, insofar as he is a rational animal (*zoon logon hechon*), is, for that very reason, a political animal (*zoon politikon*) (1253a 1-18). The founders of the modern doctrine of the State instead conceive of the political subject as an atomized individual,

free and equal. This is precisely the individual that still works as the fundamental category for the contemporary debate on politics, both for the positions that focus on the individual and for those that oppose them, either by
complicating the individual with the postmodern version of fragmented identity or by drowning it in communitarian substance. It remains nevertheless
true that, from the Greeks to the present day, to each political form conceived
by *theoria*, there corresponds a subject. To avoid the all-too Cartesian sound
of the term "subject," we could also say that each political form implies a
political approach to the question of ontology. In other words, since politics,
however one understands it, concerns itself with human beings, each conception of politics raises the ontological question, or rather, it presupposes a
political ontology. The connection is so tight that, as Giorgio Agamben
affirms, one could also say the reverse is true: "Each ontology cannot but
implicate a politics."[15]

Convinced of this close connection, Hannah Arendt claims that the political ontology of the Western tradition is, from its Greek origins onward, manifestly false. Man, whom the celebrated Aristotelian formula defines as *zoon
logon hechon* and *zoon politikon*, contradicts the basic principles of politics:
"Man is a-political. Politics is born among men, and lies therefore decidedly
outside of Man."[16] Arendt means to underscore the fact that, since it com-
bines and neutralizes the plurality of all men (and all women, it must be
added) in its concept, Man cannot be political because, within the horizon of
Man, there is no plurality and, consequently, there are no relations. In the
logic of the One, the mirror image of the logic of the Same, there is no *in-
between*, no relational space generated by action. And consequently there is
no politics. That which the Western tradition calls "politics" is in reality a
model of depoliticization that, beginning with Aristotle and, even more so,
Plato, expels the plural and relational dimension of politics; in fact, it reacts to
the contingent and uncontrollable character of this dimension. According to
Arendt, even the modern form of democracy is part of this depoliticization.
And in point of fact, it continues to decline the logic of the One through a
notion of the individual that consists in the "more or less successful repetition
of the same."[17] Although it allows for a pluralism of opinions and the parties
that represent them, the fundamental lexicon of equality negates plurality
and, consequently, politics.

It is important to stress that the Arendtian horizon of plurality should not
be confused with the theme of pluralism addressed by the branch of contemporary thought that defends the freedom of expression and the respect for
cultural differences. Plurality, for Arendt, is first of all a characteristic of the
human condition, the incontrovertible *fact* of a fundamental ontology or, if
one prefers, of a radical phenomenology. Each human being appears to oth-

ers "in such a way that nobody is ever the same as anyone else who ever lived, lives or will live."[18] From birth, which announces the newborn as a new beginning, onward, each existent appears as unique and capable of beginning new things. It is precisely this that human beings have in common: uniqueness in plurality, or rather the uniqueness that renders them plural and the plurality that renders them unique. Rejecting the foundational and universalistic logic of the subject and any other fictitious entity constructed by the tradition, Arendt takes this ontology as her point of departure for thinking politics. She therefore defines politics as the sphere of plural interaction where "with words and deeds we insert ourselves into the human world, and this insertion is like a second birth, in which we confirm and take upon ourselves the naked fact of our original physical appearance."[19] Words and deeds, both included in the Arendtian category of *action*, correspond in fact to the ability, possessed only by the human being, to express his uniqueness, or rather, to distinguish himself, to "communicate himself and not merely something."[20] Insofar as it is the sphere of action, politics adopts and fulfills the ontology of plural uniqueness. In traditional political theory, the ontology of fictitious entities—man, the individual—is functional to the centrality of the issue of order or, to use Foucault's term, of discipline, insofar as it is subjection, normalization. In Arendtian political theory, the ontology of plural uniqueness instead generates a conception of politics, which is intrinsically undisciplinable, characterized by the fragility and contingency of plural interaction, namely, action as plural action, that is, as interaction "acts into a medium where every reaction becomes a chain reaction and where every process is the cause of new processes."[21] This means that boundlessness and unpredictability are inherent to politics. In Arendtian terms, politics does not consist of forms that put subjects in order by subjecting them to a norm and excluding those who do not belong—insofar as they constitute the figure of the other, the stranger, the alien—within this normalization. Politics is a relational space—from which no one is excluded because uniqueness is a substance without qualities—that opens when unique existents communicate *themselves* reciprocally to one another with words and deeds and closes when this reciprocal communication ceases.

Consequently, we can say with Arendt that wherever this plural uniqueness is not placed in the foreground (wherever it is not welcomed, respected, set down as a value of primary and inalienable importance) there is no politics. Politics, as envisioned by the tradition, where order presupposes and organizes fictitious entities, betrays that which is most proper to politics. In this sense, totalitarianism, which amassed in the camps of human beings who were killable insofar as they were already reduced to bare life, that is, dehumanized individuals by reducing them to the reality of an automaton, is the utmost negation of politics.

Although it is not as barbaric and absolute, there is, according to Hannah Arendt, a negation of politics in each of the forms of organization that keep men together in an orderly fashion without leaving room for what she calls action. It is, in fact, worth mentioning again that, in Arendtian terms, action, beyond being a capacity for initiative, is a relational event that generates *space* for reciprocal self-revelation. With words and deeds, human beings communicate their uniqueness first of all, actively and reciprocally, in a fundamentally shared space. They communicate themselves insofar as they are unique and plural. They communicate their incommensurability inasmuch as it is absolute difference. This is why politics demands to be conceived not only as a realm that places the value of uniqueness before the traditional issue of order but that targets any residual form of order—norms, rules, agreements—to guarantee the opening of free spaces for action. In this view, then, political order does not coincide with a general form of discipline that neutralizes the risky, unpredictable, contingent, and unruly effects of plural relationality; rather, it becomes that which protects and guarantees the spaces opened by this relationality.

### 4.

The amendment of political theory proposed thus far, in terms of politicizing theory rather than theorizing politics, makes explicit reference to the position of Hannah Arendt, and it adopts both her vocabulary and conceptual framework. It is, however, worth noting that though Arendt is the first to denounce the traditional subjection of politics to the principles of *theoria*, she is not alone in conceiving politics in terms of an ontology that insists on a plurality of unique existents in relation to one another. We find a similar position today in the speculative thought of Jean-Luc Nancy. In his lexicon, which derives the name and concept of plurality from Arendt, uniqueness becomes *singularity* and relation becomes *knot*. To "democracy's empty truth and subjectivity's excessive sense," he opposes "a politics of the incessant tying up of singularities with each other, over each other, and through each other, without any *end* other than the enchainment of (k)nots."[22] Such a politics consists, "first of all, in testifying that there is singularity only where a singularity ties itself up with other singularities."[23] This is, therefore, a politics that coincides immediately with the ontological status of the being-*in*-common of singular existents: because "the singular is primarily *each* one and, therefore, also *with* and *among* all the others. The singular is a plural."[24] Contrary to Arendt, what Nancy calls politics does not therefore imply *action*, that is, it does not consist in the interaction of words and deeds, it is instead simply the way of being, the fundamental ontological condition of singular existents who are in common because they appear to one another. Rather than exhibit themselves actively, they are passively exposed: "being-in-common means that singular beings are, are presented, appear only insofar as they appear together (cum), are exposed, presented and offered to one another."[25] The political, for Nancy, corresponds precisely to the *in* of this being *in* common. Favoring, particularly in less recent works, the term "community," he in fact grounds politics in the *with*, the *among*, the *in*—which correspond, in the Arendtian lexicon, to the *in-between*—that is, in any word particle that alludes to the original ontological relation inscribed in the plurality of singular beings. Thus, according to this meaning, politics does not regard a certain, historically determined, type of relation, knot, or bond, such as, for instance, the Aristotelian *koinonia* or the contract of the doctrines of natural law, or, more generally, the law. Politics *is* the bond: a bond inscribed in the ontological status of singularity, insofar as singularity entails plurality and therefore the relation, the tying up of one to the other. The three categories that produce one another reciprocally—uniqueness, plurality, and relation—determine, according to Nancy, the *coincidence* of ontology and politics.

This coincidence is, precisely, absolute. Although he conceives it, like Arendt, in spatial terms, Nancy does not understand politics as a space that is produced contextually by the words and deeds of agents and thus as an active scene that has a local and temporal dimension. He understands it instead as the relational given of the ontological condition. This relationality has the characteristics of a tying and a spacing that extend themselves *as far as* the ontological fact of human plurality. Politics is already, at once and immediately, the existence of singular beings, tied one to the other, who share the common space of their plurality. And it is not only politics, in Nancy's texts, that gets flattened into ontology. Every disciplinary sphere—ethical, political, aesthetic, gnosiological, and so on—is in fact substantially reduced to a variable of the perspective declining in different ways the ontological theme of the knot. The question that draws in the various disciplinary horizons is precisely the *among* and the *with* of a singularity that is a plurality, or, to put it in Arendtian terms, it is the *in-between* that "relates and separates men at the same time."[26] In the lexicon of Nancy, however, this separation becomes a sharing. Existence, in fact, "*is*, only if it is shared." What binds us together, the political or the community, is the same thing that shares us.

It shares *us* is, at the same time, it shares *itself*. Symptomatically, this is also true of *logos*.

The theme of *logos* is obviously not irrelevant to the tradition of political theory. The logocentrism of politics is one of the most well-known aspects of Western culture. Concerning this, one can, in fact, point out that the traditional corpus of political theory begins, in classical Greek philosophy, with two variants that, emphasizing in different ways the ambiguous meaning that the term *logos* has in the Greek language, help to construct two extremely influential models: one of Platonic and the other of Aristotelian inspiration. Both are logocentric but while in the former *logos* is identified with a system of thought, in the latter the general meaning of *logos* as speech is preserved. With Plato, in fact, *logos* winds up coinciding with the order of signifieds, or rather, ideas insofar as they are the visible and silent objects of *theoria*. Aristotle, instead, dwells on *logos* insofar as it signifies speech, discourse, language, and thus he stresses its character of verbal communication. In other words, contrary to Plato, Aristotle does not derive the criteria of political order directly from the principles of *theoria*; instead, he takes the fictitious entity "Man" from *theoria* and defines it as a *zoon logon hechon* that is, for this reason, a *zoon politikon*. According to the *Politics* of Aristotle, Man is political because he speaks and, more precisely, because he signifies with words that which is good, useful, harmful, right, or wrong for the community (*koinonia*), that is, because he signifies the values that produce the community as order (1253a 10-18). One can understand, therefore, why the label of "neoaristotelianism" is applied to the work of contemporary supporters of democracy, who understand politics as dialogue, as an exchange of opinions, or, to use Habermas's terms, as communicative action.[27] Symptomatically, precisely for her attention to the political essence of speech, Arendt is also sometimes numbered among the neoaristotelians.

It is important to stress, however, that the intrinsic political character of speech does not consist, for Arendt, in its function of expressing that which is good, right, useful, and harmful for the community but instead consists in the ability to express and communicate to others the uniqueness of the speaker. Speaking, each human being communicates himself, the irreplaceable character of his uniqueness, the incommensurability of his singular and contingent existence. Thus, the Arendtian conception of politics functions as a radical critique both of the Platonic political theory that emphasizes the role of *theoria* and the Aristotelian one that instead valorizes the role of *logos*. In other words, the originality of Arendt's ontology, which founds itself on the plurality of unique existents, lies in her proposal of a new, absolutely antitraditional, formulation of a political theory finally understood as a politicization of theory.

As to Nancy, despite his undoubtedly antitraditional stance, the objection raised to his suggestion that ontology and politics are immediately coincident surfaces again with regard to his reflections on *logos* as knot and sharing. Glossing a famous verse of Holderlin's—"ever since we are a dialogue"— Nancy explains that we are our dialogue: "we are this among-us, that is language, and reciprocally, language is the among-us."[28] Language "itself is the insubstantial tie"[29] where the meaning of spoken words is only a secondary and consequent effect of the tie itself insofar as it is the original meaning. Every other meaning, every other process of signification, presupposes this meaning. Like Arendt, Nancy therefore privileges the relationality of *saying* with respect to the universal horizon of the *said*. He can thus affirm that the event of politics "could be called the *seizure of speech*,"[30] which should not be understood either as the democratic principle of the freedom of speech or as a plurality of "multiple wills competing to define a Sense."[31] It is, in fact, the singular entry—always singular precisely because it is spoken by someone—into the concatenation of speech, into the *legein* insofar as it is a bond. This concatenation is indissoluble, reticular, infinitely interrupted and tied again. It tends "toward the most naked function of language, toward what one calls its phatic function: the maintenance of a relation that communicates no sense other than the relation itself."[32]

Nancy's politics of the *seizure of speech* distances itself significantly, therefore, not only from the Habermasian horizon of communicative ethics but also from the Arendtian horizon that insists on the active and contextual character of relationality, of the political substance of speech insofar as it is the communication of uniqueness. In Nancy's view, speech—the practice of speaking, of engaging in dialogue, of communicating—is also reduced to a verbal figure of tying, that is, to the figure of a pure relationality that, insofar as it is the fundamental ontological condition, does not consider the concreteness of the context and does not need to be actualized. In other words, Nancy adopts the Arendtian claim that politics consists in the relation between unique existents, but he empties it of its constitutive characters of plural action and thus of interactive space. For Arendt, politics is not simply a relation, as it is for Nancy: it is a certain type of relation that is *interactive and contextual*. To put it another way, politics, understood in the Arendtian sense, does not coincide with ontology; it is instead a way of actively responding, that is, of taking charge, with words and deeds, of the ontological status of uniqueness, plurality, and relationality.

Rescuing political theory from the metaphysical fallacies of its Platonic foundation and its Aristotelian variant, Arendt allows us to radically reformulate the concept of political theory itself. In this subversion of political theory, theory and politics take on a new meaning through a politicizing of theory. *Theory* now concerns the vision of an ontology that frees itself from the traditional primacy of fictitious entities. *Politics* stresses that this ontology, far from contradicting the characters of the plural sphere of action, con-cords with them and finds in them a full realization. This is, therefore, a polit-ical theory in which the visual features of *theoria* do not perform the meaning of politics. If anything, the opposite occurs. What is at stake here is a politics that, insofar as it is the plural sphere of action and therefore the realm of con-tingency, orients the perspective from which theory "regards" ontology.

### 5.

Given that the tradition of political theory, applying the principles of the-ory to politics, has depoliticized politics, the proposal of a political theory that finally politicizes theory can also be understood as a repoliticization of politics. This proposal may appear more or less interesting or methodologi-cally plausible but, like all proposals that involve a rethinking of political the-ory, it risks remaining a mere speculative exercise if it is not confronted with the needs of the present. To deconstruct the history of political theory makes sense only if the categories used for this deconstruction aspire to respond to the current *crisis* in politics. Symptomatically, for Hannah Arendt, this was true after the experience of totalitarianism.[33] And it is true again for us today in an epoch in which the categories of modern political thought seem incapa-ble, not only of comprehending, but even of describing contemporary scenar-ios. What has happened, for instance, to the sovereign and territorial State in the era of globalization? What has happened to the disciplinary power of order, aspiring to control and homogenize individuals, in the play of the Web? What has happened to the concept of the enemy in the "war" against an international terrorism that is omnipresent? These and other questions, more or less tragic and pressing, do nothing but confirm today the rapid decline of the political categories on which modernity was founded. They prove to be obsolete, cumbersome, useless; the words of a script written for a past epoch. One perceives, at times with dismay and painful anxiety, that today a new dis-location of power is in play. But power itself, the central lemma of the entire history of political thought, now assumes forms and modes that the lexicon of the tradition no longer knows how to express.

We need a new political lexicon, a conceptuality that rejects the categories inscribed in the familiar and thus reassuring model of the modern State. As regards political theory, it is not therefore a matter of updating the canons of its disciplinary paradigms, of perfecting the methodological premises, or of adjusting the argumentative framework to rigorous principles that guarantee their scientificity. It is instead a matter of seizing the opportunity, inscribed in the present crisis, to radically rethink politics, freeing it from its traditional subjection to the depoliticizing effects of *theoria*. To put it another way, we need a new political theory that does not limit itself to reorganizing modern categories in a different way to adapt them to new scenarios but that registers their collapse to radically rethink the matrix of politics itself. Hence, the foundational role that, on the suggestion of Hannah Arendt, this new political theory recognizes in the ontology of plural uniqueness, insofar as it is opposed to traditional ontology.

This opposition is crucial. In Arendtian terms, it corresponds to the rejection of the ontology that centers itself on the question of *what-ness* of being and focuses instead on the question of *who* each one is. It is useful to point out that the question of *what-ness* does not only regard and produce fictitious entities—Man, the subject, the individual, the person—but it also concerns the problem of the so-called cultural identities based on ethnicity, religion, sexuality, class, and so on. The question, inherent to the problem of identity, asks: What does it mean to be an African American, a Muslim, a lesbian, and so forth? In the past two decades, the modern political debate has had to confront symptomatically the contradiction between the paradigm of the universal individual and the plural identities of a multiethnic and multicultural society. How does one reconcile universality with differences? The question, especially in feminist theory and postcolonial studies, often leads to a critique of the universalistic paradigm inasmuch as it is the historical product of an improper universalization of Western man, understood as white and male. In this debate within the English-speaking poststructuralist horizon, the position of Judith Butler emerges as particularly original and widely hegemonic. She thematizes identities in accordance with their inclusive or exclusive power, as effects of a performativity that "accumulates the force of authority through the repetition or citation of a prior, authoritative set of practices"; she proposes a political strategy that mobilizes these naturalized identities through a parodic and subversive repetition that makes them proliferate in an uncontrollable manner.[34] The effect of stabilization does not, in fact, concern only hegemonic identities—like those that define the subject as white, male, and heterosexual—but any identity that normalizes itself through a process of repetition. Each type of identity, as a reiterated and therefore stable response to the question of *what* someone is, arises again as a system of inclusion and exclusion, that is, it confirms the obsession of political theory with order and discipline.

Aimed at a politics of disordering subversion, Butler's ontology is therefore an ontology of permanent mobility. It nevertheless risks rendering a final and irreverent homage to the grammar of the *what-ness*, out of which the entire history of Western ontology has emerged. The Arendtian ontology that focuses instead on the question of *who* someone is therefore appears more convincing, especially now when the political model of the West is at its crisis. It is, after all, precisely this question that determines the political character of action inasmuch as it is the plural disclosure of uniqueness.

> Action and speech are so closely related because the primordial and specifically human act must at the same time answer to the question asked of every newcomer: "Who are you?" This disclosure of who somebody is, is implicit in both his words and deeds.
>
> In acting and speaking, men show who they are, reveal actively their unique personal identities and thus make their appearance in the human world, while their physical identities appear without any activity of their own in the unique shape of the body and sound of the voice. This disclosure of "who" in contradiction to "what" somebody is—his qualities, gifts, talents, and short-comings, which he may display or hide—is implicit in everything somebody says and does.[35]

The sphere of *what-ness*, here exemplified by Arendt as personal qualities and talents, can be usefully extended to the question of cultural identities. As Bonnie Honig notes, "From Arendt's perspective, a political community that constitutes itself on the basis of a prior, shared and stable identity threatens to close the space of politics, to homogenize or repress the plurality and multiplicity that political action postulates."[36] The ontology of the *who* does not do away with cultural identities and community belonging, but it does keep them from becoming the foundation of politics. The *who*, in fact, underscores the primary value of an existent without qualities, memberships, cultural identities. Above all, politics, as an interactive relation, is called on to take responsibility for this value. Politics is therefore a relational space—contextual, contingent, and groundless—that opens everywhere for everyone. The permit for entry into this space does not require membership in a group that shares an identity. Identity, in fact, must be left behind or subordinated to the genuine political character of mere relation. It is those who are present, insofar as they actively expose themselves to one another as existents clothed only in their uniqueness, who produce the local political character of the context. Responding with words and deeds to the "truth" of ontology, the plural relation decides the *proprium* of politics.

Claiming that the principal category of the political is relationality should not, however, appear as an arbitrary and, even less, a scandalous act. From a certain point of view, everything that the tradition calls politics is in fact a transfigured or, better, a disfigured form of relation. Plato calls it *harmonia* of ideas: a just conjunction concerning the noetic order, which functions as a criterion for the construction of the best *polis*. Employing the term *koinonia*, Aristotle understands it both as a natural aggregative process and, most of all, as the sphere of common meanings. The contract of natural law philosophers represents a bond that, in giving birth to the State, counters the lack of relationship inscribed in the *bellum omnium contra omnes* (Hobbes) or the potentially peaceful but practically conflicting relationship inscribed in the state of nature (Locke). These are, however, types of relations that are, precisely, disfigured: negating the plurality of unique beings, they fail to recognize that plural relationality that, as an ontological given, constitutes their very matrix. These are, that is, figures of community that immunize themselves to the contagion of relationality. The relation, in fact, far from protecting, ordering, reassuring, or disciplining, expresses that uniqueness without qualities that bind each one to the other. It places them "face to face": it exhibits the naked bond, not yet clad in cultural protections, that each time, contextually, locates unique beings in relation to one another, enacting them as plural.

### 6.

Globalization is one of the names given to the current crisis of politics. One should instead call it deterritorialization. From a certain, let us say static, point of view, the States today still conserve their territorial dimension, well-defined by borders: a space determined by political and juridical sovereignty. From another, let us call it dynamic, point of view, at present such borders nevertheless tend to disappear: the homogenizing process of globalization renders them inoperative, obsolete, superfluous. As Seyla Benhabib, who explores in depth the different sides of the problem, notes, "territoriality is fast becoming an anachronistic delimitation of material functions and cultural identities."[37] In the globalized world, the spatial imaginary changes radically.[38] The modern State, insofar as it is a territorial state, deals with borders that produce an "inside" and an "outside." The global world does not have any "outside," if not other planets still to be globalized and yet already symbolically preglobalized by the satellites that illuminate our nights like metallic heavenly bodies. Within the horizon of the State, distances render some States close and others remote. Within the global horizon everything is instead near and simultaneous. Modeled on the world of business (the market, finance, the trade mark, or, to use a term of Naomi Klein's, the *logo*), globalization travels at telematic velocities in a realm without distances, limits, or boundaries.[39] The simultaneous time of the global contracts space, annihilating its dimensions.

In a much-debated film of 1940, "The Great Dictator," Charlie Chaplin impersonates a Jewish barber who, because of his resemblance to Hitler, finds himself in the shoes of the dictator. In the most famous scene, he plays with the globe: improvising a sort of totalitarian dance, he dribbles and rolls it. The scene is useful for illustrating the difference between totalitarianism and globalization. Chaplin/Hitler, who incarnates the necessary figure of the *head* of state in the totalitarian movement, conceives of the world as *his* territory of conquest and expansion: there are countries to annex and borders to level. In the end, if the totalitarian war succeeds, there will be no more States of different colors on the globe but only one color—black, one imagines— that covers all of the lands on the surface. Instead, in the case of globalization, the States are not conquered and the borders are not leveled. They simply are no longer effective, although they remain to decorate the surface of our existing globe. Territorial and sovereign, the States still exist, we know their names and borders, we speak of them every day, but the *power* that is in play in globalization no longer rests in sovereignty or in any other feature inscribed in territory. In the global era that comes not *after* but *beyond* the Leviathan, the concept of sovereignty seems to have exhausted even its symbolic reserve. As to the figure of the *head* of state, the globalizing power, even with its actors in plain view, does not require it, just as it does not require the willful and projective subject. This power is pervasive, diffuse, decentered, reticular, and impersonal. Its machine, not by chance essentially technological, appears to run by itself.

Eluding all univocal definitions, the power that is in play in what Hardt and Negri call the capitalist imperial machine of globalization alludes first of all to a triumph of economy over politics.[40] "Economy"—this too is an old word of Greek origin—is perhaps not the most adequate term, but it serves to synthesize an interlacement of heterogeneous and complex phenomena, such as the market without borders and, ideally, without laws, the extraterritoriality of the multinational corporations, the electronic instantaneousness of the stock market, the marketing of image in the spectacular era of consumerism, the dislocation of the productive processes in the southern part of the world, the exploitation of labor in impoverished countries, the pollution of the planet, and so forth. It is instead more difficult today to indicate in detail the various phenomena that would appear under the rubric of politics. In fact, in the era of globalization, the incongruous substance of the territorial State also renders the political lexicon that is founded on it obsolete. Democracy, equality, liberty, rights, and all the categories that belong to this lexicon necessarily presuppose a territorial dimension. Citizenship itself makes no sense outside this dimension. A global citizenship is unthinkable, insofar as it is a State without borders.

*Global* is, not by chance, a neologism from the point of view of traditional political discourse, which offers the term *national* as an adjectival form of State, for comparison with the *supranational* and the *international*. The political horizon of modernity goes from the small to the large, from the national to the supranational, avoiding however, the risk of passing from *border* to *borderless*: this last term being, traditionally, nothing other than an aesthetic attribution for areas of great expanse—the desert, for example—that nevertheless belong to a State or are divided between States. From the perspective of a politics founded on territorial sovereignty, space without borders is inconceivable. Beyond every border there is always another State. The political map of modernity does not allow for a "no man's land." Western cartography makes a coherent system of the world: perhaps bipolar, divided into the two blocks that until the fall of the Berlin wall organized States in clusters, but nevertheless coherent; that is, legible in accordance with one logic only, that of the territory bounded by borders.

To tell the truth, a certain dichotomous division of the Earth also appears in the language of globalization. The most notable figure distinguishes the North from the South of the world, describing them as areas of wealth and poverty. The implied message, very much in keeping with the spirit of uniformity of the global, that unfaithful mirror of universalism, is that *with time* the impoverished countries will also become wealthy or, as one says, emerge from their current state of underdevelopment.[41] In the meantime, they are exploited as productive supplies of cheap labor. Symptomatically, this turns out to be an opportunity for exporting the model of the modern State in *zones* that are far away from the Western ones that gave birth to it. Organized as a kind of *camp* for the exploitation of slave labor, the factories of the impoverished zones of the world need, in fact, a centralized, possibly strong, political power that controls them and disciplines them. In certain circumstances and in some regions, the global economy needs sovereign States and borders but not democratic governments, or, to paraphrase Weber, the legitimate monopoly of force without the extenuating circumstance of democracy. A different need regards instead the role of borders in the West. Here, so far as the regulation of the migratory flow is concerned, the viewpoint of the global economy does not always coincide with that of a rigorously liberal and democratic politics. It depends on the circumstances. The model of the State is rigid; that of globalization tends to be elastic, uprooted, and mobile. The success of globalization cannot be separated from the mobility of commodity, capital, and people. The State is called to adapt itself to this mobility. The current scenario foresees that politics, in the course of its inevitable demise, will find its raison d'etre again in an adaptation, increasingly less negotiable and more servile, to the dictates of economy.

The decline of the territorial State continues, however, especially in the West where it was born. The extraterritoriality of globalization weakens the form and substance of the territorial State. This explains why, in the debate over the question of globalization, the *global* is not opposed to *territory* but to *local*. It concerns the well-known, apparently paradoxical, phenomenon of the so-called *glocal*: the globalization of the market and technologies sees a resurrection of identity localism that appeals to ethnic and religious roots. The identity negated by the process of deterritorialization of the global is rediscovered within a mythologization of the territorial history of local communities. A narrative that is, essentially, anti-State, or rather, antimodern, performing islands that aspire to assert themselves exclusively and thus to fight one another. Globalization and localization, through the double movement of inclusion and exclusion, seem therefore to work together for the definitive liquidation of the State: the one by frustrating the territorial cartography of sovereignty, the other by emphasizing the territorial roots of community identity.

To respond to the crisis of the present, avoiding the resurrection of premodern myths that constitute its most uncanny aspect, it would be necessary to think the spatiality of the local in different terms.[42] It would be necessary to thematize a *locality without territory*. The advent of the global, precisely because it defeats the State's logic of territory, finally frees a deterritorialized perspective on *locality*. This does not have to be thought of as a smaller portion of national territory or even a transnational "region." Most of all, it is not a zone of the world that is unified by a culture, a religion, a language, a tradition, or a belief. *Locality* is neither tribal nor communal. It is instead a place, without any homogenous or territorial substance, that can arise or disappear in any part of the globe. It is the relational space that Hannah Arendt calls precisely politics. It has been noted that this is "a space in which the terms of political representation and agency are mobilized, displaced from their locus of rigid inscription into categories, concepts and definitions; a space . . . constantly re-enacted, re-told, re-narrated."[43]

"Wherever you go, you will be a *polis*," says Hannah Arendt, quoting a famous sentence that demonstrates, in her opinion, how the political for the Greeks consists of the space that lies "between people living together for this purpose, no matter where they happen to be."[44] The *polis*, according to the Arendtian interpretation, is not physically situated in a territory. It is instead the space of appearance, always and everywhere capable of being enacted, where human beings actively show who they are. We could therefore refer to this *polis* as *absolute locality*: "absolute" insofar as it is "freed" from the territoriality of place and from the historical dimension of time that we call tradition. *Absolute locality* has neither predefined borders nor, even less, fixed or sacred borders. It extends as far as the interactive space generated by those who share it. It is a relational space that happens with the event of this interaction and, together with it, disappears. Its place and time are therefore contingent and unpredictable. "Wherever you go, you will be a *polis*": wherever there is an interactive space between unique beings, who precisely as such disclose themselves to each other, there is politics. Politics pertains to a *locality* that consists of the appearance of unique existents in their active self-exhibition, which is also a display of an incommensurable plurality. *Locality* demands plurality. Indeed, *locality* is made of the relational context of this plurality that opposes the value of uniqueness to the issue of identity.

The horizon of *locality* is not the direct fruit of the *global* but is what globalization, insofar as it is a deterritorializing and extraterritorial force, allows today to open. To put it another way, since the cartography of the States that makes of the world a coherent system has exploded and the topographic parameters that make the world a geography of borders has imploded, the world finally presents itself as a space available for the contextual and contingent advent of *absolute locality*. Emptied of communitarian substance and unbound from territory, locality can now take place any place. This does not mean that *locality*, like the knot of Nancy, is immediately everywhere, as though it were a global condition of human plurality that, for that very reason, is a political community. *Locality* is there and only there where, in any part of the globe, human beings actively show that their uniqueness is the material given, if not the absolute value, of their relation. To say it again in the language of Hannah Arendt, *locality* as a relational space does not concern *what* those who share it are but *who* they are.

Freed, at last, from the cartography of nations, the *politics of locality* prohibits placing cultural identities before the unrepeatable uniqueness of every human being. Faithful to the ontology of the *who*, locality puts *uniqueness without belonging* into play and entrusts to it only the sense of relation. Far from evoking a passivity, this implies first of all the preliminary activity of stripping away our Western, Eastern, Christian, Muslim, Jewish, gay, heterosexual, poor, rich, ignorant, well-educated, cynical, happy, unhappy, and even guilty or innocent being. The strategy of a political theory that reflects on *absolute locality* includes in fact, as its preliminary act, the deconstruction of belonging, the marginalization of qualities, the depoliticization of the *what*. What remains, because it has always been there, is *"who* are you?" as a question directed toward "you who are here": here, in the space of *locality*, contextual and everywhere capable of being enacted, a space opened by this question in which the governing principle of politics, that is, the primacy of the *who* with respect to the secondary status of the *what*, is already at work.

Despite appearances, this is not a utopian politics or even an ethics of good will. It is instead the reconfiguration of a political theory that, inspired by Hannah Arendt, locates the generative and symbolic *nucleus* of politics in the ontology of plural uniqueness. Besides offering a critique of globalization, this political theory pays a debt to the trauma of the destruction that the terrorist attacks of September 11 inflicted on the values and the security of the West. It does not, however, respond to the need for an antiterrorist strategy. It rather looks for a new sense of politics capable of taking from terrorism—and from its possible motives as well as from the logic of retaliation—all sense. There is a sociological, so to speak, and undoubtedly poignant proof of this in the behavior of the New Yorkers who, following the destruction, put up pictures of their family members killed in the Twin Towers disaster on the walls of the city. To the enormity of the terrorist attack, they responded with the exposition of a picture: the simple face of uniqueness. In the fall of 2001, which was also the definitive symbolic fall of the territorial State, the walls of New York told us first of all that the thousands who died on September 11 died *one* by *one*, and are missed *one* by *one* by their family members and by those who, looking at their faces, share their loss. Apparently, it was an emotional response, but nevertheless, from a different perspective, it was not only a far more effective political response than the appeal to the flag, but it was perhaps the most political of the responses yet offered. It underscored the fact that the fragile value of uniqueness requires a sense that contrasts with all of the senses—distorted or correct, monstrous or plausible—that the debate over the event, flags included, has so far produced on the idea of politics. This sense, it is true, is not yet the politics of *absolute locality*, but it is the figure, unfortunately tragic, of the ontological principle that constitutes this politics.

On the walls of New York, for some weeks, a map of uniqueness, plural and irreducible to any systematic reason, replaced the old order of State cartography. There were proper names, in many languages, pronounced with different accents. Behind each, a unique person that was and is now missing. The official registers have not even been able to record the deaths of some of the victims because their existence had never been registered. These were illegal immigrants: a category that is inherent to deterritorialization in the global era of the job market. The opposite of the State, globalization does not want to deal with borders and national territories at all, nor with belonging and cultures. Called or repulsed by the sirens of the global, everyone is wherever, at the moment, they find themselves. The ideal political protagonist of the politics of *absolute locality* is already precisely in this situation, beyond the ethnic ghettos that the metropolises still provide.

Without roots in territory, *absolute locality* is contextual. It does not simply want to found itself in the ontology of uniqueness nor does it want to coincide with it. *Absolute locality* always refers to unique existents who interact and are contextually present: here and now, with a face, a name, a story. *Absolute locality* convokes them, or rather, it is by them convoked, put into being. Generated as a relational space, *absolute locality* implies the proximity, of one to the other, of those who generate it. This proximity is a distance that is neither too small nor too great. It has the physical dimension of gazes and voices. It is sufficient for looking and speaking to one another. Contrary to the global, *locality* does not therefore contract space in the almost simultaneous velocity of communication afforded by electronic means. It instead takes its time for communicating. In the *politics of locality*, before communicating specific meanings—to use Arendt's terms again—those who are present in fact communicate, one to the other, first of all their uniqueness. This signifies that the value of uniqueness is the primary principle of the political scene if not the rule that decides its spatial and temporal disposition. When *absolute locality* takes place, it designs a web of plural proximities in its space. Though they appear together, these proximities communicate one to one, one each time and one at a time. Politics, and, at the same time, its symbolic power, consists of this discrete relationality of *locality*. This is to suggest that *locality*, precisely for the contagion that pertains essentially to the symbolic, has the power of multiplying itself. One, one hundred, one thousand *absolute localities* could be, a bit ironically but certainly not nostalgically, the slogan. Freed also from the logic of territory, which masked it under the concept of the individual, the ontology of uniqueness has a global extension. The politics of *locality* can take place everywhere: unpredictable and intermittent, uncontrollable and surprising.

### 7.

Politicizing theory means to overturn the tradition that instead theorized politics, but it does not mean eliminating the sphere of *sight* that is implicit in theory. Political theory, even that which orients its conceptual axis in accordance with the ontology of plural uniqueness, is always a discipline that consists of a vision and mobilizes the imagination. The vision turns, however, in this case, not to fictitious entities, but to the *datum* of the human condition: it dares to present itself as a radical phenomenology of the fundamental materiality of human beings who are incarnated singularities, existing here and now, in this way and not otherwise. The imagination turns to an *absolute locality* that is not the canonical form of the present but only a possible figuration, a simple hermeneutic principle for the political horizon, not yet present and yet already required, that comes after the epoch of the States. Obviously, political theory does not coincide with politics; it does not consist in acting politically. Political theory is theory: its disciplinary status consists in observing, seeing, and imagining. Inaugurating it, Plato constrained political theory to look upward, that is, to free itself from the *proprium* of politics to remedy its constitutive contingency with the security of order. The crisis of the State model in the era of globalization—the latest figure for the crisis of the Western political history of order—facilitates instead the theoretical gesture of looking downward. Namely, it facilitates the gesture of looking at the contingency of an agency in which plurality is the disclosure of a uniqueness that presents itself as absolute, unclassifiable, and nonorderable difference. This difference appears as disorder and chaos only from the perspective of the traditional obsession with order. Nevertheless, from a wiser point of view, it is a category that enables thinking the insubstantial reality of a political bond, capable of being enacted anywhere and supplied with a rule that affirms the primacy of the *who*. This insubstantial bond has the merit of neutralizing both the well-known conflicting potentialities of the identity bond and the normalizing effect of socially constructed identities.

The term "identity," central in many contemporary debates, has in fact, at least, a double acceptation that concerns different areas of problematization. On one hand, there is the problem of community identity. This kind of identity, when it takes an exclusionary form on the basis of religion or ethnicity, raises not so much the usual question, typical of multiethnic societies, of a democratic safeguard of differences, but rather the question of preserving the spirit of democracy itself against fundamentalism. On the other hand, there is the problem—focused on mainly by the postmodern and poststructuralist theories that insist on the performativity of language—of the various socially constructed identities that stabilize and naturalize, in accordance with a hierarchical order, the meaning of being man, woman, heterosexual, homosexual, white, black, and so on. To this twofold declination of the question of identity correspond different strategic approaches. The approach concerning the case of community identities deals with complex issues: on one hand, the community bond, when it is not exclusive and therefore in principle reconcilable with universalism, is safeguarded; on the other hand, the bond of exclusionary and fundamentalist communities, insofar as it contrasts radically with the democratic principle and the modern political tradition of the West, is opposed. The approach concerning the socially constructed identities deals with issues of a different type: as it is well exemplified by the position of Judith Butler mentioned above, the emphasis is put on a subversive strategy that attempts to mobilize, confound, and dismantle the normative matrix of identity. The inspiring principle of this subversive strategy is therefore a kind of perpetual disordering of order: perpetual because it is indebted to the constitutive mechanism of self-consolidation of order. Ancient and always new protagonist of the scene, the logic of order therefore decides the dynamics of its *other* as infinite subversion.

With respect to the two variants—here simplified in the extreme—of this problematic framework, the imagination of *absolute locality* has the advantage of hinting at a theoretical horizon that rethinks the bond, both freeing it from any identity-based substance and opposing order without paying the debt to a perpetual subversion. The interactive relation that responds to the ontology of plural uniqueness, in fact, consists in a bond that does not have either a foundation in identity or a disordering aim. There are, indeed, rules and principles inscribed in this relation: the primary value of uniqueness with respect to any community belonging, the multiple and horizontal structure of the bond, the contingency of its arising and disappearing in any place, the bare exposition of a self without qualities who depends, in the material context of *absolute locality*, on every other. The only identity permitted, in this economy of political relation, is therefore the one that one could call an altruistic identity.[45] The *other* appears here neither as an intellectual category nor as a collective entity; instead, it always has the face and the unrepeatable story of someone.

This is, after all, the radical challenge of a political theory that, abandoning the traditional vision of fictitious entities, finally politicizes theory and, as Levinas would say, compels it to look in the face of the other. The *proprium* of politics consists precisely in the regulative canon of an agency that does not betray the armless object of this gaze.

## NOTES

*Translated by John Ronan*

1. Hannah Arendt, *The Human Condition* (Chicago: The University of Chicago Press, 1958), 198.
2. Ibid., 7.
3. Ibid., 13.
4. Ibid., 23.
5. Hannah Arendt, *Between Past and Future* (New York: Penguin, 1977), 110.
6. Hans Jonas, *The Phenomenon of Life* (Evanston, IL: Northwestern University Press, 2001), 135-36.
7. Ibid., 138.
8. Ibid., 146.
9. Jacques Derrida, *Speech and Phenomena and Other Essays on Husserl's Theory of Signs*, trans. David B. Allison (Evanston, IL: Northwestern University Press, 1973); see also Adriana Cavarero, "Regarding the Cave," trans. Paul Kottman, *Qui Parle* 10 (1996): 1-20.
10. Hannah Arendt, *The Life of the Mind* (New York: Harcourt Brace, 1978), 93.
11. Ibid., 129-51.
12. Arendt, *Between Past and Future*, 115.
13. Arendt, *The Human Condition*, 13.

14. John Rawls, *A Theory of Justice* (Cambridge, MA: Belknap Press of Harvard University Press, 1971).

15. Giorgio Agamben, "Introduzione a Emmanuel Levinas," in *Alcune riflessioni sulla filosofia dell'hitlerismo* (Macerata, Italy: Quodlibet, 1996), 14.

16. Hannah Arendt, *Che cos'è la politica?*, trans. Marina Bistolfi (Milano, Italy: Edizioni di Comunità, 1995), 7.

17. Ibid., 7.

18. Arendt, *The Human Condition*, 8.

19. Ibid., 176.

20. Ibid., 176.

21. Ibid., 190.

22. Jean-Luc Nancy, *The Sense of the World*, trans. Jeffrey S. Librett (Minneapolis: University of Minnesota Press, 1997), 111.

23. Ibid., 112.

24. Jean-Luc Nancy, *Being Singular Plural*, trans. Robert Richardson and Anne O'Byrne (Stanford: Stanford University Press, 2000), 32.

25. Ibid., 91.

26. Arendt, *The Human Condition*, 52.

27. Jürgen Habermas, *The Theory of Communicative Action*, trans. Thomas McCarthy (Boston: Beacon, 1984).

28. Jean-Luc Nancy, *Luoghi Divini. Calcolo del poeta*, trans. Luisa Bonesio (Padova, Italy: il poligrafo, 1999), 71.

29. Nancy, *The Sense of the World*, 115.

30. Ibid., 115.

31. Ibid., 115.

32. Ibid., 117.

33. Hannah Arendt, *The Origins of Totalitarianism* (New York: Harcourt Brace Jovanavich, 1951).

34. Judith Butler, *Bodies That Matter* (New York: Routledge, 1993), 227; see also idem, *Gender Trouble* (New York: Routledge, 1990).

35. Arendt, *The Human Condition*, 178.

36. Bonnie Honig, "Toward an Agonistic Feminism: Hannah Arendt and the Politics of Identity," in *Feminists Theorize the Political*, ed. Judith Butler and Joan W. Scott (New York: Routledge, 1992), 227.

37. Seyla Benhabib, "Dismantling the Leviathan: Citizen and State in a Global World," *The Responsive Community* 11 (2001): 15.

38. Zygmunt Baum, *Globalization* (New York: Columbia University Press, 1998).

39. Naomi Klein, *No logo* (New York: Picador, 2000).

40. Michael Hardt and Antonio Negri, *Empire* (Cambridge, MA: Harvard University Press, 2000).

41. Dipesh Chakrabarty, *Provincializing Europe* (Princeton, NJ: Princeton University Press, 2000), 37-46.

42. See Edward S. Casey, *Getting Back into Place: Toward a Renewed Understanding of Place-World* (Bloomington: Indiana University Press, 1993).

43. Olivia Guaraldo, *Storylines* (Jyvaskyla, Finland: Sophi Academic Press, 2001), 234.

44. Arendt, *The Human Condition*, 198.

45. Adriana Cavarero, *Relating Narratives*, trans. Paul Kottman (London: Routledge, 2000), 81-93.

# 4    POLITICAL PHILOSOPHY
## AS A CRITICAL ACTIVITY

*JAMES TULLY*

## *INTRODUCTION*

Themes editor of *Political Theory* asked us to respond to the question, 'What is political theory?' This question is as old as political theory or political philosophy. The activity of studying politics, whether it is called science, theory, or philosophy, always brings itself into question. The question does not ask for a single answer, for there are countless ways of studying politics and no universal criteria for adjudicating among them. Rather, the question asks, 'What comparative *difference* does it make to study politics *this* way rather than *that*?' Political theory or philosophy not only spans three millennia of studying politics in innumerable ways but also three millennia of dialogues among practitioners over various approaches, their relative merits, and the contestable criteria for their comparison. Because there is no definitive answer, there is no end to this dialogue. Rather, it is the kind of open-ended dialogue that brings *insight* through the activity of reciprocal elucidation itself. Dialogue partners gain insight into what ruling, being ruled, and contesting rule is through the exchange of questions and answers over different ways of studying politics and different criteria for their assessment in relation to how they throw light on different aspects of the complex worlds of politics—and what counts as the 'different aspects of the complex worlds of politics' is also questioned in the course of the dialogue.[1]

With this horizon of the question in mind, I wish to respond by introducing one among many ways of studying politics and to initiate its reciprocal elucidation by comparing it with others. This practical, critical, and historical approach can be introduced by a sketch of its four defining characteristics.

First, it starts from and grants a certain primacy to practice. It is a form of philosophical reflection on practices of governance in the present that are experienced as oppressive in some way and are called into question by those subject to them. The questionable regime of practices is then taken up as a problem, becoming the locus of contest and negotiation in practice and of reflection and successive solutions and reforms in theory and policy.

Second, the aim is not to develop a normative theory as the solution to the problems of this way of being governed, such as a theory of justice, equality, or democracy, but to disclose the conditions of possibility of this historically singular set of practices of governance and of the range of characteristic problems and solutions to which it gives rise (its form of problematisation). Hence, the approach is not a type of political *theory* (in the sense above) but a species of 'practical philosophy' (politics and ethics), that is, a philosophical way of life oriented toward working on ourselves by working on the practices and problematisations in which we find ourselves.[2] However, the aim is also not to present an ethnographic thick description that aims at clarification and understanding for its own sake. Rather, it seeks to characterise the conditions of possibility of the problematic form of governance in a redescription (often in a new vocabulary) that transforms the self-understanding of those subject to and struggling within it, enabling them to see its contingent conditions and the possibilities of governing themselves differently. Hence, it is not only an interpretive political philosophy but also a specific genre of critique or critical attitude toward ways of being governed in the present—an attitude of testing and possible transformation.[3]

Third, this practical and critical objective is achieved in two steps. The first is a critical survey of the languages and practices in which the struggles arise, and various theoretical solutions are proposed and implemented as reforms. This survey explicates which forms of thought, conduct, and subjectivity are taken for granted or given as necessary, and so function as constitutive conditions of the contested practices and their repertoire of problems and solutions. The second step broadens this initial critique by using a history or genealogy of the formation of these specific languages and practices as an object of comparison and contrast. This historical survey has the capacity to free us to some extent from the conditions of possibility uncovered in the first step and so to be able to see the practices and their forms of problematisation as a limited and contingent whole. It is then possible to call these limits into question and open them to a dialogue of comparative evaluation and thus to develop the perspectival ability to consider different possible ways of governing this realm of cooperation.

Fourth, this political philosophy is practical in yet another sense. The hard-won historical and critical relation to the present does not stop at calling a limit into question and engaging in a dialogue over its possible transformation. The approach seeks to establish an ongoing mutual relation with the concrete struggles, negotiations, and implementations of citizens who experiment with modifying the practices of governance on the ground. This is not a matter of prescribing the limits of how they must think, deliberate, and act if they are to be legitimate, but, on the contrary, to offer a disclosive sketch of the arbitrary and unnecessary limits to the ways they are constrained to think, deliberate, and act and of the possible ways of going beyond them in this context. In turn, the experience with negotiation and change in practice and the discontents that arise in response provide a pragmatic test of the critical and historical research and the impetus for another round of critical activity.

These philosophical investigations thus stand in a reciprocal relation to the present, as a kind of permanent critique of the relations of meaning, power, and subjectivity in which we think and act politically and the practices of freedom of thought and action by which we try to test and improve them. Hence the title 'political philosophy as a critical activity'.

Although this type of political philosophy can be interpreted as a tradition that goes back to the Greeks and up through Renaissance humanism and counter-Reformation critical philosophy, I am primarily concerned with its three recent phases: the practice-based political philosophy of the Enlightenment (Rousseau, Wollstonecraft, Hegel, Marx, and Mill); the criticisms and reforms of this body of work by Nietzsche, Weber, Heidegger, Gadamer, Arendt, Dewey, Collingwood, Horkheimer, and Adorno; and, third, the reworking of this tradition again in light of new problems by scholars over the past twenty years. On my account, this eclectic family of contemporary scholars includes the historical approach of Quentin Skinner and the Cambridge School; the critical and dialogical hermeneutics of Charles Taylor; the extension of Wittgenstein's philosophical methods to political philosophy by Hanna Pitkin, Cressida Heyes, Richard Rorty, and others; the critical histories of the present initiated by Michel Foucault; and the critical studies of Edward Said that apply the critical methods of this tradition beyond and against its Eurocentrism.[4] In addition, this practical and historical approach oriented to testing and going beyond limits has been shaped by a continuous critical dialogue with a contrasting metaphysical and universal tradition oriented to discovering and prescribing limits. This contrasting approach stems from scholastic natural law and Kant, draws on some of the same philosophical sources, and is carried forward by many neo-Kantian political theorists today, especially the work of Jürgen Habermas.[5]

Over the past two centuries, there have been many attempts to summarize this tradition. The essay by Michel Foucault written in the last years of his life, 'What is Enlightenment?', is among the best. Within this brief text, Foucault presents a remarkable synopsis that can function as a précis of the sketch I have drawn:

The critical ontology of ourselves must be considered not, certainly, as a theory or a doctrine; rather it must be conceived as an attitude, an *ethos*, a philosophical life in which the
critique of what we are is at one and the same time the historical analysis of the limits
imposed on us and an experiment with the possibility of going beyond them (*de leur
franchissement possible*).[6]

I would now like to discuss the four defining characteristics of this philosophical *ethos*.

### PRACTICES OF GOVERNANCE

Political philosophy as a critical activity starts from the practices and
problems of political life, but it begins by questioning whether the inherited
languages of description and reflection are adequate to the task. Over the past
two centuries, the main domain of political studies has been the basic languages, structures, and public institutions of the self-contained, representative, democratic, constitutional nation-states and federations of free and
equal citizens, political parties, and social movements in an international system of states. The contending philosophical traditions of interpretation of
these practices seek to clarify the just organisation of these practices: the
ways in which modern subjects (individuals and groups) should be treated as
free and equal and cooperate under the immanent and regulative ideals of the
rule of law and constitutionalism on one hand and of popular sovereignty and
democratic self-determination on the other. Yet, over the same period, six
types of critical study have thrown this orthodoxy of practices and form of
problematisation into question.

Social-democratic theorists have broadened the range of political philosophy to include struggles over nondemocratic practices of production and
consumption, and ecological philosophers have extended the tools of conceptual analysis to our relations to the environment. More recently, feminist
political and legal philosophers have drawn attention to a vast array of
inequalities and unfreedoms in the relations between men and women
beneath formal freedoms and equalities and across the private and public
institutions of modern societies. Philosophers of multiculturalism,
multinationalism, indigenous rights, and constitutional pluralism have
thrown critical light on struggles over recognition and accommodation of
cultural diversity within and across the formally free and equal institutions of
constitutional democracies. Theorists of empire, globalisation, globalisation
from below, cosmopolitan democracy, immigration, and justice-beyond-bor-
ders have questioned the accuracy of the inherited concepts of self-contained, Westphalian representative nation-states in accurately representing

the complex, multilayered global regimes of direct and indirect governance of new forms of inequality, exploitation, dispossession, and violence, and the forms of local and global struggles by the governed here and now. Finally, postcolonial and postmodern scholars have drawn attention to the various ways our prevailing logocentric languages of political reflection fail to do justice to the multiplicity of different voices striving for the freedom to have an effective democratic say over the ways they are governed as a new century dawns.[7]

To employ Stanley Cavell's striking analysis, we can see our predicament as somewhat analogous to Nora and Thorvold in Ibsen's play *The Dollhouse*. Nora is trying to say something that is important to her, but the dominant language in which Thorvold listens and responds misrepresents the way she says it, what she is saying, and her understanding of the intersubjective practice in which she speaks. Thorvold takes it as a matter of course that a marriage is a dollhouse, and he recognises, interacts with, and responds to the problems Nora raises always already as if she were a doll, with the limited range of possible conduct this form of subjectivity entails. As a result, Thorvold fails to secure uptake of her speech act as a 'claim of reason', and so a democratic dialogue over the justice of the oppressive relations between them (which compose their practice of marriage) is disqualified from the outset. She is deprived of a voice in her political world. The first question for political philosophy today is, therefore, 'How do we attend to the strange multiplicity of political voices and activities without distorting or disqualifying them in the very way we approach them?'[8]

The six types of critical study enumerated above suggest that we cannot uncritically accept as our starting point the default languages and practices of politics and their rival traditions of interpretation and problem solving inherited from the first Enlightenment, as if they were unquestionably comprehensive, universal, and legitimate, requiring only internal clarification, analysis, theory building, and reform. If we are to develop a political philosophy that has the capacity to bring to light the specific forms of oppression today, we require an Enlightenment critical 'attitude' rather than a doctrine, one that can test and reform dubious aspects of the dominant practices and form of problematisation of politics against a better approach to what is going on in practice.

One way to proceed is to start with a broader and more flexible language of provisional description, one that enables us to take up a dialogical relation to the political problems *as* they are raised in and animate the concrete struggles of the day and then adjust it in the course of the inquiry, as the six types of critical study have begun to do. Combining thirty years of research of Quentin Skinner and the Cambridge school and of Michel Foucault and the

Governmentality school, one might take as a provisional field of enquiry 'practices of governance', that is, the forms of reason and organisation through which individuals and groups coordinate their various activities, and the practices of freedom by which they act within these systems, following the rules of the game or striving to modify them.[9]

'Government' and 'governance' in the broad seventeenth-century use of these terms and their cognates refer to the multiple, complex, and overlapping ways of governing individuals and groups. The 'practice of governance' and the corresponding 'form of subjection' of governing armies, navies, churches, teachers and students, families, oneself, poor houses, parishes, ranks, guilds, free cities, populations, trading companies, pirates, consumers, the poor, the economy, nations, states, alliances, colonies, and non-European peoples were seen to have their specific rationality and modes of philosophical analysis. By the generation of Thomas Paine, Kant, Benjamin Constant, and Hegel, the term 'government' (and 'democracy') came to be used primarily in a narrower sense to refer to the formal, public 'practices of governance' of the representative democratic, constitutional nation-state (what might be called capital 'G' Government). Political philosophy came to be restricted to reflection on the just arrangement of this narrow set of governing practices and their problems as if they were sovereign, that is, the foundation from which all others were governed and ordered through a constitutional system of laws (and the remainder could be taken over by other disciplines).

However, practices of governance in the broad sense continued to spread and multiply. The scholars of the second and third phases and the six types of critical study today strongly suggest that we are governed in a multiplicity of ways that do not derive from and cannot be deduced from the inherited traditions of interpretation of the forms of reason and organisation of the public institutions of representative democracy and the rule of law: for example, the ways a host of actors are able to govern our relations to the environment or transnational corporations try to govern their global employees, suppliers, and consumers; the ways we are led to recognise and identify ourselves as members of religions, ethnicities, nations, free and equal democracies, civilizations, and others as nonmembers; the ways of governance accompanying electronic communications, new forms of material and immaterial labour, and the desires, coded behaviour, and 'affects' of individuals and groups around class, education, gender, and race; the ways a regime of rights can empower some while excluding or assimilating others; the complex forms of indirect rule that have survived and intensified through formal decolonisation in the latter half of the twentieth century. Therefore, if our studies are to be about the real world of government, we need to start with a language of provisional description capable of illuminating practices of governance in both the narrow and broad sense.[10]

The study of practices of governance, whether narrow or broad, must proceed from two perspectives: from the side of the forms of government that are put into practice and from the side of the practices of freedom of the governed that are put into practice in response.[11] A form of government includes, first, the language games in which both governors and governed are led to recognise each other as partners in the practice, communication, and coordination of their activities; to raise problems and propose solutions; and to renegotiate their form of government, including languages of administration and normative legitimation.

Second, a form of government includes the web of relations of power by which some individuals or groups govern the conduct of other individuals or groups, directly or indirectly, by myriad inequalities, privileges, technologies, and strategies, and who are themselves subject to government by others. Relations of power in this broad sense are relations of governance, as these have developed historically in practices of governance. They are not relations of force that act immediately on unfree and passive bodies and constitute subjects without the mediation of their own thought and action. While coercion and violence can be and are employed as means, they are not to be confused with relations of power. Rather, relations of power are relations of governance that act on free agents: individuals or groups who always have a limited field of possible ways of thinking and acting in response. They are the ensemble of actions by those who exercise power that act on the actions of the governed, working by diverse means to guide and direct them to learn how to conduct themselves in regular and predictable ways—actions that aim to structure the field of the possible actions of others.

Third, as governors and governed participate in the intersubjective and negotiated relations of power and coordinated conduct, they gradually acquire a specific form of subjection or practical identity, a habitual way of thinking and acting within the assignment relations and languages of reciprocal recognition. Again, this form of being 'subject' to the languages and powers of a form of government is not to be construed as a form of identity that determines the self-consciousness and self-formation of the governed down to every detail but, rather, the diverse kinds of relational subjectivity one internalizes and negotiates through participation over time, with their range of possible conduct and individual variation. Practices of governance are thus also practices of subjectification, as, for example, members of representative democracies become citizens through participation in practices of citizenisation.

Because an intersubjective relation of power or governance is always exercised over an agent who is recognised and treated as a partner who is free, from the perspective of the governed, the exercise of power always opens up a diverse field of potential ways of thinking and acting in response. The ways subjects act on their possibilities are 'practices of freedom', and these range across three general types of case. First, individuals and groups act in accord with the rules of the practices in which they cooperate in the variety of ways of going on as usual. Even in this so-called normal activity, the ongoing conversation and conduct among the partners can modify the practice in often unnoticed and significant ways. Second, subjects raise a problem about a rule of the practice in the languages of communication and legitimation or challenge a relation of governance on the ground, enter into the available procedures of negotiation, deliberation, problem solving, and reform with the aim of modifying the practice (such as an appeal to in-house dispute-resolution procedures, courts, representative institutions, constitutional amendment, international law, or legitimate procedures of protest and ad hoc negotiations).

Third, when these institutions and strategies of problematisation and reform are either unavailable or fail because those who exercise power can subvert or bypass them, it is possible to refuse to be governed by this specific form of government and to resist, either by escape or by confronting, with a strategy of struggle, an oppressive, constitutive relation of power that is not open to challenge, negotiation, and reform (and thus is a relation of 'domination'), such as the patriarchal property relations underpinning Nora's marriage. In struggles of this kind (such as struggles of direct action, liberation, decolonisation, revolt, revolution, globalisation from below), the relations of governance are disrupted and the relatively stable interplay of partners in a practice of governance gives way to the different logic of relations of confrontation among adversaries in strategies of struggle. The powers-that-be aim to reinscribe the old regime, perhaps in a modified form, and to supplement their means of enforcement, and the governed seek to transform it and implement new relations of governance and practices of freedom.

Therefore, although political philosophers have always known that the relationship between governors and governed is some kind of unequal struggle or agonism of mutual subjection, we should be careful to distinguish among the three complex practices of freedom that are always possible, even in the most settled structures of domination (as South Africa and Eastern Europe illustrate), and that give the history of the ways humans govern themselves its freedom and indeterminacy. As Foucault summarises,

> At the very heart of the power relationship, and constantly provoking it, are the recalcitrance of the will and the intransigence of freedom. Rather than speaking of an essential antagonism, it would be better to speak of an 'agonism'—of a relationship that is at the same time mutual incitation and struggle; less of a face-to-face confrontation that paralyzes both sides than a permanent provocation.[12]

Practices of governance imply practices of freedom and vice versa.

The practices of freedom and their institutions of negotiation and reform constitute the 'democratic' side of practices of governance: the extent to which those subject to forms of government can have an effective say and hand in how they are governed and institutionalise effective practices of freedom (using 'democracy' in its narrow and broad senses corresponding to the two senses of 'government'). When subjects not only act in accord with the rules but also stand back and try to call a rule into question and negotiate its modification, they problematise this mode of acting together and its constitutive forms of relational subjectivity. This is the context in which political philosophy as a critical activity begins, especially when these voices of democratic freedom are silenced, ignored, deemed unreasonable, or marginalised.

This provisional language of description of the field of contemporary political philosophy in terms of practices of governance and practices of freedom is the first response to the limitations of our inherited languages of representation. It draws our attention to the languages in which the problems are articulated and the contexts in which the languages are employed without disqualifying new political voices at the outset. This language of description can be used to study the traditional practices and forms of problematisation of modern politics, but within a broader horizon that enables us to see them as a limited whole, as one historically specific ensemble of forms of government and practices of freedom among many, rather than as the comprehensive and quasi-transcendental framework, and so bring doubtful aspects of it into the space of questions. In so doing, this approach also discloses the multiplicity of broader practices of governance and freedom in which we are entangled that are ignored, disqualified, or misrepresented in the predominant approaches. To revert to Cavell's analogy, it frees us from prejudging a problem in a practice of marriage as a problem in a dollhouse.

## CONTEMPORARY SURVEYS

As we have seen in the Introduction, the aim of this style of political philosophy is to disclose the conditions of possibility of a historically singular set of problematic practices of governance in the present by means of two methodological steps. The first contemporary, nonhistorical step consists of two critical surveys, first of the languages and then of the practices in which the struggles arise, and various solutions are proposed and implemented or not implemented as reforms. These two surveys enable us to understand critically first the repertoire of problems and solutions in question and second the correlative field of relations of power in contestation.

The task of this first survey is not to present another solution to the problem but to provide a survey of the language games in which the problem and rival practical and theoretical solutions are articulated. There are many methods available in Anglo-American and Continental political philosophy to carry out such a task. The approach I favour draws inspiration from Wittgenstein, J. L. Austin, and the development of speech-act theory into a historical and contextual pragmatics of modes of argumentation by Terence Ball, Foucault, Quentin Skinner, Stephen Toulmin, and others.[13] Speaking and writing are viewed pragmatically and intersubjectively as linguistic activities performed by speakers and writers as participants in language games. Actors in practices of governance and theorists who present rival solutions to a shared political problem are approached as engaged in the intersubjective activities of exchanging reasons and justifications over the contested uses of the descriptive and normative concepts by which the problematic practice and its forms of subjectivity are characterised and disputed. The exchange of reasons in this broad sense of practices of argumentation is both communicative and strategic, involving reason and rhetoric, conviction and persuasion. Participants exchange practical reasons over the contested criteria for the application of concepts in question (sense), including the concepts of 'reason' and 'reasonable', the circumstances that warrant the application of the criteria, the range of reference of the concepts, and their evaluative force, to argue for their solutions and against others.

Why should political philosophers take this pragmatic approach of surveying the various theoretical solutions instead of developing a definitive theory themselves? The answer derives from two famous arguments by Wittgenstein. The first is that understanding general terms—such as freedom, equality, democracy, reason, power, and oppression—is not the theoretical activity of grasping and applying a definition, rule, or theory that states the necessary and sufficient conditions for the application of such general terms in any case. The model of applying a rule or theory to particular cases cannot account for the phenomenon of understanding the meaning of a general term and so of being able to use it and to give reasons and explanations for its use in various contexts.[14]

Second, the actual criteria for the application of a general political term are too various, indeterminate, and hence open to unpredictable extension to be explicated in terms of an implicit or transcendental set of rules or theory, no matter how complex. When we look at the uses of a general term what we see is not a determinate set of essential features that could be abstracted from practice and set out in a theory along with rules for their application. We do not find a set of features that make us use the same word for all cases but rather an open-ended family of uses that resemble one another in various ways. We 'see a complicated network of similarities overlapping and criss-crossing: sometimes overall similarities, sometimes similarities of detail' and these 'family resemblances' among uses of a concept change over time in the course of human conversation.[15]

The consequence of these two antiessentialist arguments is that under-standing political concepts and problems cannot be the theoretical activity of discovering a general and comprehensive rule and then applying it to particu-lar cases, for such a rule is not to be found and understanding does not consist in applying such a rule even if it could be found. The actual use and under-standing of political concepts is not the kind of activity that this model of political theory presupposes, that is, of 'operating a calculus according to definite rules'.[16] Rather, Wittgenstein continues, understanding consists in the practical activity of being able to use a general term in various circum-stances and being able to give reasons for and against this or that use. This is a form of *practical* reasoning: the manifestation of a repertoire of practical, normative abilities, acquired through practice, to use the general term, as well as to go against customary uses, in actual cases. Such a practical skill, like all practical abilities, cannot be exhaustively described in terms of rules, for the application of the term is not everywhere bounded by rules. A criterion that functions as an intersubjective rule for testing assertions of correct use in some circumstances is itself questioned, reinterpreted, and tested in other cir-cumstances, relative to other criteria that are provisionally held fast.

Understanding a general term thus involves being able to give reasons why it should or should not be used in a particular case, either to provoke or to respond to a dispute, being able to see the strength of the reasons given against this use by one's interlocutors, and then being able to give further rea-sons, and so on. This is done by describing examples with similar or related aspects, drawing analogies or disanalogies of various kinds, finding prece-dents, exchanging narratives and redescriptions, drawing attention to inter-mediate cases so one can pass easily from the familiar to the unfamiliar cases and see the similarities among them; thereby being both conventional and creative in the use of the criteria that hold our normative vocabulary in place. Wittgenstein illustrates his thesis with the concept of a 'game':

> Isn't my knowledge, my concept of a game, completely expressed in the explanations I could give? That is, in my describing examples of various kinds of game; shewing how all

sorts of other games can be constructed on the analogy of these; saying that I should scarcely include this or that among games; and so on.[17]

Because the criteria for the application of a term are not determinate, no set of reasons or explanations is definitive. There is always a field of possible reasonable redescriptions: illocutionary acts that evoke another consideration, draw attention to a different analogy or example, uncover another aspect of the situation, and so aim to provoke reconsideration of our considered judgments in this and related cases. These are speech acts that exercise the kind of freedom Nora tries to practice in *The Dollhouse*. Moreover, for the same reasons, the forms of argumentation in which reasons are exchanged are equally complex, and their 'reasonable' forms too are not everywhere bounded by rules but are also open to reasonable disagreement.

Accordingly, understanding and clarifying political concepts, whether by citizens or philosophers, will always be a form of practical reasoning, of entering into and clarifying the ongoing exchange of reasons over the uses of our political vocabulary. It will not be the theoretical activity of abstracting from everyday use and making explicit the context-independent rules for the correct use of our concepts in every case, for the conditions of possibility for such a metacontextual political theory are not available. When political philosophers enter into political discussions and disputes to help clarify the language being used and the appropriate procedures for exchanging reasons, as well as to present reasons of their own, they are not doing anything different in *kind* from the citizens involved in the argumentation, as the picture of political reflection as a theoretical enterprise would lead us to believe. Political philosophy is rather the methodological extension and critical clarification of the already reflective and problematised character of historically situated practices of practical reasoning.[18] Thus, we can now see why the first step should be to start from the ways the concepts we take up are actually used in the practices in which the political difficulties arise. Here we 'bring words back from their metaphysical to their everyday use' to ensure that the work of philosophy starts from 'the rough ground' of struggles with and over words rather than from uncritically accepted forms of representation of them, which may result in 'merely tracing round the frame through which we look at' them.[19]

On this view, contemporary political theories are approached, not as rival comprehensive and exclusive theories of the contested concepts, but as limited and often complementary accounts of the complex uses (senses) of the concepts in question and the corresponding aspects of the problematic practice to which these senses refer. They extend and clarify the practical exchange of reasons over the problematic practice of governance by citizens, putting forward a limited range of academic reasons, analogies, and examples for employing criteria in such-and-such a way, for showing why these considerations outweigh those of other theorists, and so on (often of course with the additional claim that these limited uses transcend practice and legislate legitimate use). A theory clarifies one range of uses of the concepts in question and corresponding aspects of the practice of government and puts forward reasons for seeing this as decisive. Yet there is always the possibility of reasonable disagreement, of other theories bringing to attention other senses of the word and other aspects of the situation that any one theory unavoidably overlooks or downplays. Political theories are thus seen to offer conditional perspectives on the whole broad complex of languages, relations of power, forms of subjectivity, and practices of freedom to which they are addressed. None of these theories tells us the whole truth, yet each provides an aspect of the complex picture.[20]

This first form of survey enables readers (and authors) to understand critically both the problem and the proposed solutions. It enables us to see the reasons and redescriptions on the various sides; to grasp the contested criteria for their application, the circumstances in which they can be applied, and the considerations that justify their different applications, thereby passing freely from one sense of the concept to another and from one aspect of the practice to another; and to appreciate the partial and relative merits of each proposal. To have acquired the complex linguistic abilities to do this is literally to have come to *understand* critically the concepts in question. This enables us to enter into the discussions of the relative merits of the proposed solutions ourselves and present and defend our own views on the matter. To have mastered this dialogical technique is to have acquired the 'burdens of judgment' (in a broader sense than Rawls's use of this phrase is normally interpreted) or what Nietzsche called the ability to reason 'perspectivally'.[21] This form of practical reasoning is also a descendent of the classical humanist view of political philosophy as a practical dialogue. Because it is always possible to invoke a reason and redescribe the accepted application of our political concepts (*paradiastole*), it is always necessary to learn to listen to the other side (*audi alteram partem*), to learn the conditional arguments that support the various sides (*in utramque partem*), and so to be prepared to enter into deliberations with others on how to negotiate an agreeable solution (*negotium*).[22]

The second contemporary survey is of the concrete practices—the relations of governance and practices of freedom—in which the problems arise and are fought over. The ways relations of power direct the conduct and shape the identities of those subject to them, and the strategies by which the subjects are able to say 'enough' and contest, negotiate, and modify these relations can be analysed in much the same way as language games can. Just as participants in any system of practices of governance think and respond within intersubjective language games, which both enable and constrain what they can do with words, so they act and contest within correlative intersubjective relations of power, which both enable and constrain the extent to which they can modify some of these while others remain immobile background relations of domination, except in struggles of direct confrontation. These surveys include the interplay of governance and freedom, the means by which the structure of governance is held in place (economic control of information, technology, and resources, the threat or use of direct or indirect military power, the organisation of the time and space of the practice, the sciences of persuasion and control, the manufacturing of consent, the techniques for internalising norms of conduct, agenda setting), and the equally diverse means by which subjects are able to resist, organise networks of support, bring the governors to negotiations, and hold them to their agreements. Just as an analytical philosophy of linguistic pragmatics has been developed to survey what can be said, an analytical philosophy of relations of power and practices of freedom has begun to be developed to survey what can be done.[23]

## HISTORICAL SURVEYS

The first survey enables students of politics to understand critically what can be said and done within a set of practices and problematisation. A genuinely critical political philosophy requires a second type of critique that enables participants to free themselves from the horizons of the practices and problematisation to some extent, to see them as one *form* of practice and one *form* of problematisation that can then be compared critically with others, and so to go on to consider the possibilities of thinking and acting differently. This second, transformative objective is achieved by means of historical or genealogical surveys of the history of the languages and practices that have been explored and understood from the inside through the first two surveys. The transition from contemporary to historical surveys turns on an argument developed in different ways by almost every member of this school of political philosophy.

When problems are raised, solutions discussed, and relations of power contested and negotiated in a problematic practice, there are always some uses of words (grammar) that are not questioned in the course of the disputation and some relations of power that are not challenged in practice. These provisionally taken-for-granted uses of the shared vocabulary function as the intersubjective warrants or grounds for what is problematised and subject to the exchange of reasons and procedures of validation in the language games, just as settled relations of power and institutionalised practices of freedom function as the intersubjective conditions of the contested aspects of governance and novel forms of freedom. The background shared understandings are the conditions of possibility of the specific problematisation. They both enable and constrain the form of problematisation. As Wittgenstein puts it,

> All testing, all confirmation and disconfirmation of a hypothesis takes place already within a system. And this system is not a more or less arbitrary or doubtful point of departure for all our arguments: no, it belongs to the essence of what we call an argument. The system is not so much the point of departure, as the elements in which arguments have their life.[24]

This loose 'system of judgements' or problematisation is neither universal nor transcendental but provisionally held in place and beyond question by all the disputation within it.[25] He calls the inherited agreement in the language in which the testing of problems and solutions takes place (testing of true and false, just and unjust, valid and invalid, reasonable and unreasonable) 'an agreement in form of life' to indicate the extent to which it is anchored in shared ways of acting as well as speaking: 'it is our *acting* which lies at the bottom of the language-game'.[26] Analogously, the corresponding uncontested relations of power that govern ways of acting function as the enabling and constraining conditions of possibility of the practice as a whole, its forms of government and contestation.

Freeing ourselves from the problematisations and practices in which we think and act is difficult because participation tends to render their shared patterns of thought and reflection and rule following and rule contesting prereflective and habitual. They come to be experienced as necessary rather than contingent, constitutive rather than regulative, universal rather than partial. As Quentin Skinner writes, 'It is easy to become bewitched into believing that the ways of thinking about them [our normative concepts] bequeathed to us by the mainstream of our intellectual traditions must be *the* ways of thinking about them'.[27] While the first two types of contemporary survey begin to disclose the unexamined conventions of the language games and the background relations of domination of the practices, the two parallel types of historical survey show how these specific forms of problematisation and practices of governance came to be hegemonic and function as the discursive and nondiscursive bounds of political reason and thereby to displace other possibilities. Skinner continues,

> The history of philosophy, and perhaps especially of moral, social and political philosophy, is there to prevent us from becoming too readily bewitched. The [historian of political philosophy] can help us to appreciate how far the values embodied in our present way

of life, and our present ways of thinking about those values, reflect a series of choices made at different times between different possible worlds. This awareness can help to liberate us from the grip of any one hegemonic account of those values and how they should be interpreted and understood. Equipped with a broader sense of possibility, we can stand back from the intellectual commitments that we have inherited and ask ourselves in a new spirit of enquiry what we should think of them.[28]

My description of the two types of historical survey can be brief because they proceed in much the same pragmatic way as the two contemporary surveys. In the first, of the hegemonic forms of political thinking about the problems and solutions, the history of their emergence and development are approached in the same manner as contemporary political theories, as responses to problems in practice at the time. Political theorists in the past are seen as questioning, testing, and challenging some of the accepted conventions of *their* age in various ways; arguing for different ways of looking at the problem and of employing the criteria of the concepts in question; showing how a concept can be extended in an unconventional yet reasonable way to solve the problem; and, in response, defending and restating the prevailing conventions in question, perhaps in novel ways. This kind of historical survey of the history of political thought shows how the mainstream system of judgments today was gradually put in place, often over centuries, as the stage setting of reflective disputes and debates, the reasons that were given for and against it, and the alternatives it displaced.

Second, these historical studies of the languages and theories of political thought are related to historical surveys of the corresponding changes in the four main, nondiscursive features of the problematic practices of governance, thereby providing a history of the practices that are the site of struggle in the present. What happens when humans are led to recognise themselves and coordinate their interaction under a new and now conventional sense of, say, 'liberty', 'discipline', or 'identity'?[29] What new institutions and relations of power are employed to induce people to acquire the appropriate modes of conduct and forms of subjectivity, and what new practices of freedom emerge and become institutionalised in response? What older practices of governance are displaced, and how are the new ones rendered legitimate, routine, and self-evident?

These philosophical studies in the history of political thought and practice have two distinct roles. They are contributions to the contextual understanding of texts in the history of political philosophy in their own right, addressed to historians of political thought and practice broadly conceived, and judged by the standards of the field. In addition, these surveys can be offered to the theorists and citizens in the disputes from which we began as further horizon-expanding reasons and redescriptions for their consideration and response.

In this dialogical role, they can be employed to acquire and exercise a critical orientation to the background conventions of the contemporary problematisation and practices that were set out in the first surveys. The acquisition and exercise of this critical attitude consists of two steps.[30]

First, on the basis of the critical understanding acquired by the two contemporary surveys, a political philosopher constructs a plausible interpretation, in a related yet novel vocabulary, of the specific *form* of problematisation and practice of governance, namely, of the specific linguistic and nonlinguistic conditions of possibility of both. This transformative step, or series of intermediate steps, provides a critical distance from the problematisation and practice by providing a new language of self-understanding, one that enables us to move, to some limited and partial extent, beyond the forms of self-understanding we have as participants within the practices and their modes of argumentation.[31]

Second, the historical surveys disclose the formation and historical contingency of this specific form of problematisation and practice and the different potential ways of organising this general kind of practice of governance that were not actualised. These histories of the present thus provide the means to criticise and evaluate the practices and ways of thinking to which we are subject by comparing and contrasting them with possible alternatives.[32] They thereby place the current struggles in a much broader field of possible responses, enabling participants to determine if some constitutive feature is the source of their oppression. This is not a critique from the vantage point of a transcendental standard or procedure of judgement, for as we have seen, such standards are internally related to the language games they purport to transcend. Rather, it is a nontranscendental yet transcending critique of the horizons of our practices and forms of thought by means of reciprocal comparison and contrast with other possible ways of being in the world. It is the general type of critique Gadamer called 'the fusion of horizons': the difficult game of putting one's horizons of thought and action into play relative to others in a question-and-answer dialogue.[33] Contemporary disputes and negotiations are thereby transformed from the limited exchange of practical reasons over reforms within a practice of governance and its modes of argumentation to a broader exchange of practical reasons over the comparative values of a range of possible practices and the relations of governance, forms of subjectivity, and practices of freedom they institutionalise.

A few examples will illustrate these two steps. Marx's *Capital* enables subjects struggling over various solutions to the problems of the conditions of work to see these struggles and debates *as* the problematisation of a specific practice of governance, a capitalist mode of production. His historical surveys then enable them to see its contingency and to compare and evaluate its features with other possible ways of governing productive activities (such as feudalism and socialism). Foucault, by recharacterising the dominant practices and traditions of intepretation of representative constitutional democracy as juridical-discursive institutions and the sovereignty model of problematisation, enables us to see many of our current political struggles and theoretical debates as moves within a historically particular set of practices of governance and mode of problematisation. Then, he contrasts this with another way of describing contemporary practices of governance (in the broad sense) as norm-governed relations of biopower that are obscured by the language of sovereignty. This survey discloses different aspects of our practices and different possible and perhaps more effective practices of freedom for consideration.[34]

Taylor's *Sources of the Self* recasts our understanding of seemingly comprehensive and mutually exclusive theories of moral and political selfhood as disclosing different aspects of a complex modern organisation of identity that moderns have come to acquire historically through participation in different practices of governance. Skinner's *Liberty before Liberalism* leads us to see the dominant way of thinking about and practicing freedom, as either negative noninterference or positive freedom, as historically contingent and partial; to compare and contrast the relative value of ways of life these promote with another form of freedom, as nondomination, that was marginalised by the ascendancy of liberalism; and to reconsider the reasons for its near eclipse.

Finally, as Wollstonecraft illustrates before the letter in *A Vindication of the Rights of Woman*, this kind of philosophical study of Nora and Thorvold's practice of marriage and its limited practices of freedom would disclose the constitutive features of this specific dollhouse form of marriage, to understand its historical formation, and to situate it in a broader field of possible forms of marriage. We would thus be in the position to secure uptake of what Nora is trying to say, to enter into a dialogue over the injustices of its relations of domination and forms of subjectivity, and to consider the concrete practices of freedom by which it could be transformed.[35]

## POLITICAL PHILOSOPHY AND PUBLIC AFFAIRS

Political philosophy as a critical attitude starts from the present struggles and problems of politics and seeks to clarify and transform the normal understanding of them so as to open up the field of possible ways of thinking and acting freely in response. These investigations are addressed to political philosophers and scholars in related disciplines, and they are tested in the multidisciplinary discussions that follow. However, insofar as they do throw critical light on contemporary struggles over oppressive practices of governance, they are addressed to the wider audience of citizens who are engaged in the struggles and seek assistance from university research. This is a communicative relationship of reciprocal elucidation and mutual benefit between political philosophy and public affairs.

On one hand, such studies throw light on the features of the practice in which a problem arises and becomes the site of struggle and negotiation, enabling the participants to become more self-aware of the conditions of their situation and the range of actions available to them. On the other hand, the experiments of the participants in negotiating, implementing, and reviewing concrete changes in practice provide a pragmatic, concrete test of the studies and their limitations. By studying the unanticipated blockages, difficulties, and new problems that arise in the cycle of practices of freedom—of negotiations, implementation, and review—political philosophers can detect the limitations and faults of their initial account, make improvements, and exercise again, on the basis of the new problems, this permanent critical *ethos* of testing the practices in which we are governed.[36]

To conclude, let me present one final difference it makes to study politics in this way. If political philosophy is approached as the activity of developing comprehensive theories, the questions of politics tend to be taken up as problems of justice, of the just way to recognise free and equal citizens and for them to govern their stable institutions of constitutional, representative democracy. This has been the dominant answer to the question 'what is political theory?' over the past two centuries. The subaltern school I have outlined is respectfully sceptical of this orientation and of the presupposition that there are definitive practices of free governance and theoretical solutions to their problems.

Consequently, this alternative answer to our question is oriented to freedom before justice. The questions of politics are approached as questions of freedom. What are the specific practices of governance in which the problems arise and the practices of freedom by which they are raised? And what are the possible practices of freedom in which free and equal subjects could speak and exchange reasons more freely over how to criticise, negotiate, and modify their always imperfect practices? This is a permanent task of making sure that the multiplicity of practices of governance in which we act together do not become closed structures of domination under settled forms of justice, but are always open to practices of freedom by which those subject to them have a say and a hand over them.

## NOTES

*I would like to thank Cressida Heyes, Cheryl Misak, David Owen, Paul Patton, Quentin Skinner, Charles Taylor, and Stephen White for comments on earlier drafts of this chapter.*

1. An exemplar of this kind of question-and-answer dialogue for both Islamic and Western cultures is Plato's dialogues. For a contemporary reformulation, see Hans-Georg Gadamer, *Truth and Method* (New York: Continuum, 1999), 362-81. For the distinction between the logic of a dialogue of questions and answers and one of problems and solutions that I use below, see idem, *Truth and Method*, 376-77. For a history of dialogical political philosophy from Socrates to Hobbes's argument against it and his assertion of an influential style of monological political theory, see Quentin Skinner, *Reason and Rhetoric in the Philosophy of Hobbes* (Cambridge, UK: Cambridge University Press, 1996).

2. There are of course many other types of political theory. I am using this specific type as an object of contrast. For the history and renaissance of practical philosophy, see Stephen Toulmin, *Return to Reason* (Cambridge, MA: Harvard University Press, 2001); Alexander Nehemas, *The Art of Living: Socratic Reflections from Plato to Foucault* (Berkeley: University of California Press, 2000); Charles Taylor, *Philosophical Arguments* (Cambridge, MA: Harvard University Press, 1995), 1-60; Bernard Williams, *Ethics and the Limits of Philosophy* (Cambridge, MA: Harvard University Press, 1985).

3. For studies in the history of the critical attitude, see Michel Foucault, "What Is Critique?" in *The Politics of Truth*, ed. Sylvère Lotringer (Los Angeles: Semiotext(e), 1997), 23-82; Michel Foucault, *Fearless Speech*, ed. Joseph Pearson (Los Angeles: Semiotext(e), 2001).

4. See James Tully, ed., *Meaning and Context: Quentin Skinner and His Critics* (Cambridge, UK: Polity, 1988); Quentin Skinner, *Regarding Method* (Cambridge, UK: Cambridge University Press, forthcoming); James Tully, ed., *Philosophy Is an Age of Pluralism: The Philosophy of Charles Taylor in Question* (Cambridge, UK: Cambridge University Press, 1994); Ruth Abbey, *Charles Taylor* (Teddington, UK: Acumen, 2000); Taylor, *Philosophical Arguments*; Cressida Heyes, ed., *Wittgenstein and Political Philosophy* (Ithaca, NY: Cornell University Press, forthcoming); Cressida Heyes, *Line Drawings: Defining Women through Feminist Practice* (Ithaca, NY: Cornell University Press, 2000); Richard Rorty, *Philosophical Papers*, 2 vols. (Cambridge, UK: Cambridge University Press, 1991); Gary Gutting, ed., *The Cambridge Companion to Foucault* (Cambridge, UK: Cambridge University Press, 1994); Michel Foucault, *The Essential Works of Foucault*, 3 vols. (New York: New Press, 1994, 1997); Edward Said, *Culture and Imperialism* (New York: Knopf, 1993); Edward Said, *Reflections on Exile* (Cambridge, MA: Harvard University Press, 2000). Richard Rorty, J. B. Schneewind, and Quentin Skinner, eds., *Philosophy in History* (Cambridge, UK: Cambridge University Press, 1984), is a landmark text in the 'third phase' of this tradition.

5. For the dialogue between these two traditions, see Samantha Ashenden and David Owen, eds., *Foucault contra Habermas: Recasting the Dialogue between Genealogy and Critical Theory* (London: Sage, 1999); David Couzens Hoy and Thomas McCarthy, *Critical Theory* (Oxford, UK: Blackwell, 1994); Michael Kelly, ed., *Critique and Power: Recasting the Foucault/Habermas Debate* (Cambridge, MA: MIT Press, 1994); Stephen K. White, ed., *The Cambridge Companion to Habermas* (Cambridge, UK: Cambridge University Press, 1995).

6. Michel Foucault, "What Is Enlightenment?" in *The Politics of Truth*, ed. Sylvère Lotringer (Los Angeles: Semiotext(e), 1997), 101-34, at 133. The various versions of this article are collected in this volume.

7. For these trends in recent scholarship, see James Tully, "The Unfreedom of the Moderns in Comparison to their Ideals of Constitutional Democracy," *Modern Law Review* (forthcoming, March 2002).

8. Stanley Cavell, *Conditions Handsome and Unhandsome* (Chicago: University of Chicago Press, 1990), 101-26. For a helpful commentary, see David Owen, "Cultural Diversity and the Conversation of Justice," *Political Theory* 27, no. 5 (1999): 579-96.

9. For the Governmentality school, see Mitchell Dean, *Governmentality: Power and Rule in Modern Society* (London: Sage, 1999); Nikolas Rose, *Powers of Freedom* (Cambridge, UK: Cambridge University Press, 1999); and Graham Burchell, Colin Gordon, and Peter Miller, eds., *The Foucault Effect: Studies in Governmentality* (Chicago: University of Chicago Press, 1991). For the Cambridge school, see references at note 4 above.

10. For more on this sketch of practices of governance, see James Tully, "Democracy and Globalization," in *Canadian Political Philosophy: Contemporary Reflections*, ed. Ronald Beiner and Wayne Norman (Toronto, Canada: Oxford University Press, 2000), 36-63.

11. See Michel Foucault, "What Is Enlightenment?" 129-30, and his further discussion of practices of governance and practices of freedom in "The Ethics of the Concern for Self as a Practice of Freedom," in *The Essential Works of Foucault*, vol. 1, 281-302. My sketch of the five features of practices of governance and freedom draws in part on these articles. I have discussed them in relation to other authors in this tradition in "To Think and Act Differently," *Foucault contra Habermas*, 90-142.

12. Michel Foucault, "The Subject and Power," *The Essential Works of Foucault*, vol. 3, 326-49, at 342. My presentation of practices of freedom draws on this article, the changes in 'The Ethics of the Concern for the Self as a Practice of Freedom'. I have discussed this account of freedom in "To Think and Act Differently," 130-39. See also Clarissa Hayward, *Defacing Power* (Cambridge, UK: Cambridge University Press, 2000), 161-79; and James C. Scott, *Domination and the Arts of Resistance* (New Haven, CT: Yale University Press, 1990).

13. Ludwig Wittgenstein, *Philosophical Investigations*, ed. G.E.M. Anscombe (Oxford, UK: Blackwell, 1968); J. L. Austin, *How to Do Things with Words* (Oxford, UK: Oxford University Press, 1962); Gadamer, *Truth and Method*; Hanna Pitkin, *Wittgenstein and Justice* (Berkeley: University of California Press, 1973); J.G.A. Pocock, *Virtue, Commerce, and History* (Cambridge, UK: Cambridge University Press, 1985), 1-36; Tully, *Meaning and Context*, 29-134, 231-89; Terence Ball, James Farr, and Russell Hanson, ed., *Political Innovation and Conceptual Change* (Cambridge, UK: Cambridge University Press, 1989); Stephen Toulmin, *The Uses of Argument* (Oxford, UK: Oxford University Press, 1958); Toulmin, *Return to Reason*; John Shotter, *Conversational Realities* (London: Sage, 1993); Douglas Walton, *The New Dialectic: Conversational Contexts of Argument* (Toronto, Canada: University of Toronto Press, 1998); Iris Marion Young, *Intersecting Voices* (Princeton, NJ: Princeton University Press, 1997), 38-74.

14. Wittgenstein, *Philosophical Investigations*, secs. 81-85. For this interpretation of Wittgenstein's arguments, see James Tully, "Wittgenstein and Political Philosophy," in *Wittgenstein and Political Philosophy*, ed. Cressida Heyes (forthcoming); and *Strange Multiplicity: Constitutionalism in an Age of Diversity* (Cambridge, UK: Cambridge University Press, 1995), 103-15.

15. Ibid., secs. 65-67. For the relation of this line of argument to deconstruction, see Henry Staten, *Wittgenstein and Derrida* (London: University of Nebraska Press, 1986).

16. Ibid., sec. 81.

17. Ibid., sec. 75, compare sec. 71.

18. Compare David Owen, "Orientation and Enlightenment: An Essay on Critique and Genealogy," in *Foucault contra Habermas*, 21-44, and references in note 2.

19. Wittgenstein, *Philosophical Investigations*, secs. 116, 107, 114. It is interesting to note that Isaiah Berlin recommended that political philosophers abandon their abstract analysis and get back to the way words are actually used in the struggles of the day at the very beginning of his famous Oxford lecture in 1958. Isaiah Berlin, "Two Concepts of Liberty," in *Four Essays on Liberty* (Oxford, UK: Oxford University Press, 1977), 118-72, at 118-21. Yet his critical and historical survey of two uses of 'liberty' in twentieth-century struggles has been abstracted from practice and treated as two 'theories' of liberty. For recent pleas to ground the study of freedom in the practices of freedom to which I am indebted, see Wendy Brown, *States of Injury: Power and Freedom in Late Modernity* (Princeton, NJ: Princeton University Press, 1995), 3-29; and Rose, *Powers of Freedom*, 1-14.

20. Albert R. Jonsen and Stephen Toulmin, *The Abuse of Casuistry: A History of Moral Reasoning* (Berkeley: University of California Press, 1988), 293.

21. For this broader interpretation of Rawls as a member of this tradition of political philosophy, see Anthony Laden, *Reasonably Radical: Deliberative Liberalism and the Politics of Identity* (Ithaca, NY: Cornell University Press, 2000). For Nietzsche, see Friedrich Nietzsche, *Human All Too Human*, trans. R. J. Hollingdale (Cambridge, UK: Cambridge University Press, 1986), 9.

22. Skinner, *Reason and Rhetoric*, 14-16, 138-80.

23. See Arnold I. Davidson, "Introduction," *Foucault and His Interlocutors* (Chicago: University of Chicago Press, 1997), 1-20; Rose, *Powers of Freedom*, 1-98; and references in note 12.

24. Ludwig Wittgenstein, *On Certainty*, trans. Denis Paul and G.E.M. Anscombe (Oxford, UK: Blackwell, 1974), sec. 105.

25. Ibid., secs. 140-44.

26. Wittgenstein, *Philosophical Investigations*, secs. 240-42; idem, *On Certainty*, sec. 204.

27. Quentin Skinner, *Liberty before Liberalism* (Cambridge, UK: Cambridge University Press, 1998), 116.

28. Ibid., 116-17. The classic example of this first type of historical survey is Quentin Skinner, *The Foundations of Modern Political Thought* (Cambridge, UK: Cambridge University Press, 1978).

29. See, respectively, Skinner, *Liberty before Liberalism*; Foucault, *Discipline and Punish: The Birth of the Prison* (New York: Pantheon, 1977); and Charles Taylor, *Sources of the Self: The Making of the Modern Identity* (Cambridge, MA: Harvard University Press, 1989).

30. For a careful analysis of these steps, see David Owen, "Genealogy as Perspicuous Representation," in Heyes, *Wittgenstein and Political Philosophy*.

31. For example, Foucault's characterisation of classical debates on ethics in terms of a problematisation consisting of four main dimensions enables us to achieve a certain distant for the debates as a whole. Michel Foucault, *The Use of Pleasure* (New York: Pantheon, 1985), 14-25. For his invention and careful development of the concept of a problematisation and its relation to practices, see idem, *Foucault Live* (Los Angeles: Semiotext(e), 1996), 413-14, 421-22, 462-3; and *Fearless Speech*, 74, 171-73.

32. The technique of comparative critique rather than transcendental critique, while famil-
    iar to this entire tradition, is reformulated in a novel way by Wittgenstein, *Philosophical
    Investigations*, secs. 122, 130-31. For its genesis, see Raymond Monk, *Ludwig
    Wittgenstein: The Duty of Genius* (London: Jonathan Cape, 1990), 298-327.
33. Gadamer, *Truth and Method*, 306-7, 374-75. See Richard Rorty, "Being That Can Be
    Understood Is Language," *London Review of Books* 22, no. 6 (2000): 23-25; and Taylor,
    *Philosophical Arguments*, 165-81.
34. Foucault, *Discipline and Punish*; idem, *History of Sexuality: Volume I* (London: Pen-
    guin, 1978). See Dean, *Governmentality*, 98-113; and Owen, "Genealogy as Perspicu-
    ous Representation." For an extension of this kind of contrast of sovereignty and
    biopower to the problematisation of globalisation, see Michael Hardt and Antonio
    Negri, *Empire* (Cambridge, MA: Harvard University Press, 2001). Edward Said's criti-
    cal studies, especially *Culture and Imperialism*, bring to light the imperial horizons of
    the literature that has shaped Western sensibilities for two centuries and what has been
    and is being said and done in response.
35. Mary Wollstonecraft, *The Vindications*, ed. D. L. Macdonald and Kathleen Scherf
    (Peterborough, Ontario, Canada: Broadview, 1997).
36. Compare Foucault, "What Is Enlightenment?" 126, 133, and idem, *Essential Works*, vol.
    1, 321-28. The evolving reciprocal relationships between many schools of political the-
    ory and philosophy (both historical-critical and neo-Kantian) and concrete struggles
    constitute a complex global network of research and communication. The six types of
    multidisciplinary critical study mentioned earlier have spearheaded this renaissance of a
    Socratic relation to the public good broadly conceived. For example, the historical and
    theoretical knowledge of these scholars has enabled them to throw a broader and more
    critical light on the forms of oppression in an era of globalisation—inequality, exploita-
    tion, domination, racism, deliberative democratic deficits, and rights' abuses—and on
    the practices of freedom that might be effective in response. I have discussed these rela-
    tionships further in "Democracy and Globalization" and "The Unfreedom of Moderns."

# 5     AT THE EDGE

*WENDY BROWN*

> Here lies the vocation of those who preserve our understanding of past theories, who sharpen our sense of the subtle, complex interplay between political experience and thought, and who preserve our memory of the agonizing efforts of intellect to restate the possibilities and threats posed by political dilemmas of the past.
>
> —Sheldon S. Wolin, "Political Theory as a Vocation"

> In the same way in which the great transformation of the first industrial revolution destroyed the social and political structures as well as the legal categories of the ancien regime, terms such as sovereignty, right, nation, people, democracy, and general will by now refer to a reality that no longer has anything to do with what these concepts used to designate—and those who continue to use these concepts uncritically literally do not know what they are talking about.
>
> —Giorgio Agamben, *Means without Ends: Notes on Politics*

> Looking obliquely at the edges of things, where they come together with other things, can tell you as much about them, often, as can looking at them directly, intently, straight on.
>
> —Clifford Geertz, "The Near East in the Far East"

Contemporary critical theory teaches that identity is created through borders and oppositions. The outside constructs the inside and then hides this work of fabrication in an entity that appears to give birth to itself. Thus to inquire "What is political theory?" is to ask about its constitutive outside as well as its techniques of dissimulating this constitution. What does political theory position itself against and by what discursive means? What does it imagine itself not to be, to be different from? What epistemological, stylistic, and ontological conceits denote its significant others, its scenes of alterity?

Explicit answers to these questions have varied over the several millennia of political theory in the West. For Socrates, the epic poets and the sophists contoured the edges of political theory; for Machiavelli, it was Christian moralists; for Hobbes, the scholastics; for Nietzsche, moral theorists; for Weber, political ideologues; for Arendt, social and economic theory; for Sheldon Wolin, methodism; for Isaiah Berlin, science. This partial list reminds us that what is cast out is also that which rivals or displaces the enterprise or that contains the specter of its colonization. What defines political theory for any epoch or thinker is also conceived, at least in part, as threatening its dissolution. This becomes even clearer when we leave the consideration of epistemological concerns for ontological ones: across its disparate modalities, political theory takes its bearings from a tacit presumption of the relative boundedness and autonomy of the political. The existence of political theory qua political theory has depended heavily on defining the political as distinguishable (if not distinct) from the economic, the social, the cultural, the natural, and the private/domestic/familial. Nor does content exhaust this project of differentiation: political life is also tacitly circumscribed by its theorists in terms of a distinct ethos or sensibility, differentiated (albeit not necessarily sequestered) from the emotional, the psychic, the erotic, the poetic, the literary, and at times, the moral. For political theory to claim singularity and claim propriety over a territory of concern, it must set itself off from these other domains, practices, and sensibilities. But like political theory's epistemological others, each laps at the shore of the political, promising to subvert or undo it if certain policing measures are not undertaken.

All of which is to say the familiar: if the very existence of political theory depends on contingent designations of what is not political and what is not theoretical, then political theory is a fiction, constituted by invented distinctions and a range of rivalries and conceits, all of which are mutable and puncturable and vary across time and place, not to mention investment and interest. To identify political theory's contrived nature, however, does not reduce or devalue the enterprise; rather, it helps to set the stage for considering the possibilities and challenges it faces in a particular time and place. An understanding of what political theory arrays itself against today, how it differentiates itself from what is intellectually proximate to it, and what wolves it fears at its door, may help us grasp not only what political theory imagines itself to be and to be for, but what anxieties and uncertainties it has about this identity and what limits it places on itself to maintain coherence and purpose in the face of its potential undoing.

Antiessentialist perspectives and an appreciation of the fictional quality of knowledge categories are not the only insights from late modern critical theory relevant to our problem. There is also, for example, the matter of marked and unmarked signifiers. What is political theory . . . today? To pursue the question without the temporal qualifier would be to eschew not only the contingency of identity production but its relentlessly historical quality. To pursue the question without the temporal qualifier is already to take a stance within the battle for political theory's future, one that aims for hegemony and refuses to avow its own dependencies and unconscious strategies. To let the temporal qualifier remain unspecified is also to propose to consider the nature and purpose of political theory in terms that disavow its historically constructed and contingent nature from the start and thus to try to resurrect a truth undone by the enterprise of theory itself. So, then, what is political theory today . . . where? in the Anglo-American intellectual world? in western Europe or its eastern step-sibling? outside the metropoles of modernity? in the academy? in the streets? (whose streets?) To leave these matters unspecified is to remain blinkered to the long elite past of political theory as well as the saturation by colonial European and postwar American hegemony that has conditioned the identity and contents of recognized political theory in the more recent past. It is also to sustain, unreconstructed, the legacies of these pasts in the answer. And if we stipulate our question, "What is political theory today in the American academy?" we still need to ask about the work of that tiny verb, "is." Are we searching for the soul of an existing practice or a possible one? Are we asking what we do now, how we signify to others (which others?), or what we might become?[1] And if we are not forthrightly blending normative desire into description—if we really endeavor to describe our activity rather than our own particular investments in it—what sleights of hand are we engaged in then?

Still thinking about what contemporary critical theory might suggest about the question of "What is political theory?" we learn from identity critique to inquire, What animates and invigorates this particular attempt to designate and distinguish a collective practice or way of life? What might be feared or hoped for here that stipulated identity is imagined to resolve or provide? If identity always entails a certain cessation in what Plato called 'becoming', if it is always an attempt to consolidate being over becoming, if it is always a foreclosure of desire with ontology, of yearning with naming (of an "I want," in which the wanting incessantly deconstructs the I, with an "I am," in which the I fantasizes itself as immune to being undone by desire), of indeterminacy with a hardened list of attributes—if, in short, identity is always both a fall and a set of foreclosures, it may be instructive to attend to the anxieties or sufferings precipitating the call for identity resolution at this particular moment. What vulnerability to the inchoate, the impure, or the unknown appears to be untenable and in need of reprieve? What pressures on political theory to yield its boundaries or reach beyond itself appear radically imperiling to the enterprise and its trench workers?

Of course it is impossible, in a single essay, to take the measure of all that these questions open up, but we may nonetheless feel their disruptive presence as we pursue a narrower set of questions. One way to do this involves considering contemporary challenges to the identity of political theory through the frame of border politics. Which of modern Western academic political theory's constitutive borders are currently weakening or eroding, from what sources, and with what consequences for the enterprise? Where are these erosions producing fertile transformations of political theory's objects of study, self-understanding, and articulations with other disciplinary approaches? And where are these changes the occasion of a reactive identity formation—manifesting either as anxious efforts to reconsolidate rapidly liquifying objects of analysis, or as fierce policing of widening gaps in porous boundaries? And where might we see both transformative and reactive processes going on at once?

In what follows, I will not consider every border or every strand of what has become an ornately subdivided field. I will not look closely, for example, at the changing boundary between philosophy and political theory organizing the territory and concerns of moral political thought, or that between new historicism and political theory configuring historicized interpretations of canonical works of theory. And I will not much consider the border between political theory and the discipline of political science, or political theory's particular and peculiar border with what has come to be denominated as formal theory. Certainly each of these could be the site of a productive inquiry. But I want to begin more broadly, with consideration of a set of late modern developments that have created substantial challenges for the particular strand of political theory addressed to contemporary political life and its possibilities, whether in a conserving, diagnostic, or prescriptive vein. These developments have historical-material wellsprings that in turn generate certain intellectual responses, both across academic thought and specifically within the profession of political theory. Provisionally and somewhat awkwardly, I will denote these late modern challenges to political theory as "world-historical," "intellectual," and "professional" and sketch each briefly.

## WORLD HISTORY

World history, the ungainly term by which is signified the emergence of certain forces and the transformation of certain orders of existence that exceed any locally or nationally instigated events, offers a host of challenges to the boundedness and autonomy of politics. Here is how it goes today: nation-state sovereignty recedes while *economic* forces and transnational institutions come to the fore as major global actors; *culture* patently shapes political identity and drives political conflict and affiliation; *nature* emerges as an intensely agentic political force and politicized field, neither immune to human construction nor absent a politics of its own; the *bodily*, the *ethnic*, and the *sexual* have erupted as dense sites of local, national, and international conflict; the *domestic* withers to its smallest possible dimensions and content, where it is denaturalized by relentless commodification and erupts as a province of power saturated with relations of inegalitarianism, domination, and exploitation; the *social* or the *civic*, rather than the state, is increasingly figured as the domain of democracy—social movement is the name for popular political mobilization and civil society is the designated sphere for political association, participation, and virtue (its absence is denoted as a "crisis" for democracy); and finally, historically specific *global* powers are understood to have diverse *local* effects, hence the temporally contingent and the local become sites for theorizing and enacting democratic resistance to these powers.

These developments—whether regarded as effects of globalized capitalism or of late modernity more broadly—are significant for political theory; indeed, they are almost (but not quite) deadly in their significance. With them, the traditional outcasts from the political as it has been widely conceived in Western political thought—economics, culture, nature, the bodily, the domestic, the social, the civic, and the local—come home to roost. In this return, they dilute the distinctiveness, the hypostasized purity of political theory, just as surely as the last half-century's migration of the colonials to the metropoles has irreversibly undone the conceit of (pure) (European) Man. It is difficult to choose the most apt postcolonial metaphor here: have these phenomena forced an encounter with the inherent hybridity or impurity of the political, or have they disseminated and hence unbounded the political? Or both? Perhaps different developments function differently, some producing hybrids, as in the fusion of certain cultural and political phenomena or the expansion of the politicized economy, while others figure the dissemination of the political, for example, the construal of many facets of domestic life—from child care to domestic violence to the definition of marriage—as political and legal concerns. What is common within this variety is the potential identity crisis for political theory threatened by these developments. If, for example, democratic political life is increasingly understood as negotiated at temporally contingent and spatially local levels, what happens to the universal and transhistorical signature of political theory? If politics is in culture and culture is relentlessly political, what denotes the boundary between political theory and anthropological or other kinds of cultural theory, including theories of art, music, film? If the public/private distinction is in part ideological and functions to obscure the saturation of the private sphere by power and convention, then what is the difference between feminist theory devoted to theorizing this saturation and political theory? Indeed, what, other than anxiety about loss of identity and place, animates the drawing of a line between feminist theory and political theory, between theories of culture and theories of politics, between social or political economic theory and political theory? What remains of the *generic* of political theory other than an obvious and anxious power move to demote these other kinds of inquiry to subgeneric status? What would be the function of this move other than to preserve a realm itself undone by history?

## INTELLECTUAL MIGRATIONS

The intellectual migrations affecting the boundaries around political theory are occasioned in part by the world historical developments listed above but contain their own contingencies as well. The work of thinking about political matters theoretically has lately been undertaken in disciplines as far removed from each other and from political science as art history, anthropology, rhetoric, geography, and literature. To a degree, this is an effect of the late modern dissemination of the political described above; when culture appears as suffused with politics, anthropologists and art historians inevitably become political theorists even as political theorists take up culture as an object of analysis. However, the intellectual dissemination of political theory beyond the bounds of philosophy and political science also issues from a consequential rethinking of power over the past half century.

In the nineteenth century, Marx challenged the boundaries of political theory with his discovery of power in the social and specifically economic realm. The blow this argument delivered to the line between political and social theory could be repelled only by refusing Marx's insistence on the primacy of the economic, which was exactly Arendt's move, in a different vein, Foucault's, and of course the move of bourgeois liberals. In the past forty years, however, the disciplinary challenge has come from another direction, one more difficult for political theory to repel because it concerns not merely the venue but the very conceptualization of what Weber called "the lifeblood of politics": power. Recent Continental thought—not only in philosophy but also that of structuralist and poststructuralist linguists, anthropologists, semioticians, literary theorists, psychoanalysis, and historians—has radically reconceived the operations, mechanics, circulation, logics, venues, and vehicles of power. On one hand, power has been discerned in relations between words, juxtapositions of images, discourses of scientific truth, microorganizations of bodies and gestures, in social orchestrations of pain and pleasure, sickness, fear, health, and suffering. On the other hand, these reconceptualizations have devastated conventional formulations of power—those that cast power as merely negative or repressive, as commodifiable and transferable, as inherently related to violence or to law. Understandings of power have also been transformed and enriched by work in feminist theory, postcolonial theory, critical race theory, and queer theory: no longer is it possible to reduce stratification by gender, sexuality, race, or ethnicity to semiotic or biological essences on one hand, or mere effects of law, policy, or social prejudice on the other. Rather, as effects of power, these formations highlight the manifestation and circulation of power carried in imagistic and discursive representations, in psychic subjection, in spatial organization, in the disciplining of bodies and knowledges. They concretize the Derridean and Foucauldian insights into power's normative actions and effects. They make it difficult if not impossible to return to simple equations of power with sovereignty, rule, or wealth.

In addition to the reformulations of power discussed above, there is another matter concerning power that is significant for political theory today, namely, the status of capitalism in our thinking. For a number of reasons, capitalism is not much on political theory's agenda today. First and most important, it appears unchallengeable. Second, it is difficult to make the case for viable alternatives, either for their viability or for the possibility of achieving them. Third, over the past century and a half, in many ways capitalism has become steadily less odious and more pleasurable for the majority populations of the First World; gone are the scenes of the masses laboring at starvation wages for the wealth of the few, except in the Third World. Capitalist commodity production is also ever more oriented to the pleasures of the middle-class consumer, and the middle class is ever more oriented by its own pleasures. Thus, writes Agamben, "while the state in decline lets its empty shell survive everywhere as a pure structure of sovereignty and domination, society as a whole is . . . irrevocably delivered to the form of consumer society, that is, a society in which the sole goal of production is comfortable living."[2] Capitalism charms rather than alienates us with its constant modifications of our needs and with its production for our mere entertainment, and we are remarkably acclimated to its production of algorithmic increases in the rates of redundancy and replacement of technologies. Fourth, however cynically or superficially, First World capitalism has developed an ethical face: it recycles, conserves, and labels; it divests itself of genetically modified organisms and monosodium glutamate, and caters to kosher, vegetarian, and heart-healthy diets; it refrains from testing on animals and develops dolphin-safe tuna nets; it donates fractions of its profits to cancer research and reforestation and sponsors Special Olympics, Gay Pride, summer Bach festivals, and educational supplements for the underprivileged. Save for occasional revelations about heinous sweatshop practices or dire devastations of pristine nature, it has largely lost its brutish reputation as a ruthless exploiter and polluter. With the aid of the media that it also sponsors, it has effectively transferred this reputation to images of power mongering, desperate, ignorant, or fundamentalist sites in the Third World—the Taliban, Castro, the People's Republic of China, the rubber tappers of the Brazilian rainforest. Fifth, these changes in capitalism itself are complemented by recent left intellectual tendencies that deflect from capitalism as a crucible of unfreedom and inegalitarianism. When the seeming perdurability of capitalism, the absence of compelling alternatives, its devotion to consumer pleasures, and its ostensibly improved conscience are combined with increased theoretical attention to other orders of injustice—those targeted by multiculturalist politics—capitalism slips into the background as an object of critique or political concern. Sixth, the rise of professionalism (about which more below) in political theory and the apolitical nature of much theory and theoretical exchange means that this backgrounding goes largely uncontested even by those who consider themselves to be on the cultural left. Finally, the repair of most Marxists to their own journals and conferences (this, too, a symptom of professionalism), and the extent to which many Anglo-American Marxists have substituted "postmodernism" and "identity politics" for capitalism as the chief target of their wrath and analytical attention, means that the Marxist project of illuminating the place of capitalism in political and social life has pretty much vanished from the orbit of political theory.

Yet if capitalism has all but disappeared as a subject and object of political theory (notwithstanding routine drive-by references to "globalization"), capitalism is and remains our life form. Understood not just as a mode of production, distribution, or exchange, but as an unparalleled maker of history, capital arguably remains the dominant force in the organization of collective human existence, conditioning every element of social, political, cultural, intellectual, emotional, and kin life. Indeed, what for Marx constituted the basis for a critique of capital deeper than its exploitation and denigration of labor, deeper than the disparities between wealth and poverty it organized, is that capital is a larger, more creative, and more nearly total form of power than anything else in human history yet fundamentally escapes human control. It was this, in Marx's view, and not its inegalitarian distribution of wealth, that rendered capital such a profoundly antidemocratic historical force: too little is ours to craft or control as long as this force organizes and produces our world; too little can be ordered according to democratic deliberation about human need, gratification, or enhancement—not our work, our values, our fortunes, our enmities, our modes of education, our styles of love, the content of our suffering. This is not to say that capital is the only significant social power afoot in the contemporary world. We have learned otherwise from Nietzsche, Freud, Weber, du Bois, de Beauvoir, Fanon, Foucault, and their respective contemporary legatees. While importantly supplemented by these teachings, however, Marx's insight into capital's awesome power to drive human history and contour agentic possibility is not diminished by them.

No one could have predicted how the force of this insight would multiply between Marx's time and the present. Our problem today, however, is less with its intensification than with what to do with it when both the science of history and the revolutionary impulse that Marx counted on have collapsed, when the validity of the critique persists but there is nothing to be done about it. For Marx, the depth of the critique was matched by the depth and reach of the redemptive promise. Today this promise is almost fully extinguished. That the most powerful undemocratic force in human history appears here to stay—this is the fundamental left and liberal predicament today, a predicament that haunts our theoretical and political practices concerned with freedom, equality, justice, and more.

This haunt is not the only consequence of failing to engage the powers of capitalism in our work. Rather, our averted glance here also prevents us from grasping the extent to which the dramatic alterations in the configuration of the political discussed under the rubric of "world history" are themselves effects of capitalism and not simply of secularization, disenchantment, or contingent human invention. To paraphrase from the *Communist Manifesto*, capitalism is a world-class boundary smasher: there is nothing it cannot penetrate, infiltrate, rearrange, hybridize, commodify, invent, or dissolve. The movement of capital is largely responsible for the extent to which boundaries have been erased, in late modernity, between activities or spheres historically bearing at least a modest distinction from one another in terms of space, style, organization, or function, for example, the university and the corporation, sex and technology, or the political and the cultural. Thus, to theorize the politics of recognition, the sexual order of things, the nature of citizenship, or the reconfiguration of privacy, without taking the measure of their historically specific production by capitalism, is literally not to know the constitutive conditions of one's object of analysis. It is not to be able to grasp the powers organizing life in our time and hence to risk ontologizing this organization and reifying its effects. Finally, to the degree that potential transformations are figured in abstraction from the powers delimiting possibility, it is to make political theory into fantasy play.

## PROFESSIONALIZATION

Political theory might be defined in general terms as a tradition of discourse concerned about the present being and well-being of collectivities. It is primarily a civic and secondarily an academic activity. In my understanding this means that political theory is a critical engagement with collective existence and with the political experiences of power to which it gives rise.[3]

The practice of political theory has probably never been as professionalized as it is today, a phenomenon certainly shaped by external forces but heartily taken up from within political theory's ranks, and even from the most young and hip among its ranks. By professionalization, I mean in part the organization of a practice whose referent is itself, whose audience and judges are one another, and whose existence is tallied and certified by conferences, journals, prizes, recruitments, and other markers of recognition conferred according to established hierarchies and norms. I also mean the orientation of those within the profession to these markers and the setting of an agenda of inquiry by them. But the *Oxford English Dictionary* provides a fuller sense of the pejorative implications of professionalization: a profession is, in the widest sense, "any calling or occupation by which a person habitually earns his living" but appears to derive from that aspect of the word "profess" referring to "the promise or vow made by one entering a religious order, hence the action of entering such an order."[4] Moreover, as Weber emphasized in his essays on politics and science as vocations, the professional is distinguished not simply by degree of expertise in relation to the amateur but is one who, in the words of the dictionary, "makes a profession or business of any occupation, art, or sport generally engaged in as a pasttime." Thus, the dictionary entry continues, "professional" is a term "disparagingly applied, to one who 'makes a trade' of anything that is properly pursued from higher motives, as a *professional politician.*"[5] The notion of entry into a religious order, with all the implicit oaths, vows, hierarchy, norms, and gatekeeping such entry entails, combined with the conversion of an intrinsically worthy endeavor into an instrument of personal or financial gain give some indication of what may be at stake and especially what may be the costs of the growing professionalization of political theory.

Most severe among these costs is the steady attenuation of political theory's orientation both to political life and to politically interested intellectuals outside the discipline. Debates in the profession are more often framed by internal quarrels—communitarian versus liberal, Habermas versus Foucault—than by problems or events in the political world, and the value of our contributions to these debates is brokered by degrees of recognition within the profession, a brokering whose outcome is largely predetermined by established hierarchies and networks. We are thus vulnerable to the very charge most often leveled against our most methodologically oriented political science colleagues: explanatory or normative power in the political world is rarely the referent for our work nor the index of its worth.

The growing Balkanization of political theory, and a relative sanguinity about this Balkanization among political theorists, can also be understood in terms of the forces of professionalization.[6] If professional recognition for a particular kind of work is scarce or unavailable in one subcaste of political theory, then it is easy enough to declare a new field or new juxtaposition of fields, anthologize a group of theorists in this area, inaugurate a new journal or professional association, and/or found a new American Political Science Association section. Ironically, such breakaway efforts, which are themselves the effects of professionalism, are often misrecognized by those who undertake them as antiprofessional political projects, with the consequence that the work of building a new institutional and intellectual niche in the profession is framed as a struggle in the front lines of a real-world political skirmish. Of course knowledge is always political and politics always involves battles over knowledge claims, but the stakes of these narrowly professional battles (predominantly but not exclusively matters of employment, advancement, and above all, signification within and recognition by a minuscule readership) surely do not exhaust the possibilities for political theory's articulation with political life.

The current professionalization of political theory is overdetermined. It is configured in part by contemporary pressures to professionalize and commodify every vocation, indeed every pasttime, no matter how countercultural (think of the "professional" skateboarder, rapper, or body piercing artist), and the corporatization of every aspect of public and private enterprise, including the university. But if these were its only sources, at least some political theorists—those who consider themselves opposed to the commodification and corporatization of everyday life—would be more likely to resist than abet the process. Yet such resistance is rare, thus raising the question of whether professionalization serves as a bulwark against felt worldly impotence on one hand, and against identity erosion and loss of secure territory for political theorists on the other, in short, as partial insulation against some of the boundary-eroding, identity-dissolving forces of the world historical and intellectual terrain shifts discussed above.

Our political world today is full of power, forces, and events but rather short on collective action. There are exceptions, of course—the Velvet Revolution, Tiananmen Square, even World Trade Organization protests—but as suggested in the discussion of capitalism above, the contemporary political world is largely organized by enormous forces and institutions controlled by no one and immensely difficult to challenge. We live this paradox daily in small and large ways: the world is radically disenchanted and at the same time the metaforces structuring it and the metadynamics moving it are in no one's hands, and pace Marx, stand little chance of coming under individual or collective human command. This does not necessarily complicate the work of political critique and diagnosis, but it severely problematizes the aspect of critical political theory oriented to the question, "What is to be done?" For those who insist on a tight, even seamless connection between diagnosis and action, who require that the action remedy the illness as defined by the theory, the situation becomes especially thorny: a political world immune to large-scale augmentation by human action is a world inevitably frustrating to critical political theorists. And so we take flight: into moral theory, which mostly works in abstraction from the concrete powers organizing political life, into ethics and aesthetics, in which relations with the other and with the world are generally theorized without strong reference to contemporary orders of power, into an ironic *amor fati* extended toward the world, or into pure critique. Or we simply retreat into the profession, where impassioned arguments and position taking need not resonate with the contemporary political landscape.

A second phenomenon weakening resistance to professionalization pertains to the boundary erosion around political theory discussed above. If the boundaries around political theory appear particularly porous and contestable today, this is a problem not only for the identity of the field but for the identity of individual political theorists. If a scholar of English literature writes brilliantly on Hobbes's *Leviathan*, if cultural anthropologists are currently the most incisive theorists of nationalism, if scholars of gender and race have developed genuinely new perspectives on social contract theory, if geographers have some of the most astute insights into the political implications of the transformations of time and space wrought by post-Fordist capitalism, then who am I and who is my constituency or reading audience? Indeed, if the disciplinary boundaries really disintegrate, what obscurity lies in wait for us in a world much vaster than a small cadre of colleagues whose card of entry to the order is modest mastery of approximately two dozen great books and fluency with a small number of watchwords: justice, liberty, power, obligation, constitutions, equality, citizenship, action, government, rule, polity? And what better way to secure ourselves against this impending identity crisis and potential obscurity than ever more public, organized, and policed recognition and certification of who and what we are?

* * * * *

I want to consider now these three domains in which political theory's boundaries are negotiated—the domain of the world, the domain of intellectual life, and the domain of the profession—as harboring three different forces exerted on and in the field of political theory. The world historical developments I have outlined are primarily dispersive in their effect on our subject matter; they corrode the boundaries between zones of human existence that have historically produced the ontological autonomy of the political and thus disperse the political itself. The intellectual developments, especially by disturbing conventional formulations of power and contesting conventional locales of power, disseminate the currency of the field and also parallel the world historical effects by dispelling the boundaries historically constitutive of the epistemological autonomy of the field. The professionalizing tendencies, while engaging some of these effects, mostly run in the opposite direction, constricting and narrowing the reach of the field and its qualified participants. In addition, professionalization invariably entails a turn away from the political world and even from a potential intellectual audience for political theory outside of its own membership. In short, we have, on one hand, dispersive, disseminating, and dispelling forces, and, on the other, a constricting and containing force.

A vibrant future for political theory depends in part on developing contrapuntal relations to the three sets of forces contouring and agitating its boundaries. Counterpoint, whether in music, painting, or verbal argument, is more complex and productive than simple opposition and does not carry the mythological or methodological valence of dialectics. Counterpoint is a deliberate art, at once open ended and tactical, that emanates from an antihegemonic sensibility and requires at least a modest embrace of spectral multiplicity to be comprehended. Counterpoint involves, first, the complicating of a single or dominant theme through the addition of contrasting themes or forces; it undoes a monolithic element through the multiplication of elements. Second, counterpoint sets off or articulates a thematic by means of contrast or juxtaposition; it highlights dominance through a kind of reverse othering. I want to insist on the value of counterpoint, in both of these senses, for the multifold project of renewing political theory's political concerns, renovating its identity, and developing its capacity to intervene in the restructuring of intellectual life. In short, counterpoint might be a late modern strategy for bringing to light and resisting certain forces that otherwise contour our practices. Following are some of the ways this contrapuntal strategy might work.

It is crucial that political theorists learn to move and work in the larger and less clearly demarcated, disciplined, and territorialized fields of thought and existence opened by recent world history and intellectual redistricting. Yet if political theory is concerned with the human negotiation of the powers, governance, and values of collective life, then it remains our task to discern and cultivate the distinctive spaces and idioms in which such negotiation can occur. This means, I think, taking the measure of the recent world historical and intellectual dispersion and dissemination of the political without simply capitulating to it, naively celebrating or abetting it. Indeed, it means drawing (nonabsolute) distinctions on behalf of distinctively political life and doing so against the very historical tide that is washing them away. In part an intervention in the political and intellectual world, it is also the case that the renewal of our identity as political theorists lies here, in coming to terms with the contemporary conditions of political life and political theory and self-consciously cultivating agency and identity from within these conditions.

Let me try to introduce more precision here. If the political is signaled by the presence of any human relations organized by power, which is one important way to signal it, especially if one seeks to demystify or denaturalize a particular order of domination, then it is inevitable that we would find the political everywhere today—in cultural, familial, economic, and psychosexual relations, and more. But if the political is alternatively signaled by the distinct problematic of negotiating the powers and values of enduring collectivities, which is another important way to signal it, especially if one seeks to attend to the prospects for democracy in late modernity, then the political cannot simply be indicated by the presence of power.[7] The intellectual tendencies of the last quarter century have been toward the first formulation, while conventional political theory clings hard to the second. The first renders almost everything political (and renders all theory political theory); the second radically delimits the scope of the political and tends not to see the politicalness of many of its own predicates—knowledge, language, kinship, nature, gender, regulatory norms, and more. What if we were to tack between these perspectives, retaining the emphasis on collectivity while expanding our sense of the reach and operations of power that collectivities harbor and through which collective life can be studied—the complex subjects and subjectivities, the rich range of discourses and practices comprising them?

Let us approach the same problem through the phenomenon of politicization and the dissemination of the problem of power in late modernity. To speak of politicizing something generally carries one of two meanings: either it entails corrupting a process or domain of activity with issues of interest or advantage, as in "the job search became so politicized that hiring the best candidate wasn't even a possibility," or it involves revealing relations of power in something ordinarily conceived in other terms, as in "feminist theory has politicized gender, showing it to be an effect of power rather than a natural phenomenon." What is common to these seemingly disparate usages is that politicization introduces power where it was presumed not to exist before. But in the wake of late-twentieth-century thought, especially Foucault, we now know power to be everywhere in the human universe, which means that, quite literally, everything pertaining to human existence can be politicized. Does this make everything pertaining to human existence the subject of political theory? (Does Plato triumph after all?) It is this move that I am counseling against, suggesting instead that we carve a distinction between the politicization of particular relations and endeavors, for example, science or canon formation or sex, and the bearing of this politicization on the political where the latter is understood as the distinct problematic of the values and powers binding collectivities. This is not to say politicization is irrelevant to the political—far from it. As Marx politicized private property, as feminists and gay activists have politicized marriage, an understanding of the exclusions and injuries performed by depoliticized forms of domination or regulation—those shrouded in discourses of the natural or the neutral—is crucial material for political theorists. But theoretical politicization of any activity or relation is not the same as theorizing the political, just as the presence of power, precisely because it is everywhere, cannot be equated with the problem of how we do and ought to order collective life.

If the world historical and intellectual disseminations of the political may be simultaneously thematized and offset by a self-conscious and strategic reterritorialization of the political on the part of political theory, the conservative, narrowing, and constraining effects of professionalism on political theory require a different kind of counterpoint. Here, deliberate and careful transgression, risk, and interdisciplinary adventurousness are in order— these are the strategies that will facilitate erudition in the organizing features of our time and make us worldly rather than narrow in our political theoretical approach to them. These are also the strategies that will educate us in the characteristics of language and rhetoric, and the techniques of reading and thinking, that have been developed so richly outside the discipline and are essential to our work. It is here, in our choice of research materials, colleagues, and audience, that we can most artfully confront the identity dissolution of political theory incited by the disseminating effects of the world historical and intellectual configurations of our time. It is here that we may most productively consort with those who are not our kind—those from other fields and with other foci—and not only be stretched by but also recover a sense of the project of political theory through the encounter.

Political theory aimed at critically apprehending our contemporary condition, I am suggesting, needs to engage closely without surrendering to the contemporary dissemination of politics, power, and theory. Our historically constitutive terms and questions—about power, action, political institutions, freedom, stability, change, membership, equality, obligation, domination, and justice—will indubitably continue to organize our work and identity, even as other terms are added. But while we allow these terms and questions to be reconfigured by the world historical changes and the intellectual developments that have so dramatically altered their meanings from what they were a century or twenty-five centuries ago, we can also reassert the singular value of political theory by recovering our constitutive orientation to the problem of how collectivities are conceived and ordered in the contemporary world, a world that poses as a most urgent and open question what kinds of collectivities currently or will next order and contain humanity. Thus, the problems of rule, sovereignty, and legitimacy, which persist as important problems, will contend on the one side with the loss of stable sovereign entities—states or subjects—and on the other with the discovery of other modalities of power that rival sovereignty in the ordering of collectivities. Questions about justice, our founding and enduring question, cannot presume a temporally stable, transcendental, undifferentiated concept of man; cannot presume the cultural neutrality of liberal (or any other) values; and cannot elide economic, familial, sexual, gendered, or racial orders of power that bear on what is just. Questions about the nature of the political cannot presume its radical independence from the cultural, the economic, and, above all, the technological. Questions about the relation of public and private must take the measure of the "politics" discovered in the private realm by a quarter century of feminist theory, of the complex hybridizations of public and private produced by contemporary capitalism, and, of course, of the fantastic reconfigurations of the meaning and experience of public and private induced by contemporary digital technologies. Questions about membership and citizenship will take the measure of the unstable, composite, dynamic, and often incoherent nature of contemporary collectivities at the international, national and subnational level; they must grapple with the slackening of the state-citizen tie and the awkward, multiple, and often fractious nature of other, especially transnational, claims on membership and forces of subjection, fealty, or obligation. Can citizenship be thought apart from generations-long belonging to a stable nation-state and hence independently of state sovereignty, law, constitutions or ethnic-religious homogeneity? What genealogical rupture in the mutually constitutive state-citizen relation does this thought require?

As I have suggested, political theory (or political science for that matter) is not the field that has most knowledgeably, carefully, or artfully explored the late modern transmogrifications in the configurations of social, political, economic, and cultural life invoked in the formulations above any more than it is the field that has developed the richest understandings of language, interpretation, and argument.[8] Although some contemporary political theory nods to the charred ground of conventional citizenship in its attempt to theorize "culture," "group rights," "difference," and "language," for example, much contemporary theorizing about citizenship remains linked to social contractarian accounts of the state, society, and individual on one side, or to attempts to move liberal principles of individualism and altruism toward an abstract cosmopolitanism or "parallel polis" on the other. Certainly, there is no need for political theorists to conduct primary research on the restructuring entailed in globalization, but to theorize the implications of this restructuring, we must go to the work that exhumes and examines it—in anthropology, cultural studies, political economy, geography, media studies. As political theorists, we do not need to develop original theories of rhetoric, semiotics, or interpretation, but to be effective readers of texts—events, canonical works, or historical developments—and to be as rigorous and self-reflexive as possible in the construction of our own arguments, we need to consult the fields that do make these studies, especially literary, rhetorical, and visual theory. If we do not make these crossings, we literally make ourselves stupid, about this world and the knowledges that will incisively apprehend and criticize it. This imperative, of course, also renders our contemporary task enormous, requiring as it does an expanded erudition that is wide and not only deep.

But this interdisciplinary traveling is only one antidote for the condition we find ourselves in today, a combination of theoretical and historical conservatism, hyperprofessionalism, and a certain remoteness from the world. If we are to survive the current erosions of our identity with more than a profession intact, we also need to introduce counterpoint to the antipolitical tendencies of professionalism. This would involve cultivating a political orientation for our work, foregrounding concern with the question of how collective life is ordered, what powers and possibilities it harbors, what prospects exist for advancing the values we argue that it should feature. No matter how much boundary crossing we do at the level of knowledge, it is only this turn that will renew the identity of political theory amidst current challenges. Such a turn not only implies replacing professionalism with the political world for sources of incitement and even potential audience, it involves close theoretical engagement with the powers now organizing political life, especially those of capitalism, with which I have suggested contemporary political theory has often been disinclined to engage.

But in this effort to reverse political theory's retreat into professionalism and to reorient it toward politics, we must also beware of capitulating to a certain pressure on theory itself today—to apply, to be true, or to solve immediate real-world problems. This is a pressure that must be resisted if the future of political theory is to approximate or even carry a trace of the richness of its past. This pressure has several sources, but the current "information phase" of capital is crucial: as information itself is unprecedentedly commodified and at the same time becomes the most significant commodity, this commodification and this significance effectively diminish the value of all thought not readily commodified. Hence, the intensifying demand on and in the universities, even on the humanities and arts, for knowledge that is applicable and marketable. This, combined with steadily growing corporate sponsorship of university life, overtly and indirectly incites us to turn against the autonomous value of theory; consciously and unconsciously, we are threatened with a terrifying degree of academic marginalization, perhaps even extinction, if we submit theory to this emerging table of values.

Why can't theory meet the demand for applicability or usefulness without being sacrificed? What is it about theory that is destroyed by such a demand? The question of theory's nature and purview today is fiercely contested; even as a question, it is markedly fragmented—no two disciplines or subfields mean the same thing by theory nor value it in the same way.[9] Within political science alone, the appellation of theory has been appropriated for an extraordinary range of work—from rational choice and game theory to cultural and literary theory to analytic philosophy to hermeneutics to historical interpretations of canonical works. But in all cases, just as politics and political theory define themselves against and through their hypothesized Others, theory, too, takes its definition through differentiation, whether from empiricism, method, science, storytelling, the arts, history, truth, experience, poetry, observation. That these alterities are what create and circumscribe theory is not the problem. Rather, it is a contemporary anxiety about theory's difference as such, and in particular about its enigmatic and other-worldly character, that we would do well to allay rather than submit to.

Theory is not simply different from description; rather, it is incommensurate with description.[10] Theory is not simply the opposite of application but carries the impossibility of application. As a meaning-making enterprise, theory depicts a world that does not quite exist, that is not quite the world we inhabit. But this is theory's incomparable value, not its failure. Theory does not simply decipher the meanings of the world but recodes and rearranges meanings to reveal something about the meanings and incoherencies that we live with. To do this revelatory and speculative work, theory must work to one side of direct referents, or at least it must disregard the conventional meanings and locations of those referents. Theory violates the self-representation of things to represent those things and their relation—the world—differently. Thus, theory is never "accurate" or "wrong"; it is only more or less illuminating, more or less provocative, more or less of an incitement to thought, imagination, desire, possibilities for renewal.

There is another reason that theory cannot be brought to the bar of truth or applicability. Insofar as theory imbues contingent or unconscious events, phenomena, or formations with meaning and with location in a world of theoretical meaning, theory is a sense-making enterprise of that which often makes no sense, of that which may be inchoate, unsystematized, inarticulate. It gives presence to what may have a liminal, evanescent, or ghostly existence. Thus, theory has limited kinship with the project of accurate representation; rather its value lies in the production of a new representation, in the production of coherence and meaning that it does not find lying on the ground but that, rather, it forthrightly fashions. Similarly, theory does not simply articulate needs or desires but rather argues for their existence and thus literally brings them into being. As theory interprets the world, it fabricates that world (*pace* Marx! especially Marx!); as it names desire, it gives reason and voice to desire and thus fashions a new order of desire; as it codifies meaning, it composes meaning. Theory's most important political offering is this opening of a breathing space between the world of common meanings and the world of alternative ones, a space of potential renewal for thought, desire, and action. And it is this that we sacrifice in capitulating to the demand that theory reveal truth, deliver applications, or solve each of the problems it defines. In responding to the pressures of professionalism, then, a double counterpoint is necessary to offset political theory's deflected attention to contemporary political life and its anxiety about its "difference" from other modes of inquiry, its remove from the empirical, from facticity, from accurate representation, from truth. While perhaps contradictory at first blush, the project of retrieving the world as an object of theory and of recuperating the value of theory as a distinctive form of figuring the world not only both resist current troubling influences on the discipline but are compatible in the project of identity renewal for political theory: they connect our work to political theory's rich canonical past while honing it for the work of understanding a singular present.

* * * * *

Political theory, in addition to losing many of its territory markers in recent decades, has tacitly ceded sovereignty over its own subject matter. This condition, I have suggested, is the consequence of (1) a dissemination of power and politics, a dissemination about which political theory must become erudite and in which it must intervene; (2) political theory's relative failure to be enriched by interpretative and rhetorical techniques developed elsewhere in the humanities and interpretative social sciences; (3) political theory's attenuated relation to the subject of political life understood as the negotiation of power in collectivities; and (4) challenges to theory's intrinsic worth that press it in the direction of applied social science. Recovery of our identity in the face of disseminated theories and practices of politics is hinged to recovery of our value. Recovery of our value in turn depends on the acquisition of fluency in the complexities of power and language as they have been adumbrated outside the discipline, as well on cross-cutting the currents of professionalism to draw our questions and cares from political life, broadly construed and at least partially to insulate theory from the relentless commodification and capitalization of knowledge. A tall order? It is possible that the human world has never been so difficult to fathom, to theorize, to imagine justice for, to render just. Our theoretical blankets of comfort have perhaps never been thinner, nor redemption more faint. We should not be astonished that our work is so hard.

## NOTES

*Thanks to Robyn Marasco for research assistance and to Stephen White, Judith Butler, and Gail Hershatter for their critical readings.*

1. Foucault's return to Kant's question, "Was Ist Aufklarung?" is a rich instance of the strategy of admixture here. See Michel Foucault, "Was Ist Aufklarung?" in *The Foucault Reader*, ed. Paul Rabinow (New York: Pantheon, 1984).
2. Giorgio Agamben, *Means without End: Notes on Politics* (Minneapolis: University of Minnesota, 2000), 113.
3. Sheldon Wolin, *The Presence of the Past* (Baltimore: Johns Hopkins University Press, 1989), 1.
4. *Oxford English Dictionary* (New York: Oxford University Press, 1971), 1427, 1428.
5. Ibid., 1428.
6. Here I refer to the division of political theory into distinct strains: liberal democratic thought, Arendtian-inflected democratic thought, (liberal) communitarian thought, neo-Nietzschean and poststructuralist thought, Habermassian thought, Straussian thought, Marxist thought, moral political philosophy, psychoanalytic thought, and still others harder to name. While there is crossover terrain and there are also crossover artists, for the most part, each strain has its own subcanon, its own roster of stars and rising stars, its own groundbreaking and self-endorsed monographs and anthologies, its own newsletters and conferences.
7. Some of the most interesting contemporary philosophers of the political reject both of these formulations of the political. See, for example, Jacques Ranciere, "Ten Theses on Politics," *Theory & Event* 5, no. 3 (2002), retrieved from http://muse.jhu.edu/journals/theory_and_event/, or consider Giorgio Agamben's recent insistence that "politics is a force field, an intensity, not a substance" and that this force field is delimited by the "friend/enemy" relation (seminar, Princeton University, October 15, 2001). I find these accounts provocative, if not fully convincing, and above all appreciate their incitement to theoretical conversation about what we mean by politics and the political today.
8. The general intellectual impoverishment of political theory on these developments is apparent in a wide range of topics. For example, an anthropology graduate student remarked in a seminar I recently taught on political theories of tolerance that culture is more reified and less theorized in the work of most contemporary democratic theorists addressing multiculturalism than it was for anthropologists in the nineteenth century. Treated as a kind of primal, transhistorical, and subrational good, assumed to be espe-

cially cherished and valued by oppressed minorities, culture is generally counterposed to liberalism and cosmopolitanism, both of which are presumed to be relatively cultureless.

9. At the moment when the very possibility of apprehending the "real world" has been challenged by postfoundationalist analysis and by the insistence on the embodiment of all description in discourse, every utterance can now potentially qualify as a theoretical one.

10. These thoughts were developed in the context of a seminar on Jean Laplanche's *Seduction, Translation and the Drives* offered by Judith Butler at Princeton University in November 2001. Working from my notes, I am uncertain which of these thoughts are Butler's, which are her reading of Laplanche's remarks about the nature of theory, and which are my own thoughts in response to Butler and Laplanche. So this paragraph must stand as collaboratively written, if unintentionally so.

6       GLOBALIZING POLITICAL THEORY

*ROLAND BLEIKER*[1]

**M**odern political thought has traditionally revolved around debates that
are central to life within the nation state. But processes of globalization have
weakened the significance of state boundaries and engendered new transnational dilemmas, from global terrorism to economic interdependence and the
cross-territorial flow of refugees. Have these and other phenomena changed
the world to the point that new concepts and theories are required to deal with
the political, as Adriana Cavarero suggests,[2] or is it, following George
Kateb,[3] primarily a matter of updating and extending the canon? I would like
to explore a path that leads somewhere between these two poles. Political theory still provides rich and highly relevant sources to grapple with the dilemmas of globalization, but these sources can remain relevant only if their users
too embark on a more active global journey.

The issues at stake may become clearer if confronted with a puzzle that
unites all the multifarious aspects of globalization: the rapid loss of certainty.
Perhaps one can even speak of a loss of meaning, if one understands meaning, as Zaki Laïdi does, in terms of stable political foundations as well as a
sense of unity and common purpose, a telos, so to speak.[4] We now live in a
world of gray zones, transgressions and multitudes—a world in which "ends
collide," as Stephen White noted in the introduction to this volume.[5]

Two ensuing challenges stand out as particularly important. The first is
how to deal with difference, be it of an ethnic, racial, gendered, cultural, religious, political, ideological or any other nature. The loss of certainty has lead
to a widespread search for stability in old and seemingly stable identities,
which have often been politicized in a hostile juxtaposition to what is different from them. Examples abound, ranging from ethnic conflict in Rwanda,
Bosnia, Kosovo or East Timor to increasingly frequent manifestations of
xenophobia in much of the western world. The task here consists of concep-

tualizing otherness within and across national boundaries in a way that optimizes possibilities for respectful, or at least nonviolent, relationships between identity and difference.

A second major challenge of globalization consists of articulating foundations in a world where the nation state has ceased to be the sole and perhaps even prime site of political legitimization. A great variety of crucial projects, from determining the direction of global economic governance to defending human rights, require transnational, ethical-political foundations. But how to create them in the absence of a universally accepted institutional structure is far from clear. Here too the problems created by the loss of certainty have been avoided through a reassertion of often problematic essences, be it in the form of religious fundamentalism, liberal triumphalism or the good-versus-evil rhetoric that characterized the U.S. response to the terrorist attacks of September 2001. Diverse and even opposed as these political approaches may be, they all stake a claim to uncontested universal validity. They all express a desire to reestablish the sense of order and certitude that existed during the Cold War: an inside/outside world in which, according to U.S. President George W. Bush, "you are either with us or against us."[6] The task here consists of accepting the politically and historically contingent nature of foundations, but doing so in a way that still retains possibilities for affirmative judgments and for grounding political projects, sometimes even universal ones, in a perpetually contested transnational realm.

Neither of these challenges is necessarily new. Nor are the phenomena that have precipitated them. Processes of globalization go back at least to Marco Polo, and so does the fear of uncertainty. Periods of instability have often led to antagonistic articulations of identity against difference, as for instance in Germany during the 1930s. Likewise, the problem of foundations is as old as politics itself. But for most of the modern epoch these challenges arose and could be met within relatively stable institutional frameworks provided by the nation state. That is no longer the case today, as many of the most difficult disputes take place in an inherently contested transnational realm. The challenges that these disputes pose are of a qualitatively different order, akin perhaps to what occurred during two pivotal moments in western history, the period following the decay of the Greek polis in the 5th century B.C. and the collapse of the theocratic order in the transition from the medieval to the modern period. In both of these transitions, just as today, a deeply entrenched order disintegrated and people were inevitably confronted with the task of legitimizing political projects on new and highly uncertain grounds.

Political theory offers various possibilities for engaging the challenges ahead, perhaps more so than the discipline of international relations, which has tended to either ignore or essentialize questions of identity and foundations. The most influential contributions to international relations scholarship, particularly in North America, remain framed by the debate that gave rise to the respective academic discipline: the dispute that was waged between liberals and realists in the period between the two World Wars. There are heated arguments on various important issues but both traditions of thought are surprisingly similar in their fundamental assumptions. They revolve around an image of a global system dominated by nation states and one key structural feature, that of anarchy: the absence of a central regulatory authority.[7] The international is portrayed as a realm of threats and dangers. While liberals believe that some of these perils can be mediated through international cooperation, the standard realist response is to protect state sovereignty, order and civility at the domestic level by promoting policies that maximize the state's military capacity and, so it is assumed, its security. That this very practice only increases everyone else's insecurity is evident, not least through extensive realist attempts to theorize the respective dilemmas. Far less certain, though, is whether realist theories and policies remain adequate, and ethical for that matter, at a time when process of globalization have transformed the very nature of the global system and its most influential actors.

Between further theorizing international relations and internationalizing political theory the latter may thus be a more promising route. Or it does, at least, provide an alternative mode of engagement, one that is not obliged to retrace the boundaries of worn-out disciplinary quarrels. A variety of approaches have already begun to engage the global in ways that lead neither to structural platitudes nor to a fatalism that generates, justifies and then masks its own conflictive logic.[8] Political theory can make an important contribution to these debates, but to do so it must become more active in addressing the pressing problems of our time. The lack of communication between theorists and practitioners is notorious. When urged to comment on the key political challenges of his day, Heidegger, for instance, responded that he could not help, that it is not the task of thinking to make public statements on moral and practical issues.[9] But doing just that has nevertheless been a central concern of many theorists and philosophers, from Machiavelli (how to govern the newly emerging modern state) to Arendt (how to deal with the holocaust legacy) and Rawls (how to establish principles of justice in a liberal state). A revival of this practice is needed, not to deliver indisputable policy recommendations, but to provide insight and options to an audience larger than academic specialists: insights into the construction, nature and implications of existing political constellations; and options to visualize, explore and possibly ground alternatives to them.

This essay will begin with a further specification of what is at stake in the process of globalization. Subsequent sections take up questions of identity and foundations. I end with suggestions about the type of mindset that could help us face both challenges. Central here is that political theory should press not only beyond the state but also beyond the canon of western thought. An active, dialogical and sustained engagement with nonwestern traditions is essential to understand and engage the key dilemmas of our time.

A brief disclaimer is in order before the journey can begin. I do not offer solutions. I only identify challenges and fields of engagement that seem promising. I advance the ensuing explorations through what could be called a moderate Nietzschean approach: a position that accepts the contingency of knowledge and politics, but refuses to equate such situatedness with an inability to advance critique or decide on political action. I am not suggesting that this is the only way of tackling the dilemmas of our day. But I believe it is one that offers rich insights and the flexibility necessary to engage global challenges that may remain as elusive as they have become important.

## GLOBALIZING UNCERTAINTY

Globalization is an omnipresent and unruly phenomenon. Its manifestations are as diverse as its interpretations are contestable.[10] One could, borrowing from Adorno, say that the concept of globalization always lags behind itself, for "as soon as it is applied empirically it ceases to be what it claims it is."[11] Some see globalization primarily as an economic process. Others view it as a more radical series of events, emerging from cross-territorial interactions of people, technology, money, images and ideas. The increasing volume and scale of these flows, Arjun Appadurai argues, has produced "interactions of a new order and intensity."[12] Paul Virilio, likewise, believes that we are currently witnessing a revolution in global relations, comparable to the fundamental impact of changing mass transportation in the 19th century and means of telecommunication in the twentieth. This transformation revolves around the use and regulation of speed, which signifies the relationship between time and space. Space has decreased in importance, Virilio claims, and time has taken over as the key criterion around which global dynamics revolve.[13]

Globalization has led to various cross-territorial interactions that render the existing political and mental boundaries increasingly anachronistic. Nation states are no longer the only player in a world where financial, productive, cultural and informational dynamics have come to disobey, transgress, and challenge the deeply entrenched principle of sovereignty. Globalization is gradually eroding not only the privileged position of the state but also, and perhaps more importantly, the discourses that have come to justify this privileged standpoint. Jürgen Habermas, when analyzing the role of global markets, refers to a legitimacy crisis of the nation state.[14] States have, of course, never been as sovereign as they appear.[15] Nor have they lost their central position in domestic and global politics.[16] But a great variety of cross-territorial actors and factors, from multinational corporations to media networks and protest movements, are becoming increasingly influential. This is why several authors draw attention to what they believe is an increasing "deterritorialisation" of the world: processes that call into question the very spatial organization of the state and interstate system, that is, the key pillars of "state sovereignty, territorial integrity and community identity."[17] Consider one of many possible implications: Virilio predicts that the globe will no longer primarily be divided spatially into North and South, but temporally into two forms of speed, absolute and relative. The "haves" and "have-nots" are then sorted out between those who live in the hyperreal shrunken world of instant communication, cyberdynamics, and electronic money transactions—and those, more disadvantaged than ever, who live in the real space of local villages, cut off from the temporal forces that drive politics and economics.[18]

Loss of human control is one of the most widely perceived effects of eroding sovereignty. Such feelings are, of course, not new. The modern project itself can be seen as an attempt to suppress ambiguity through various ways of asserting control over the world.[19] But causes and manifestations of uncertainty today have taken on new and inherently transnational dimensions. We hear of a nation state that is no longer able to uphold the spheres of justice and civility its boundaries were supposed to protect. We hear of a global market, whose random dynamics are increasing the gap between rich and poor. We hear of an economic system increasingly run by multilateral institutions and multinational corporations: big unaccountable structures whose strategic leitmotifs and decision making principles reflect the imperatives of short-term capital, rather than the long-term concerns more attuned to the protection of average people and an already stretched global ecosystem. There is no lack of voices that draw attention to these problems. The so-called antiglobalization movement is perhaps the most vocal expression of discontent. But globalization itself can hardly be opposed. It is neither reversible nor, for that matter, would such a reversal necessarily be desirable. Globalization has engendered as many positive aspects as it has precipitated problems. What can be challenged, though, are the prevalent political approaches to globalization, such as the neoliberal trust in free-market economics. Whether or not the respective policies should be challenged is, of course, an entirely different question. But it is a question that must be posed and debated publicly. This is why Vandana Shiva urges us to view globalization not as something inevitable, but, at least in part, as a constructed narrative, "a political project which can be responded to politically."[20] And this is precisely where political theorists come into play: they can offer valuable insights into the nature and direction of globalization.

## THE PROBLEM OF IDENTITY

Globalization has engendered widespread fear not only about the absence of certainty, control and participation, but also about the loss of identity. For centuries, the state has promoted, legitimized and protected identity constructs, particularly those essential for the process of nation building. The state provided mythological and institutional frameworks that separated self from other, inside from outside, safe from threatening.[21] But the state is being undermined in various ways, not least through processes of fragmentation and disintegration that accompany globalization.[22] These phenomena pose serious threats to many established identities and communities. The resulting anxieties have produced reactions that defend particular identities and cultural traditions against everything that threatens them. The loss of meaning is then countered by political discourses that find coherence and stability in the past, as in ethnic or religious roots that distinguish one social group from another. In many cases the reassertions of identity have taken on nationalist tones. From Rwanda to Fiji, from Sri Lanka to Bosnia, from Kosovo to East Timor, from Kashmir to the Middle East, the political manipulation and mobilization of identity led to widespread violence, even instances of genocide. States in the process of disintegration are by no means the only places where the loss of control is compensated for through a hostile defense of identity against difference. In much of the affluent and seemingly secure western world the fear of uncertainty has led to a rise of xenophobia. The reemergence of far-right political parties across Europe is only one manifestation of this trend.

Problems of identity and difference have always been central to political life. They can be located at the heart of modern politics: in practices of national security, for instance, which are based on the very idea that safety and order can only be created by constituting as potentially threatening anything that lies outside the designated inside-zone. Michael Shapiro illustrates this problematique from an unusual but revealing perspective. He shows that in tribal societies, such as the Hurons or the Aztecs, warfare was an important, even vital activity through which a sense of collective identity was forged and maintained.[23] Many prestate societies did not hide this aspect of war, but celebrated it proudly and publicly. Shapiro argues that this ontological dimension of warfare is equally important in today's state societies, except that its presence is concealed by a language that has rationalized war as if it were a mere response—necessary and pragmatic—to an objective external threat. But warfare today is far more than a utilitarian policy: it is integral to the constitution of our identity. Hidden behind a pragmatic understanding of war is an ontological justification of state violence in which the cultural production of an enmity, an antagonistic Other, is essential for the maintenance of a body politic and a coherent societal whole.[24] But with the gradual erosion of this body politic (the nation state), the discourses that have sustained it appear more and more inadequate, and this at the very same time as they are being reinforced and held up as the sole response to the very forces that have already rendered them anachronistic.

While not new, tensions over competing identities are becoming increasingly transnational. Even seemingly local issues, such as conflicts around different identifications in a Bosnian village, are intrinsically linked to a variety of regional, national, transnational and global dynamics, ranging from party politics to the impact of worldwide television networks and the practice of humanitarian intervention. An adequate response to such challenges must thus take into account the impact of globalization. But there is no panacea for doing so. Tensions between identity and difference in an ongoing situation of genocide are, for instance, of a different order—and require different solutions—than those that occur in an otherwise well-functioning multicultural democracy. Without doing injustice to these disparities it is nevertheless possible to locate broad mindsets with which the task of meeting the respective challenges can be approached.

A way out of the globalized and self-generating cycle of identity and violence begins with recognizing the constructed nature of identifications and the conflicts that issue from them. Once the artificial demarcations of identity have become internalized in language, school curricula, political institutions, moral discourses and the like, their mythical origin appears more and more real until the ensuing world-views, and the conflicts they generate, seem inevitable, even natural. We begin to "lie herd-like in a style obligatory for all," Nietzsche would say.[25] To recognize the constructed dimensions of identity is not to deny their existence or to devalue their importance. Identities are essential for our individual and social existence. They give people a sense of belonging. They provide political communities with the coherence necessary to articulate and advance common projects. William Connolly recognizes that such standards of identity and responsibility are essential for political life, even if they do injustice to what is excluded through their application.

Identities, he argues, are neither fictitious nor naturally given. They simply are indispensable.[26] But they do not automatically lead to political problems. Connolly believes that the most serious cause of fragmentation and violence today stem not from interactions with difference, but from doctrines and movements that suppress it by trying to reinstate a unified faith in one form of identification.[27]

The task ahead consists of articulating identity in less antagonistic ways and in rendering these articulations politically acceptable. Political theory offers a multitude of possibilities to contribute to this project. Some use Nietzsche or Heidegger as a starting-point to theorize the relationship and responsibility to otherness. Others find inspiration in Levinas and his attempt to develop an ethics of responsibility that refuses to encompass difference into the same. Ethics then becomes a question of developing a relationship to alterity that displays understanding of and respect for the other's different identity performances.[28] This is not to say that acceptance of and tolerance towards alterity can eliminate conflicts between different identifications. Rather, the challenge is, as Paul Ricoeur puts it, to "bring conflicts to the level of discourse and not let them degenerate into violence."[29] In an ideal scenario, such a discursive engagement with difference should even go a step beyond tolerance, for tolerance assumes a superior standard against which anything else is to be judged. Accepting alterity, by contrast, would entail affirming one's identity in a way that permits a dialogical and empathetic relationship with difference. Some even argue that such an engagement is most crucial precisely at those moments when the other's position poses a fundamental danger to one's own values.[30] But the world does not always offer ideal scenarios. An unconditional acceptance of otherness cannot—and indeed should not—always work in practice. There are moments when the assertion and imposition of one identity over another becomes desirable, perhaps even politically indispensable. The struggle against fascism is one example where there is, at least from today's perspective, widespread consensus about refusing to accept, or even tolerate, diverging identification patterns. But even in such extreme cases, successful and fair solutions to political challenges are more likely to emerge if positions are not dogmatically asserted, but carefully justified through a critical and self-reflective understanding of the tensions between identity and difference.

## THE PROBLEM OF FOUNDATIONS

If political theory is to engage the global dilemmas of identity and difference, then these debates have to be extended into a postnational context. But doing so is an intricate task, and not only because the transnational realm lacks an institutional framework that can ground alternative conceptions of the political. A sustained engagement with the difference problematique would require a fundamental rethinking of deeply entrenched political mindsets and practices.

An acceptance of difference is often associated with postmodern theories, and thus with a fateful fall into a nihilist abyss. International relations scholars are particularly concerned that heeding such theoretical voices would open up the floodgates to relativistic ravings according to which "anything goes" and "any narrative is as valid as another."[31] Upon closer reading such strong warnings often indicate less an opposition to identity issues than a fear of not being able to articulate and ground specific value commitments and the political projects that issue from them. The perception is perhaps similar to the dilemma Stephen White located in Heidegger's work: "extraordinary insights into the responsibility to otherness, matched by deeply flawed insights into the responsibility to act."[32] But do Heidegger's philosophical contributions actually preclude the grounding of specific political engagements? He certainly shied away from this task. And his problematic relationship to Nazism has been widely cited as proof that his ideas, and Nietzschean thought in general, are inherently problematic. Without minimizing the political and philosophical implications of Heidegger's link to fascism, the dangers of totalitarian thought and practice can be eliminated neither through a denial of difference nor through a simple affirmation of seemingly natural and foundational values. Indeed, a brief historical comparison reveals that the major challenge ahead is not relativism, difficult as it may be, but the search for foundations that can be recognized as just and politically acceptable even in a disputed postnational context.

The world today may well stand at a crucial historical juncture similar to the one Europe faced in the transition from the medieval to the modern period. The first transition has been characterized by the recurring inability to come to terms with what Nietzsche called the death of God: the disappearance, at the end of the Middle Ages, of a generally accepted world view that provided a stable ground from which it was possible to assess nature, knowledge, common values, truth, politics; in short, life itself. Connolly offers one of the most illuminating contemporary interpretations of the long struggle in a modern world where there is no longer a God that serves as a unifying center for humanity. He shows that while successive attempts to ground certainty in other external sources run into grave difficulties, the insistence that such foundations must be found has remained a prominent modern theme.[33] For Renaissance humanists the quest for essences centered around attempts to elevate "man" to the measure of all things. During the Enlightenment it was trust in science and universal reason. For romantics it was the belief in a dei-fied Self, and for Marxists it consisted of faith in history's teleological dimen-sion. Jean-François Lyotard portrays the contemporary quest for founda-tional authority as an attempt to ground and legitimize knowledge in reference to a grand narrative, a universalizing framework that aims at eman-cipating the individual by mastering the conditions of life.[34]

While the central moral and political authority of the papacy had been lost for good, the modern state was at least able to provide a strong institutional framework through which the recurring quest for foundational certainty could be politically implemented and masked. But in the age of globalization the state is gradually loosing its concealing power. The ensuing political seepage into the transnational reveals that the lack of stable foundations is not an epistemological flaw that can be attributed to misguided postmodern rav-ings, but an empirical fact: a political challenge that calls for engaging and innovative insights, not metaphysical deflections.

How, then, is it possible to define norms, set policy priorities and advance justice in a world that lacks both a broad political consensus and an institu-tional framework that can generate, legitimize and uphold any possible com-promise among clashing interests? The purpose of political theory is not to advance definitive answers to these difficult questions. Doing so is the task of politicians and requires assessing the unique circumstances that surround each decision. The challenge for political theory consists, rather, of identify-ing and exploring the type of mindset that most likely leads to appropriate and fair practical results. Such a journey begins with recognizing the dangers entailed in elevating a majoritarian position to the level of uncontested truth, no matter how insightful, logical and morally imperative this compulsion appears. Any political position or system, whether universalized or local, whether anchored in an essentialized claim or a historically contingent legiti-mization, rests on a structure of exclusion that accompanies efforts to separate right from wrong, good from evil, moral from immoral.

Making choices, drawing lines and defending them are inevitable in a world of clashing interests. But to remain adequate, legitimate and fair, we must set out the political foundations that justify our choices in full aware-ness of their political function. They need to be submitted to periodic scrutiny and readjustment. Judith Butler speaks of the contingent nature of founda-tions. But for her, the recognition that power pervades all aspects of society does not necessarily lead into a nihilistic abyss. It merely shows that political closure occurs through attempts to establish foundational norms that lie beyond power. Likewise, to reopen this political domain is not to do away with foundations as such, but to acknowledge their contingent character, to illuminate what they authorize, exclude and foreclose.[35]

Instead of accepting the politically contingent nature of their positions, many approaches to the theory and practice of international relations depoliticise the choices they make by viewing them through a set of foundational norms. Examples of such practices can be found across the entire political spectrum. Consider the recent rise of fundamentalism: authentic foundational norms are reasserted in the face of a rapidly fading sense of certainty. The respective political movements, be they based in Christian, Islamic or any other religious identifications, are widely discredited, even vilified, by dominant secular political forces. And yet, the very battle against the dangers of radical fundamentalism is fought in a strong fundamentalist spirit itself. Look at how the US response to the terrorist attacks on New York and Washington has been advanced in a rhetoric of "good" versus "evil." One can read this reaction as a desire to return to the familiarity of dualistic and militaristic Cold War thinking patterns. The illusion of safety is sought in the desire to reestablish the sense of certitude that existed prior to September 11. Most people, including the author of this essay, readily agree that defending democratic principles against terrorist threats is a worthwhile endeavor. It is, indeed, essential. Whether or not a foundationalist approach is helpful to this task is an entirely different question. Various analysts strongly challenge this assumption. Douglas Klusmeyer, Astri Suhrke and Roxanne Euben, for instance, believe that employing the rhetoric of good and evil prevents both serious investigations into the problem of terrorism and, perhaps more importantly, innovative solutions to addressing it.[36] Evil is a term of condemnation for an inherently irrational phenomenon. It can neither be fully comprehended nor addressed, except through state-based and militaristic forms of intimidation and retaliation, which are hardly adequate to meet the increasingly complex and transnational security challenges of our time.

The reflective qualities of political theory can carve out the intellectual space necessary to recognize the consequences of foundational closure. But critique is, of course, not enough. We also need viable alternatives to foundationalism. Defending them may even require a momentary closing of dialogue and thinking space. It certainly requires taking decisions, which is one of the most difficult and frightening tasks, as Kierkegaard already knew, for the consequences of decisions can, by definition, not be calculated at the moment they are taken.[37] Otherwise there would be nothing left to decide. That is, indeed, the very essence of a decision: a leap of faith beyond the known and the empirically knowable.

Political theory can make the leap into the unknown territory of globalization less frightening. The debate about foundations offers concrete help, even though it has been framed in unnecessarily dichotomous terms. On one side are radical Nietzschean theorists whose suspicion of totalizing thought and foundational norms is equated with a deconstruction of the very project of modernity. Representative here is the later Wittgenstein, Heidegger, the early Frankfurt School, much of contemporary French philosophy and so-called postmodern thought. Adorno, Horkheimer, Foucault, Lyotard, Derrida, Spivak and Rorty are among those viewed as key contributors. On the other side of the spectrum we find those theorists for whom the main challenge consists of reviving, rather than abandoning Enlightenment values. Their ambition lies in theorizing the normative or procedural preconditions necessary for the protection and advancement of civilized life. Habermas and Rawls are seen as particularly representative of this more universally inclined and optimistically perceived tradition. But a growing number of authors theorize the rich middle ground between these two opposing poles. Pierre Bourdieu and Richard Bernstein, for instance, see the central opposition that characterizes our time, the one between objectivism and relativism, as largely misleading.[38] For them, and for an increasing number of contemporary political theorists, there are no either/or extremes. They recognize that we must take political decisions, but that we do not need to choose between an ultimate faith in stable foundations and a relentless fall into a nihilist abyss.[39]

The potential for exploring the middle ground between objectivism and relativism may become clearer if we draw a distinction between foundationalism and universalism. The former inevitably leads to political closure while the latter has become necessary in an age of globalization. Many of the most pressing problems of our day can no longer be solved at the level of the nation state. These problems are of a transnational nature. They have transnational causes and require transnational solutions. Global decision making, application and legitimization has thus become a political imperative. But contrary to Lyotard, the ensuing universalized engagement does not necessarily lead to a totalizing grand narrative. One could even argue, as Andrew Linklater has, that the very acceptance of difference, which lies at the heart of the postmodern project, does in itself contain a universal claim.[40]

## POLITICAL THEORY AS GLOBAL DIALOGUE

There is, of course, a big gap between recognizing the need for global solutions and finding agreement on how to reach these solutions, not to speak of what they actually are. Democracy offers perhaps the most widely accepted model for global decision making. But democracy, as we know it, is closely intertwined with the institutions and territorial boundaries of the nation state. How to extend its application into the transnational realm is far from clear, although the desirability of such a move is underlined by the growing literature on cosmopolitan democracy.[41] Even if practically feasible, such a universalized democratic framework could be ethically viable only if it remains sensitive towards the contingency not only of the respectively created norms and political solutions, but also of the very procedures that have led to them. A global democratic practice thus needs to be self-reflective about its own values, most notably about the fact that democracy is a product of western historical experiences. This is not to say that democratic values are exclusively western. There are as many opponents of democracy in the West as there are proponents of it in the rest of the world.

Accepting the challenge to apply democracy to global issues is to extend understandings of democracy, contested and contestable as they are, beyond models and institutions into a procedural realm; a move that is meanwhile well accepted, or at least intensely discussed, among political theorists.[42] Habermas's discourse ethics is perhaps the best known procedural framework that tries to meet such a challenge.[43] But his communicative approach is as strongly rooted in western traditions as are the democratic principles he seeks to extend. Habermas and most other political philosophers have relied almost exclusively on western examples and sources of insight. One could argue, as many have done, that globalization is above all a process of westernization, and that it is thus essential to investigate the very sources of this evolution.[44] True, perhaps, at least to some extent. But that is only part of the story. Although western institutions and mindsets have spread throughout the globe, an undifferentiated universal assessment of them suppresses not only valuable insights, but also local differences. It fails to appreciate the fragmentation and contradictions, the practices of resistance that arise precisely as a reaction against homogenization. Appadurai is one of many postcolonial theorists who acknowledge the global influence of western ideas while, at the same time, revealing how "different societies appropriate the materials of modernity differently."[45]

In an age of globalization, political theory can remain relevant only if its practitioners embark on an active dialogue with nonwestern modes of thought, perhaps even with nonmodern ones as well. An engagement with the legacy of ancient Chinese philosophy illustrates the potential that could emerge from what Roxanne Euben calls "comparative political theory."[46] This is only one example of many, and it can be sketched out here only in the most rudimentary terms. But consider how for Taoists the process of understanding political problems, and of choosing between goals or options, is as much an instinctive as a rational process. Before making an apparently conscious decision, intuitional factors have often already shaped the outcome of the decision–making process. One of Chuang-tzu's well-known passages acknowledges the limits of perception, knowledge and communication:

> Chuang-tzu and Hui Shih were strolling on the bridge above the Hao river.
> "Out swim the minnows, so free and easy," said Chuang-tzu.
> "That's how fish are happy."
> "You are not a fish. Whence do you know that the fish are happy?"
> "You aren't me, whence do you know that I don't know the fish are happy?"[47]

Rather than resigning into a relativist defeatism, Taoists embarked on an affirmative path by supplementing rational analysis with insights derived from detached awareness, instinct, wisdom, and spontaneity. A.C. Graham sums up the ancient Chinese attitude to reason more generally as follows: "reason is for questions of means; for your ends in life listen to aphorisms, example, parable and poetry."[48]

Such positions obviously stand in contrast to most prevailing western assumptions. Here too, Habermas is a good comparative example. Although he is skeptical about the possibility of justifying our ends solely by rational means, Habermas's procedural trust in reason is as prominent and unwavering as his commitment to universalism. For Habermas, modernity must rely on reason because of very specific historical circumstances, namely the need to ground authority out of itself, rather than by way of borrowing from or rejecting the ideas of a passed period.[49] Reason occupies a different role in China, where the urge to break with tradition has historically been much weaker than the desire to draw from the wisdom of past rulers, philosophers and poets. One of the most notable recent exceptions to this tendency is, of course, the Communist revolution. But many of the earlier cultural features remain embedded in the Chinese language and thus continue to shape social and political attitudes. As opposed to most Indo-European languages, Chinese does not have an existential word like "to be," which refers to both the existence and the nature of a thing or a person. From a Chinese perspective "you know not the essence of a thing, but what name fits it," stresses Graham, one of the foremost scholars of Chinese thought and grammar.[50] Such semantic features reveal that any form of linguistic representation expresses a relationship between objects and human-made names, which are by definition open to disagreement and change. "Things do not know that they are the 'that' of other things; they only know what they themselves know," Chuang-tzu would say.[51] In a similar vein, the Korean language has, in comparison to most European languages, a far greater and more complex vocabulary to express emotional perceptions, states and relations. Given these linguistic traditions, it is not surprising that some East Asian scholars object to the strong rational base of Habermas's concept of communicative action, even while supporting his overall search for a procedural ethics that can be applied globally.[52]

Recognizing these cultural differences is not to draw a stark line between East and West. That is, indeed, precisely the problem. Habermas, for instance, makes too much of the distinction between a secularized and individualistic West on the one hand and a communitarian Asian or a fundamentalist Islamic tradition on the other.[53] The contours between East and West are much more blurred. Look at how Taoists refuse to think in the form of dichotomies: opposites are considered complementary because neither side can exist by itself. Since any concept, such as the West, can exist only by virtue of its opposite, the East, both are an inseparable and interdependent unit in which one element is necessary for the articulation and existence of the other. Says Chuang-tzu: "Because of the right, there is the wrong, and because of the wrong, there is the right. Therefore the sage does not proceed along these lines (of right and wrong, and so forth) but illuminates the matter with Nature. This is reason."[54]

And reason is, indeed, a good illustration of the interconnection of opposites, for despite its prominent antirational stance, there is also a strong rationalist tradition in Chinese philosophy. In fact, many of Chuang-tzu's stories are a direct reaction to the rationalism of the later Mohists.[55] Likewise, the critique of reason has for long been a central theme of western philosophy, from Sophism to Romantic poetry and poststructural philosophy. Some authors, such as Heidegger, even drew their critique, at least in part, from Taoist texts.[56]

Searching for cross-cultural meeting points, and taking them beyond stereotypical images of the other, is essential to meet the challenges of globalization. Each cultural tradition contains rich debates about issues that are central to social and political life. These debates go far beyond the cliches that are often used to present conflicts between different religious or secular identifications as unavoidable. The latest prominent example of such an essentialist construction of conflict is Samuel Huntington's much discussed treatise on the clash of civilizations, which revives the realist fear of an anarchical international system, except that it locates the inevitability of conflict not in the interaction of security-seeking states, but in the confrontation of incompatible cultural identities.[57] Such a conflict-prone stance, which continues to guide policy making in many parts of the world, can and should be replaced with cultural dialogues that draw on commonalties and develop from them the type of understanding, respect and tolerance needed for the articulation of a nonviolent relationship between identity and difference. It is obvious that such harmonious engagements will always remain an ideal, rather than a perpetual end-state. But the principle of cross-cultural dialogue should be elevated to a more central political principle, if only because there is sufficient evidence to point towards strong linkages between violence and the breakdown or absence of dialogue.[58]

A return to reason and cosmopolitan democracy, via the crucial influence of Kant, exemplifies how comparative political theory may engender more sensitive forms of universalism. Much like other classical philosophers, Kant has been used by western international relations scholars in a rather self-serving way. Whereas Machiavelli, Hobbes and Rousseau were selectively appropriated to justify a set of already formed realist interpretations, Kant is held up as the prime inspiration for cosmopolitanism. The Kant that is remembered here is mostly the Kant of the categorical imperative and of the treatise on *Perpetual Peace*. A great number of otherwise very disparate authors thus present Kant as the quintessential philosopher of the Enlightenment, the prime advocate of reason: the one who refuses to justify the means by their ends, the one who rejects instrumental approaches to politics in favor of an ethics that revolves around universally accepted principles.[59] But this is, of course, not the only Kant. References to the three *Critiques*, for instance, are strikingly absent from international relations scholarship. And it is precisely there that sources for a more culturally attuned global dialogue could be found.

Kant can then be seen as offering not only the foundations for cosmopolitanism but also a critique of the problematic but semantically concealed western assumption that our knowledge of the world is located in the objects we seek to understand. Because all attempts to reveal something a priori about them had failed, Kant suggested that knowledge of objects was not structured primarily by their a priori existence, but by the nature of our perception of them.[60] He drew attention to what happens if these epistemological limits are ignored and if knowledge is measured solely by its correspondence to external appearances. A few dominant forms of insight, usually those emerging from reason, are then given the power to coordinate and synchronize a variety of otherwise rather disparate faculties, such as imagination, memory and understanding. As a result, many of the nonrational insights so valued by Chuang-tzu, such as instinct and spontaneity, are either dismissed as irrational or become reduced to *supplementing* the rational intellect. By examining how the beautiful and the sublime generate an inherent tension between imagination and reason, Kant sought to find ways for allowing each faculty to cultivate its unique insights and passions.[61] Even though some detect strong assumptions about a standard western subject in the Kantian notion of the sublime,[62] the three *Critiques* offer the epistemological tolerance necessary to appreciate and engage with insights and knowledge practices from different cultural traditions.

Drawing attention, by way of example, to the problematic links between rationality and culture is not to deny or devalue the crucial role of reason, but to explore the full potential of a culturally attuned global dialogue. Ensuing alternatives are not necessarily better than those emerging from reason. Nor can they discover authentic insight underneath the appearance of representation. But they can draw attention to the very act of representing and its political consequences. A legitimization of alternative knowledge-forms, such as the parables and stories valued in Chinese philosophy, would broaden our political options, even though the respective insights can never be codified into a fixed set of rules and norms. A brief essay-length exposé cannot outline how such a promotion of cross-cultural dialogue and sensibilities would translate into concrete responses to specific policy challenges, as for instance the threat of global terrorism. But one can assume that the respective approaches would neither be couched in a dualistic good-versus-evil rhetoric nor be based on military means alone. Instead of isolating problems and attributing them solely to the immediate perpetrators of terrorist acts, a Taoist approach would, for instance, focus on patterns, rather than causes of disharmony. It would present problems in a correlational and holistic manner, considering violence as part of a larger set of political dilemmas that include issues such as cultural perception, inequality and poverty. What ensuing policy positions would look like, and whether or not they would be desirable, is of course open to debate. Other cross-cultural engagements may well offer more convincing insights, commonalties and political options. But such cross-cultural debates must be promoted and waged if cosmopolitan approaches to global problems are to avoid foundational closure and new forms of imperialism.

### CONCLUSION

I have identified two key challenges posed by globalization, both being linked to the loss of certainty that accompanies the acceleration of speed and the gradual weakening of state sovereignty. The dual challenge consists of dealing with difference, be it of an ethnic, religious or any other nature, and of establishing foundations in an increasingly influential but contested transnational context. These are, of course, not the only challenges ahead. But many others, from terrorism to poverty, are in one way or another intertwined with the dilemmas of identity/difference and the problem of foundations. I have suggested that despite its historical association with the nation state, political theory still offers rich and highly relevant resources to tackle the challenges of globalization. The key, I argued, lies in taking responsibility for political decisions by refusing to essentialize questions of identity and foundations. The dilemmas of globalization force us to confront the fundamental challenge of how to live with proliferating diversity, how to accept the contingent and contestable nature of foundations, while still retaining the possibility of articulating, justifying and advancing political projects that can decide between right and wrong, moral and immoral.

The complex and increasingly far-reaching challenges of globalization call for as many different insights and approaches as possible. The dilemmas that currently haunt world politics are far too serious not to employ the full register of human perception and intelligence to understand and deal with them. This is why political theory should reach beyond the western canon into a cross-cultural global dialogue, which is essential for establishing common ground, or at least an atmosphere of trust and tolerance, in conflict situations that may otherwise seem intractable.

While cultivating such an open attitude one must also recognize that the pressures of globalization call for specific and immediate political commitments and actions, some requiring global application and justification. The ensuing political projects need to be grounded in foundations that inevitably discriminate. Even a resort to a procedural, self-reflective and culturally sensitive ethics cannot avoid such practices of exclusion. They are as inevitable as they are desirable. Politicians and diplomats, being faced with the pressure of finding principled responses to immediate challenges, will undoubtedly push towards foundational closure. Quite rightly so, for many problems require determined actions. Political theory can offer a much needed counterweight to this imperative, for the foundations of a just world order, whatever they may be, can remain adequate and fair only if its norms and procedures are submitted to periodic scrutiny and adjustment.

## NOTES

1. I would like to thank Martin Leet, Don Moon, Barbara Sullivan and Stephen White for their insightful comments. My gratitude also goes to the Alexander von Humboldt Stiftung, for giving me the opportunity to spend a research year in Berlin, and to Claus Offe, for hosting my stay.
2. Adriana Cavarero, "Politicizing Theory," in this volume, p. 60.
3. George Kateb, "The Adequacy of the Western Canon," in this volume, p. 30.
4. Zaki Laïdi, *Un Monde privé de Sens* (Paris: Fayard, 1994), 15.

5. Stephen K. White, "Pluralism, Platitudes and Paradoxes: Western Political Thought in a New Century," in this volume, p. 2.

6. "You are either with us or against us," CNN, 6.11.2001.

7. See D. A. Baldwin, ed., *Neorealism and Neoliberalism: The Contemporary Debate* (New York: Columbia University Press, 1993); Charles W. Kegley, ed., *Controversies in International Relations Theory: Realism and the Neoliberal Challenge* (New York: St. Martin's, 1995).

8. For a recent overview of these critical debates and the mainstream positions they engage, see Scott Burchill et al., *Theories of International Relations* (Houndmills: Palgrave, 2001).

9. Martin Heidegger, "Nur noch ein Gott kann uns retten," interview conducted in 1966, reprinted in *Der Spiegel*, 11.11.2002, 142.

10. See, for instance, Ulrich Beck, *Was ist Globalisierung* (Frankfurt: Suhrkamp, 1997); David Held and Anthony McGrew, eds., *The Global Transformations Reader: An Introduction to the Globalization Debate* (Cambridge: Polity Press, 2000); James H. Mittelman, ed., *Globalization: Critical Reflections* (Boulder, Col: Lynne Rienner, 1996); Jan Aart Scholte, *Globalization: A Critical Introduction* (Basingstoke: Macmillan, 2000).

11. Theodor W. Adorno, *Negative Dialektik* (Frankfurt: Suhrkamp, 1992), 154.

12. Arjun Appadurai, *Modernity at Large: Cultural Dimensions of Globalization* (Minneapolis: University of Minnesota Press, 1996), 27-37.

13. Paul Virilio, *Vitesse et Politique* (Paris: Éditions Galilée, 1977).

14. Jürgen Habermas, *Die postnationale Konstellation: Politische Essays* (Frankfurt: Suhrkamp, 1998), 120.

15. Stephen D. Krasner, *Sovereignty: Organized Hypocrisy* (Princeton: Princeton University Press, 1999).

16. Thomas Bernauer, *Staaten im Weltmarkt: Zur Handlunsfähigkeit von Staaten trotz wirtschaftlicher Globalisierung* (Opladen: Leske und Budrich, 2000).

17. Gearóid Ó Tuathail, *Critical Geopolitics: The Politics of Writing Global Space* (London: Routledge, 1996), 228-30; Appadurai, *Modernity at Large*, 37-38.

18. See Paul Virilio, *La Vitesse de Libération* (Paris: Galilée, 1995); and Jerry Everard, *Virtual States: Globalization, Inequality and the Internet* (London: Routledge, 1999).

19. See Zygmunt Bauman, *Modernity and Ambivalence* (Oxford: Polity, 1991).

20. Vandana Shiva, "This Round to the Citizens," *The Guardian*, 8.12.1999.

21. See Benedict Anderson, *Imagined Communities: Reflections on the Origin and Spread of Nationalism* (London, Verso, 1983).

22. Ian Clark, *Globalization and Fragmentation: International Relations in the Twentieth Century* (Oxford: Oxford University Press, 1997).

23. Michael J. Shapiro, *Violent Cartographies: Mapping Cultures of War* (Minneapolis: University of Minnesota Press, 1997), 67.

24. Ibid., 41-72.

25. Friedrich Nietzsche, "Über Warheit und Lüge im aussermoralischen Sinn," in *Erkenntnistheoretische Schriften* (Frankfurt: Suhrkamp, 1968), 103.

26. William E. Connolly, *Identity/Difference: Democratic Negotiations of Political Paradox* (Ithaca: Cornell University Press, 1991/2002), 12.

27. William E. Connolly, *The Ethos of Pluralization* (Minneapolis: University of Minnesota Press, 1995), xxi-ii.

28. See, for instance, Emmanuel Levinas, *Time and the Other*, trans. R. Cohen (Pittsburgh: Duquesne University Press, 1987) and, for applications in the international realm,

Shapiro, *Violent Cartographies*, as well as, David Campbell, "The Deterritorialisation of Responsibility: Levinas, Derrida, and Ethics after the End of Philosophy," *Alternatives* 19, no. 4, December 1994.

29.  Paul Ricoeur, "Imagination, Testimony and Trust," in R. Kearney and M. Dooley, eds., *Questioning Ethics: Contemporary Debates in Philosophy* (London: Routledge, 1999), 12.

30.  Roxanne L. Euben, *Enemy in the Mirror: Islamic Fundamentalism and the Limits of Modern Rationalism* (Princeton: Princeton University Press, 1999), 16.

31.  Øyvind Østerud, "Antinomies of Postmodernism in International Studies," *Journal of Peace Research* 33, no. 4, November 1996, 386.

32.  Stephen K. White, *Political Theory and Postmodernism* (Cambridge: Cambridge University Press, 1992), 11.

33.  William E. Connolly, *Political Theory and Modernity* (Ithaca: Cornell University Press, 1993/1988).

34.  Jean-François Lyotard, *La Condition Postmoderne: Rapport sur le Savoir* (Paris: Les Editions de Minuit, 1979), 7-9.

35.  Judith Butler, "Contingent Foundations: Feminism and the Question of 'Postmodernism,'" in J. Butler and J. W. Scott, eds., *Feminists Theorize the Political* (New York: Routledge, 1992), 3-7.

36.  Douglas Klusmeyer and Astri Suhrke, "Comprehending 'Evil': Challenges for Law and Policy," *Ethics and International Affairs* 16, no. 1, 2002, 37; Roxanne L. Euben, "Killing (for) Politics: Jihad, Martyrdom, and Political Action," *Political Theory* 30, no. 1, 2002, 4.

37.  Søren Kierkegaard, *Fear and Trembling*, trans. A. Hannary (London: Penguin, 1985). See also Jacques Derrida, "Hospitality, Justice and Responsibility," in Kearney and Dooley, *Questioning Ethics*, 66-67.

38.  Pierre Bourdieu, *The Logic of Practice*, trans. R. Nice (Stanford: Stanford University Press, 1980); Richard Bernstein, *Beyond Objectivism and Relativism Science, Hermeneutics, and Praxis* (Oxford: Basil Blackwell, 1983).

39.  Axel Honneth, *Das Andere der Gerechtigkeit: Aufsätze zur praktischen Philosophie* (Frankfurt: Suhrkamp, 2000); Martin Leet, *Aftereffects of Knowledge in Modernity: Politics, Aesthetics and Individuality* (Albany, NY: State University of New York Press, forthcoming 2003); Stephen K. White, *Sustaining Affirmation: The Strength of Weak Ontology in Political Theory* (Princeton: Princeton University Press, 2000).

40.  Andrew Linklater, *The Transformation of Political Community* (Cambridge: Polity, 1998).

41.  Richard Falk, *On Humane Governance* (Cambridge, Polity, 1995); Habermas, *Die postnationale Konstellation*; David Held, *Democracy and the Global Order: From the Modern State to Cosmopolitan Governance* (Cambridge: Polity, 1995); and *Theory, Culture and Society* 19, no. 1-2, 2002, special issue on Cosmopolis.

42.  John S. Dryzek, *Deliberative Democracy and Beyond: Liberals, Critics, Contestations* (Oxford: Oxford University Press, 2000).

43.  Jürgen Habermas, *Theorie des kommunikativen Handelns*, two vols. (Frankfurt: Suhrkamp, 1988).

44.  Hedley Bull and Adam Watson, eds., *The Expansion of Universal International Society* (Oxford: Clarendon Press, 1984); Anthony Giddens, *The Consequences of Modernity* (Stanford: Stanford University Press, 1990); and Serge Latouche, *The Westernization of the World*, trans. R. Moorris (Cambridge: Polity, 1996).

45.  Appadurai, *Modernity at Large*, 17

46. Euben, *Enemy in the Mirror*, 9.
47. Chuang-tzu, *Chuang-tzu: The Inner Chapters*, translated by A.C. Graham (London: Unwin Paperbacks, 1986), 123.
48. A. C. Graham, *Disputers of the Tao: Philosophical Argument in Ancient China* (La Salle: Open Court, 1989), 7. See also B. I. Schwartz, *The World of Thought in Ancient China* (Cambridge: Harvard University Press, 1985); Qing Cao, "Selling Culture: Ancient Chinese Conceptions of the Other in Legends," S. Chan, P. Mandaville and R. Bleiker, eds., *The Zen of International Relations: IR Theory from East to West* (Houndmills: Palgrave, 2001), 202-21.
49. Jürgen Habermas, *Der philosophische Diskurs der Moderne* (Frankfurt: Suhrkamp, 1985), 13-58; and "Conceptions of Modernity and Critical Theory," in Han Sang-jin, ed., *Habermas and the Korean Debate* (Seoul: Seoul National University Press, 1998), 177-79.
50. Graham, *Disputers of the Tao, 222.* See also 155, 177 and 389-428.
51. Chuang Tzu, "The Chuang-tzu," 182-83.
52. See Ryu Honglim, "Justifying Discourse Ethics in the Public Sphere," in Han, *Habermas and the Korean Debate*, 266.
53. Jürgen Habermas, "Theory and Praxis Revisited," in Han, *Habermas and the Korean Debate*, 16.
54. Chuang Tzu, "The Chuang-tzu," 182-83.
55. Graham, *Disputers of the Tao*, 137-212
56. Otto Pöggeler, "West–East Dialogue: Heidegger and Lao–tzu," and Paul Shih–yi Hsiao, "Heidegger and our Translation of the Tao Te Ching," both in G. Parkes, ed., *Heidegger and Asian Thought* (Honolulu: University of Hawaii Press, 1990).
57. Samuel P. Huntington, *The Clash of Civilizations and the Remaking of the World Order* (New York: Simon & Schuster, 1996).
58. Michel Wieviorka, "Le nouveau paradigm de la violence," *Cultures et Conflits: Sociologie Politique de l'International*, no. 29/30, Summer 1998, 15.
59. See, for instance, W. B. Gallie, *Philosophers of Peace and War* (Cambridge: Cambridge University Press, 1978); Ekkehart Krippendorff, *Die Kunst, nicht regiert zu werden: Ethische Politik von Sokrates bis Mozart* (Frankfurt: Suhrkamp, 1999); and Linklater, *The Transformation of Political Community*.
60. Immanuel Kant, *Kritik der Reinen Vernunft, Vorrede zur zweiten Auflage* (Stuttgart: Reclam, 1996), 28-29.
61. Immanuel Kant, *Kritk der Urteilskraft* (Frankfurt: Suhrkamp, 1974). This short and necessarily inadequate interpretation of Kant is based on a Deleuzian reading. See Gilles Deleuze, *Difference and Repetition*, trans. P. Patton (New York: Columbia University Press, 1994); *La Philosophie critique de Kant* (Paris: Presses Universitaires de France, 1963); and Paul Patton, *Deleuze and the Political* (London: Routledge, 2000).
62. Gayatri Chakravorty Spivak, *A Critique of Postcolonial Reason: Toward a History of the Vanishing Present* (Cambridge, Mass.: Harvard University Press, 1999).

# 7    TRAVELING THEORISTS AND TRANSLATING PRACTICES

*ROXANNE L. EUBEN*

He who does not travel will not know the value of men.

الي ما جال ما يعرف بحق الرجال.

Travel, you will see the meaning [of things].

جل ترى المعاني.

—Moroccan Proverbs[1]

T here is much at stake in the attempt to define political theory. How political theory is conceived—as an academic field, a canon of books, a set of interrogatives, or a practice of inquiry—determines who participates in its ongoing "Great conversations," in what locales theorizing may be said to transpire, and what counts as political theory properly understood. The following chapter advances a conception of theorizing as an inherently comparative enterprise by recuperating the Greek practice of *theôria*, precursor to the English word "theory," and the association between the acquisition of political wisdom and the experience of travel it presupposes. In this context, travel becomes both a metaphor and a practice for the pursuit of knowledge about others and oneself by way of literal and imaginative contrasts with seemingly alien lands, peoples and institutions. As recent work in anthropology, cultural and postcolonial studies has shown, an unqualified emphasis on travel collapses important distinctions between those who can and cannot travel, and those for whom mobility is a matter of survival rather than leisure. My use of travel, however, is an attempt to ground the acquisition of knowledge in those inescapable, ordinary, yet transformative if inevitably flawed practices of translation so often occasioned by exposures to the unfamiliar. So understood, travel in search of knowledge is not only a practice of translation but a *term* of translation,[2] a bridge across traditions separated by culture or time in which the link between mobility and wisdom, as well as the corruption or loss it risks, are explicit.

In the following pages, travel opens up a particular realm of comparative inquiry by bringing into sharp relief similar practices between "the West"[3] and Islam, cultural constellations increasingly portrayed as hermetically sealed and constitutively antagonistic "civilizations." The Islamic emphasis on *talab al-'ilm* (pursuit of knowledge) I develop below shows that travel in search of wisdom, curiosity about what is strange, the capacity for critical distance and the domestication of otherness latent in all practices of translation are not the monopoly of the West. Such "civilizational" borders are thus doubly permeable, traversed by travelers from many directions whose wanderings disclose commonalities in the cross-cultural production of knowledge. Importantly, when informed by a hermeneutic approach, taking travel as both a practice and term, translation registers rather than effaces the untranslatable, preserving strangeness while pluralizing the locations, genres and cultures in which theorizing may occur.

## I. THEORY AND THEÔRIA

In his monumental history of India (1817), British philosopher James Mill devotes over two-thirds of the preface to refuting the charge that a man who has never visited the subcontinent or learned its languages is unsuited to the task of writing Indian history. Mill insists that what some might regard as parochialism is in fact a virtue, for his critical faculties and judiciousness require insulation from the "partial impressions" and distortions characteristic of first-hand sense perception. He writes, "Whatever is worth seeing or hearing in India, can be expressed in writing. As soon as everything of importance is expressed in writing, a man who is duly qualified may obtain more knowledge of India in one year in his closet in England, than he could obtain during the course of the longest life, by the use of his eyes and ears in India."[4]

Mill's defense of insularity has many precedents and progeny within and beyond the so-called West. Yet as early as *The Epic of Gilgamesh* (transcribed 1900 BCE), the pursuit of knowledge and the attainment of wisdom has been linked to travel and direct experience of the radically unfamiliar. Gilgamesh, the mythic Sumerian traveler and ruler, "was the man to whom all things were known: this was the king who knew the countries of the world. He was wise, he saw mysteries and knew secret things, he brought us a tale of the days before the flood. He went on a long journey, was weary, worn-out with labour, returning he rested, he engraved on a stone the whole story."[5] Indeed, the very roots of the Western tradition are often traced to the world of Homer, whose epic poem *The Odyssey* promises its listeners tales of a hero who is a "man who has traveled a great deal; he has seen the cities of men and learned their minds."[6]

The association between travel and experience is, of course, common-place, and is reflected in the etymological roots of the Indo-European words for travel, from the proximity of the German *Erfahrung* (experience) and *irfaran* (to travel, in Old High German) to the ways in which "experience" itself connotes a "passage through a frame of action."[7] The connection between travel and knowledge is perhaps less commonplace and, from a per-spective such as Mill's, deeply suspect. Yet Mill's ostensibly solitary reflec-tions on the history of India are dependent upon the first-hand experiences of others, and so at once presuppose and conceal the mutual implication of knowledge and autopsy (here in the Greek sense of the word, to see with one's own eyes). This association is quite explicit, however, in the Greek practice of *theôria*, the etymological precursor to the English word "theory". In George Rawlinson's translation of Herodotus, *theôria* is rendered only as "to see the world," yet *theôros* has multiple meanings, including a spectator, a state delegate to a festival in another city, and someone who travels to consult an oracle.[8] Theôria is itself a compound of different etymological possibili-ties: the first half of the word suggests both vision (*thea*, meaning sight/spec-tacle) and God (*theos*), while *-oros* connotes "one who sees."[9] Unsurprisingly, then, *theôrein* is the verb meaning "to observe," and is con-nected to both sightseeing and religious emissaries. This etymology posits a link among *theôria*, travel, direct experience and vision, but it is in Herodotus's *Histories* that such practices are tied specifically to the achieve-ment of knowledge: in one of the earliest known uses of the word *theôria* in the ancient world, Herodotus describes Solon the Lawgiver's journey from Athens for the sake of *theôria*, and explicitly links theory and wisdom (*sophia*) to travel across vast terrain (1.30.2). Herodotus reiterates the associ-ation among theory, travel and knowledge when he describes Anacharsis the Scythian (4.76.2) as one who "had traversed much of the world on a *theôria* and throughout this had given evidence of his great wisdom."[10]

Herodotus provides a bridge between the Greek practice of *theôria* and the English word 'theory,' most often understood as the systematic investiga-tion and attainment of knowledge. But it is Plato who specifies the implica-tions of this practice, and the knowledge such travel makes possible, for the course of political life. In book 12 of *The Laws*, the character of "the Athe-nian" contends (951c) that only men of good repute over the age of 50 will be allowed to travel abroad for the purposes of observing other practices and peoples, and then for a period of no more than ten years (the exact length of Solon's journeys). Such sojourns are not only permissible but necessary, Plato writes, for without these carefully selected travelers, the polis "will never in its isolation attain an adequate level of civilization and maturity, nor will it succeed in preserving its own laws permanently, so long as its grasp of them depends on mere habituation without comprehension." (951b).[11] Such travelers must be rigorously examined upon their return, however, the knowledge they bring home carefully vetted by those presumably capable of distinguishing between wisdom and contamination. Without specifying precisely how to differentiate between subversive and useful knowledge from afar, the Athenian concludes that if the *theôros* is improved by his journeys, he shall be honored both in life and in death. But should it be shown that the *theôros* has been corrupted by his travels, the examiners may forcibly remove him from influence, either by death or isolation (952a-c).[12]

Plato's grim warning about the risks of travel for both the *theôros* and his polis is echoed in the story of Herodotus's Anacharsis, whose attempt to introduce a foreign religious practice upon returning to his native Scythia occasioned his violent death (4.77). Such narratives do indeed seem to "articulate a general truth about the dangers involved in contact between different societies,"[13] but this passage in the *Laws* also discloses the (literally) conservative dimension to the activity of the theorist, one with roots in the etymological connection between the suffix -*ôros* in *theôros* and "one who watches over, guards."[14] This is because travel and *theôria* are here rendered not only as practices of observation but also vehicles of wisdom and *political* wisdom in particular: exposures to other lands and the comparisons they make possible facilitate an epistemological journey from habit to knowledge upon which the survival and excellence of the polis depends. The image of political wisdom this passage thus evokes is not the Philosopher-King's solitary contemplation of the eternal but rather the figures of Solon and Gilgamesh, the ancient Sumerian traveler-King, whose wisdom derived from observation of more worldly things and places.[15]

I want to argue that Herodotus and Plato's *Laws* disclose an often unacknowledged connection between the Greek practice of *theôria*, and the attainment of knowledge in general and political wisdom in particular. Without collapsing the distinction between *theôria* and theory, such linkages are nevertheless suggestive of an argument different from that advanced by Mill. For if we take Herodotus and the *Laws* seriously, theorizing is a practice intimately and explicitly connected to the comparative insights first-hand observation often provides, political wisdom a function of direct yet agonistic engagement with the world. So understood, theory is not the opposite of the political, actual, practical, empirical and everyday, but rather entails a journey to a perspective that makes visible the larger patterns and connections that inform our and others' lives. In this context, 'travel' at once signifies a literal movement across lands and cultures, and an epistemological and imaginative journey, in Nietzsche's words, to "the other shore," to worlds less familiar, and in terms of which a traveler comes to understand his or her own. What this means, of course, is that theory is not only embedded in actual practices and experiences, but that theorizing is an inherently comparative enterprise, an often transformative mediation between knowledges and practices both familiar and unfamiliar.

As the *Laws* suggests, a practice of theorizing so rooted in the messiness of human affairs is potentially double edged: while exposures to other ways of living and arranging collectivities makes possible the knowledge necessary for both politics and political excellence, it is also and simultaneously rife with hidden dangers and risks. This is less because direct experience and autopsy are inherently corrupting, but rather because the consequences for politics of the knowledge thereby gained are radically indeterminate. Unlike atoms of inert (noble) gases that collide and part unchanged, exposures to different and often alien lands, institutions and practices may well transform those who travel, those who are visited, and those who remain behind. For inasmuch as travel occasions comparisons, and comparisons entail translation between what is unfamiliar and familiar, such journeys make possible not only greater awareness of other worlds but also a perspective of critical distance from home and the often unexamined commitments and attachments 'home' entails. Most obviously, awareness of unfamiliar lands can serve and has served as a precursor to imperialist ventures, ancient and modern; it has also served as the grounds on which such ventures and conceits of cultural superiority are challenged. Less obviously, such distance unsettles the presumption that familiar political arrangements are natural, inevitable, and inherently coherent. Yet here too the outcome is highly unpredictable: it may engender either deeper allegiance or radical skepticism toward inherited political practices and cultural shibboleths. As Plato knew well, those who gather knowledge from afar render urgent questions to which there is no definitive *a priori* answer: "[a]re these travelers ambassadors of certainty or of doubt? Do they confirm or destabilize notions of cultural identity? Do they make room for the 'other,' or do they put it in its place?"[16]

## II. "SEEING THE ENTIRE WORLD AS A FOREIGN LAND"

It has been suggested that to "travel and observe is characteristically Greek."[17] Yet from Bacon's characterization of travelers as "merchants of light," to Montesquieu's description of his fictional Persian travelers as searchers after wisdom, to Nietzsche's contention that "we must travel, as old Herodotus travelled" in part because "[i]mmediate self observation is not

enough, by a long way, to enable us to learn to know ourselves,"[18] it is clear
that the links between theory, travel and knowledge is a subterranean premise
of Western political and social theory long after the classical era.[19] It is thus
perhaps no accident that a remarkable range of histories and political treatises have been composed under conditions of voluntary or coerced exile, of
physical and intellectual distance from "home" and the attendant press of
everyday affairs. Speaking in particular of coerced exile, Edward Said captures the broader import of the experience of dislocation: to be of but no longer in one's own cultural home creates an "agonizing distance" from what
was once second nature, an experience of loss often productive of extraordinary moments of insight.[20]

A classic case in point is Machiavelli, who wrote *The Prince* while in exile
from Florence in 1513 and refers to it in the dedication as part of the many
cruelties suffered at the hands of the Medici's. Yet in the same dedication,
Machiavelli exhorts the prince to recognize the enlargement of vision made
possible by dislocation, likening the task of an informed ruler to that of landscape painters who "station themselves in the valleys in order to draw moun-
tains or high ground, and ascend an eminence in order to get a good view of
the plains."[21] Herodotus traveled extensively after he left Halicarnassus, and
the observations about Greeks and non-Greeks occasioned by his journeys
comprise a substantial portion of the *Histories*. Thucydides endured twenty
years of exile from Athens following his reputed failure to save Amphipolis,
yet such homelessness occasioned, in his words, the "leisure" necessary to
access both sides of the war, the result of which was a history containing
"exact knowledge of the past," a "possession for all time" rather than an exag-
gerated or rhetorically excessive story pitched to "win the applause of the
moment."[22] In an account of his own famous nineteenth-century travels,
Alexis de Tocqueville exhorts his countrymen to look to America, not "in
order slavishly to copy the institutions she has fashioned for herself, but in
order that we may better understand what suits us; let us look there for
instruction rather than models," and likens a theorist to a "traveler who has
gone out beyond the walls of some vast city and gone up a neighboring
hill . . .the city's outline is [now] easier to see, and for the first time he grasps
its shape."[23]

The examples abound. Thomas More wrote Book II of his *Utopia* in 1515
while living in Flanders on a commercial embassy from England; Thomas
Hobbes composed both *De Cive* and *Leviathan* during his eleven year stay in
Paris; "A Letter Concerning Toleration" was written while John Locke was in
exile in Amsterdam; and although Rousseau identifies himself as a "citizen
of Geneva" in the *Second Discourse*, his life after he was locked out of the
city gates at age 16 was characterized by homelessness, political, geograph-

ical and spiritual. Importantly, such instances are not confined to European peoples: for example, Ibn Khaldûn—born to a family itself in exile from Andalusia because of the Christian Reconquista—retreated with his family to a remote area of Tunis after a series of ultimately unsuccessful political interventions. During the ensuing four years of self-imposed exile he wrote the *Muqaddimah* (finished in 1377), the Introduction to a much longer history of the world that sought to discern an underlying pattern connecting all discrete historical events. Jamal al-Din al-Afghani [al-Asadabadi] (1839–1897), one of the most influential proponents of pan-Islamic unity, forged his arguments against imperialism in a condition of perpetual itinerancy far from his native Iran (indeed, Afghani intentionally hid his origins as a Shi'ite Iranian, preferring to be thought of as a Sunni Afghan).[24] Ayatollah Ruhollah Khomeini's famous work on Islamic government was fully developed during his protracted exile from Iran.[25] And Edward Said, "specular border intellectual"[26] par excellence, has stitched together by argument and example of both the pain and privilege of homelessness: that "unhealable rift forced between a human being and a native place, between the self and its true home . . .[a] crippling sorrow of estrangement" that also makes possible the "privilege" of having "not just one set of eyes but half a dozen, each of them corresponding to the places you have been."[27] Said elaborates:

> While it perhaps seems peculiar to speak of the pleasures of exile . . .[s]eeing the "entire world as a foreign land" makes possible originality of vision. Most people are principally aware of one culture, one setting, one home; exiles are aware of at least two, and this plurality of vision gives rise to an awareness of simultaneous dimensions, an awareness that—to borrow a phrase from music—is *contrapuntal*. For an exile, habits of life, expression, or activity in the new environment inevitably occur against the memory of these things in another environment. Thus both the new and the old environments are vivid, actual, occurring together contrapuntally. There is a unique pleasure in this sort of apprehension, especially if the exile is conscious of other contrapuntal juxtapositions that diminish orthodox judgment and elevate appreciative sympathy.[28]

In these instances, images of exile, distance, loss, travel, discovery, vision and knowledge overlap and intertwine. The valorization of wandering, rootlessness and perpetual itinerancy has often served to privilege a position of what Michael Walzer has called radical detachment, intellectual and emotional, characteristic of representational or correspondence theories of knowledge. Yet it is my contention that these many examples reveal an agonistic engagement with the world best expressed in the language of *dislocation* rather than *detachment*, an inescapably rooted estrangement akin to what Walzer has characterized as the "ambiguous connection" of those "in but not wholly of their society."[29] Negotiating the extremes of rootlessness and parochialism, the language of dislocation brings into view the mutual implication of home and abroad, mobility and place, critical distance and engagement that captures, for example, how it is that Tocqueville's account of his travels to America are also reflections on France, and Ibn Battuta's fourteenth-century account of the Maldives simultaneously articulate the contours of his connections to his North African home.

### III. EXPOSURES AND CLOSURES

In the context of a postcolonial world grown smaller by the advent of globalization and the rapid movement of peoples, ideas and information it entails, travel as both a metaphor and practice of seeking knowledge about what is either unfamiliar or unrecognized has increasingly taken center stage in a variety of disciplines. In the context of what is often termed late modernity in particular, "it is easy to see why notions of mobility, fluidity, provisionality and process have been preferable to alternative notions of stasis and fixity."[30] Consequently, anthropologists, cultural and literary theorists, scholars of globalization and postcoloniality are increasingly speaking of deterritorialization and mining experiences of displacement such as nomadism, tourism, diaspora, exile, and migration as "contact zones,"[31] sites that articulate the preconditions and implications of cross-cultural encounters.[32] Such scholarship has foregrounded not only the virtues of mobility but also its closures and exclusions. Abstracted from concrete contexts, the category of 'travel' collapses crucial distinctions between, at one extreme, the power, privilege and leisure that makes voluntary mobility (such as tourism) possible and, at the other, the pogroms, poverty, sex traffic and slave trades that have transformed entire peoples into immigrants, refugees, fugitives, chattel.[33] Moreover, travel as a metaphor for the search for knowledge has been criticized for valorizing mobility and aloofness over the concrete attachments to particular cultures and places arguably central to human life.[34] This is because the association of travel, imagination, curiosity, knowledge and reflexive self-understanding simultaneously produces an image of the people who do not or cannot travel, whether they are those 'left behind' or those 'exotics' at the end of the journey. If immobility is implicitly linked to stasis, inertia, narrowness and complacency, those who do not travel come to be characterized by an absence of curiosity, lack of philosophical reflectiveness, or both.

Much attention has been given, for example, to the intersection of travel and gender privilege: the travel metaphor tends to code the pursuit of knowledge as a distinctively male activity, for certain kinds of mobility are historically associated with men, while the 'domain of women' is often linked to particular places of home and hearth.[35] Indeed, what counts as travel—what James Clifford ironically refers to as "good travel," that which is "heroic, educational, scientific adventurous, ennobling"[36] —is rarely the movement of servants, slaves, beggars, concubines, mistresses and wives.[37] Travel is gendered, but not only because women have historically traveled far less than men. The very rhetoric of travel is "shot through with metaphors that reinforce male prerogatives to wander and conquer as they please" [38] and so, as Janet Wolff argues, the "gendering of travel (as male) both impedes female travel and renders problematic the self-definition of (and response to) women who *do* travel."[39] The connection between theory and spectatorship/sightseeing has thus elicited from a variety of quarters a powerful critique of vision— a "systematic suspicion of the apparent transparency and naturalness of vision"[40]—the result of feminist analyses of the objectivating "male gaze," a deepening skepticism toward positivism and the ideal of detached, impartial knowledge it enshrines.[41]

Moreover, the link between literal and figurative mobility, critical distance and philosophical reflection also tends to code "heroic" travel as a distinctively Western activity: just as women are often rooted literally and metaphorically to the home left behind, peoples of the so-called non-West are often those to whom men travel rather than travelers themselves, objects rather than agents of 'discovery.' At times gender may be mapped onto geography and culture, resulting in the feminization of non-Western peoples located at the end of the voyage: thus a French traveler could describe Japan as "opened to our view, through a fairy-like rent, which thus allowed us to penetrate into her very heart."[42] The epistemological implication of coding "heroic" travel as Western is made explicit in Jürgen Habermas's contention that "[t]o gain distance from one's own traditions and broaden limited perspectives is the advantage of Occidental rationalism."[43] As Pratap Mehta points out, the underlying premise of Habermas's account is that members of other cultures are "prisoners of their mythic worldviews, their culture possesses them rather than they *it*."[44] This is perhaps nowhere more evident than in both scholarly and popular accounts of Islam. Despite the fact that large populations of Muslims live in Europe, Islam is one of the fastest growing religions in the United States, and there is a mutual cultural and intellectual debt between Europe and Islam dating back centuries, in popular imagination, Islam is often associated with a world "over there," home of an explosive anti-Western rage, the front line of conflict in a post-Cold War world increasingly defined by a clash of civilizations between 'the West and the Rest.'[45] In a post-September 11 world in particular, the most ubiquitous image of Muslim travel is the mobile *mujahid* (fighter of *jihad*) who moves from Saudi Arabia to Pakistan to Afghanistan to Africa to the United States and back with terrifying speed and ease. The deadly purposes of *al-Qaeda* have mobilized a broader anxiety that when non-Westerners—and Muslims in particular—captured by their "mythic worldviews" *do* travel, it is less to learn than to disrupt and destroy.

Some contemporary scholars of the Middle East reinforce rather than trouble the presumption that adherents of Islam are by definition captured by a particularly narrow worldview inimical to critical reflection. In *The Muslim Discovery of Europe*, for example, Bernard Lewis contends that Europeans sought to acquire Arabic and knowledge of the politics, culture and economics of Muslim lands not only to fulfill the practical demands of commerce and diplomacy but also to "gratify the boundless intellectual curiosity unleashed by the Renaissance."[46] By contrast, Lewis repeatedly notes the lack of curiosity or desire for knowledge among Muslims about languages, literatures, religions or cultures beyond Islamic lands, a narrowness attributable to the Muslim world's "belief in its own self-sufficiency and superiority as the one repository of the true faith and—which for Muslims meant the same thing—of the civilized way of life."[47] Travel accounts by merchants, diplomats and other Muslims provide much of Lewis's historical data, but in general the extensive literature about Muslim travels, both literal and imaginative, is attributed to a "great appetite for wonders and marvels" as distinct from a desire for knowledge.[48] It is only under duress that a Muslim world in the shadow of Western power begins to show interest in matters European, but then only for purely practical purposes.[49] Lewis concludes that it "was not until Renaissance and post-Renaissance Europe that a human society for the first time developed the sophistication, the detachment and, above all, the curiosity to study and appreciate the cultures of alien and even hostile societies."[50]

By contrast, anthropologist Mary Helms has shown that curiosity about cultural others, as well as an emphasis on the intrinsic value of knowledge gleaned from travel to "geographically distant places," is common to a remarkably wide array of preindustrial cultural traditions and practices.[51] Further complicating Lewis's claims, it will become clear in the following pages that *within* Western traditions, encounters with what is foreign has been accompanied as much by anxiety and ambivalence as curiosity. And while it is true that historical sources do not reveal a great interest in cultures and peoples outside of Muslim lands on the part of government officials prior to the colonial era, what such apparent official lack of interest says about the curiosities of ordinary Muslims or Muslims in general is debatable.[52] But what is perhaps most striking in Lewis's argument is the almost offhand remark in which he draws a distinction between an "appetite for wonders and marvels" and genuine knowledge: here the line between history-as-knowledge and fiction-as-fantasy is fixed and bright, a reiteration of the age-old epistemological distinction Cicero drew between history, which aims at truth, and poetry, the purpose of which is pleasure.[53] For Lewis, this epistemological distinction maps onto a civilizational divide between modern Islam and Christendom in particular. Muslims gather factual information about the unfamiliar for purely instrumental purposes, but their curiosity is reserved for the fantastic. By contrast, the pursuit of knowledge about others for its own sake—knowledge which is, to borrow from Clifford, scientific and ennobling—is a distinctively European phenomenon.[54]

## IV. ISLAM, TRAVEL, AND TALAB AL-'ILM

A sharp divide between knowledge, truth and history on the one hand and fantasy, wonder and pleasure on the other misses the ways in which curiosity itself connotes a drive to know about what is novel or strange; the pursuit of knowledge for its own sake is often characterized in terms of desire or love of wisdom; and the very project of history is increasingly described as the privileging of one interpretation of the past over other possible interpretations. As many philosophers of social science have pointed out, knowledge is not solely a matter of one-to-one correspondence between interpretation and "linguistically naked" things-in-themselves—between what, for example, Herodotus says about Scythia and what archeological research suggests Scythians actually were.[55] In the human sciences in particular, knowledge is a hermeneutically informed endeavor, an open-ended inquiry mindful always of the embeddedness of both scholars and subjects in linguistic and cultural worlds that constitute, constrain and enable self understanding and understanding of others. Knowledge, then, is not only that which meets the positivistic criteria of correspondence, but is also what is revealed in the translating practices of the traveler who purveys and represents what is unfamiliar by way of comparison with what is familiar, an activity that simultaneously discloses and articulates the shifting boundaries and content of other and self.

So understood, it is my contention that the connection between travel and knowledge is not confined to any particular culture or epoch and, as two recent edited volumes on Muslim travel amply demonstrate, is particularly prevalent in both Muslim doctrinal sources and historical practice.[56] In a general sense, as Franz Rosenthal points out, the "ancient use of travel as a metaphor to describe man's sojourn on earth was widely accepted in Islam," and is in evidence in several Qur'anic suras, including one (5:18) which states that "Allah's is the Sovereignty of the heavens and the earth and all that is between them, and unto Him is the journeying (*masīr* / مصير)."[57] Some Sufi mystics would transform the metaphorical rendering of life as a journey into an embrace of perpetual homelessness, an exhortation to live as a stranger through constant travel.[58] More specifically, however, the Qur'an repeatedly exhorts its readers to "travel on the earth and see" (3:137; 6:11; 12:109; 16: 36; 29:20; 30:9; 30:42) both how the end comes to the unjust and "how He originated creation" (29:20).[59] And sura 22:46 asks: "Have they not traveled in the land that they could have the heart to understand, and ears to hear?"

Al-Suyuti records a narrative in which Muhammad is said to have exhorted his followers to seek knowledge as far as China.[60] Several accounts of the words and deeds of Muhammad (*ahadith*-plural of *hadith*) link travel to God's pleasure, including one in which Anas b. Malik reported that the Prophet said, "Those who go out in search of knowledge will be in the path of God until they return," and another which states that the search for knowledge can serve as expiation for past deeds.[61] A hadith of Ibn Majah states:

> God makes the path to paradise easy for he who travels a road in search of knowledge, and the angels spread their wings for the pleasure of the seeker of knowledge. All those in heaven and earth will seek forgiveness from those who pursue knowledge, even the serpents in the water. The learned person is superior to the worshipper just as the moon has precedence over the rest of the stars.[62]

The knowledge (*'ilm*) here is unquestionably religious, but a hard and fast distinction between secular and religious knowledge misses the scope of *'ilm*. Within the terms of Islam, all human knowledge—whether of things divine or purely mundane—ultimately derives from God, and thus all potential objects of human knowledge are themselves aspects of divine creation.[63] Of course the scope of what humans can know is clearly delimited by the Qur'an, which repeatedly invokes God's omniscience, cautioning believers to remember that "God knows, but/and you do not know" (3:66). Yet when joined to the exhortation to travel and learn, the invocation of God's omniscience serves not to arrest human inquiry but to insist upon its limits; it prescribes humility rather than ignorance. The insistence that only God knows the secrets of the universe presupposes, as does hermeneutics (for different reasons), the finitude of human understanding—and, by extension, that wisdom may reside not only in what one knows but also, as Socrates argued, in the recognition of what one does not know.

The translation of *'ilm* as knowledge and learning broadly understood[64] is supported by Rosenthal's evocative suggestion that in pre-Islamic Arabia the root of *'ilm* was originally connected to the concept of "way signs," or "signposts," those "characteristic marks in the desert, which guided [the Bedouin] on his travels and in the execution of his daily tasks" and that constituted "the kind of knowledge on which his life and well-being principally depended."[65] Indeed, Michael Karl Lenker contends that the *rihla* (a genre of Arabic travel literature) reflected secular and religious concerns alike and concludes that as a "motive for travel, [*talab al-'ilm*] surpassed in significance all other incentives including the pilgrimage itself," and was often seen as a "lifetime mission rather than a short term goal motivated by practicality."[66]

This rendering of *talab al-'ilm* illuminates the ways in which pilgrimage, the religious journey *par excellence*, has in practice shaded into quests of a more mundane nature, occasioned the emergence or transformation of political and social identities, or served as a cultural marker over which governmental and popular forces discursively struggle.[67] Far from signaling some radical epistemological difference between cultural traditions, then, *talab al-'ilm* recalls the many connotations of the Greek *theôria* in which religious embassies, pilgrimage, sightseeing, knowledge and observation of others are closely connected, and may in this sense be continuous with practices of pilgrimage in other cultural traditions, for example, *darśan* in Hinduism.[68] Indeed, an early meaning of *theôros* was an envoy dispatched to consult the Delphic Oracle and so "from the very beginning the theorist was sent to bring back the word of a god."[69] The sense in which the Greek practice of *theôria* could in this way become a "divine vocation" is thus mirrored in the identification in Islam of travel with "pious activity," the achievement of which was thought to constitute a "sign of divine approval and munificence."[70]

The scope of *'ilm* in the exhortation to travel in search of knowledge is reflected in the extensive and varied types of Muslim travel, every one of which may entail both physical movement and spiritual transformation: the *hajj* (pilgrimage to Mecca), *hijra* (emigration), *rihla* (travel in pursuit of knowledge) and *ziyara* (visits to shrines). Any single journey, moreover, might incorporate all four of these purposes.[71] Of course, the motivations for actual Muslim travel over the centuries range well beyond these formal categories—some travelers undertook journeys for such mundane and less religiously specific purposes as job-seeking, diplomatic missions for sultans, desire for status, or just plain wanderlust—and wanderers throughout the *Dar al-Islam* [Abode of Islam] included beggars, slaves, soldiers, crooks and "low-class entertainers," as well as pilgrims, merchants, students, poets and fortune-hunters.[72] In short, travel in pursuit of knowledge may be said to constitute a central teaching of Islam although its terms and categories can never capture the varieties of historical practice.[73] Sanctioned by divine exhortations, tied to the promise of *baraka* ("the blessings both in this world and the next which would come from visiting holy places and obtaining the blessings of saintly men"),[74] and nourished by a complex and cosmopolitan civilization "which in the fullest sense owed its vibrancy to constant movement,"[75] travel in pursuit of knowledge is more than merely a recurrent theme in Islam, but rather an ethos.[76]

## V. THE DOUBLE-EDGED NATURE OF TRAVEL

The foregoing suggests that what are often called Western and Islamic traditions, both past and present, share an emphasis on the connection between travel and the pursuit of knowledge. What this means is that despite the ways it may elide important distinctions of privilege and marginality, power and powerlessness, travel here operates as a bridge that opens a realm of comparative inquiry across culture and history without presupposing any particular content. Importantly, this focus discloses not only a transcultural association of mobility and knowledge but also a remarkable range of common anxieties and ambivalences occasioned by travel. Such anxieties are tied in part to the inevitable risks a traveler may court—Ibn Khaldûn lost his family and all his belongings in a shipwreck and Ibn Battuta was robbed and barely outran the Black Plague—risks reflected in the etymological connection of "travel" to "travail" by way of its roots in the Latin *trepalium*, an instrument of torture.[77] Indeed, as Helms suggests, the prestige a traveler may enjoy is often dependent upon the inaccessibility of what is faraway and the danger associated with reaching it.[78] Moreover, as the passage in Plato's *Laws* details, there is an ever present possibility that the knowledge a traveler brings home will occasion disaster, as when Herodotus's Crœsus misunderstands the message of the Oracle at Delphi, assuming that the empire he was prophesied to destroy would be that of Persia rather than his own.[79]

The traveler also courts the psychic, physical, social and economic miseries separation from home may entail. Thus, a late-fifteenth century English guidebook for pilgrims warns against the dangers of "shrewes," the "blody fluxe," robbers and the ever present possibility of death from corrupt air and water.[80] Medieval Arabic literature links travel not only to renewal, opportunity, a broadened perspective and a useful education, but also to poverty, to the humiliation and loss of prestige entailed by the abandonment of familiar connections with family and friends, and to the homesickness and loneliness of the stranger who, "far away from his town and people is like a runaway bull which is a target for every hunter."[81] Travel, in short, signals estrangement from the moorings which impart solidity and definition to human life; a loss, not just of a familiar place but of a world comprised of family, friends, customs and institutions, which both nurtures and sustains its inhabitants. Thus it is that the Socrates of *The Crito* envisions the Laws of Athens speaking to him as parent to child, reminding him of why he did not "travel abroad [*theôria*, 52b] as other people do," and delineating the moral and practical futility of attempting to take refuge elsewhere when his own fellow-citizens have condemned him to death.

Inasmuch as travel makes possible and often reflects a desire for new experience and knowledge,[82] there are also those who have identified a latent affinity between travel and disorder, who see in all that is unprecedented or innovative the potential for disruption of stable boundaries, conventional arrangements, settled customs or established authority. In Arabic, for example, the word for innovation, *bid'a*, is the same word for heresy. And in Muslim scholarship of the "manuscript age," for example, the association between novelty and danger meant that, as Rosenthal writes, "the ultimate success of new ideas, which did not fit in with the dominant systems of thought, was unusually uncertain. If a new idea did not find the approval of a comparatively large group of scholars in a comparatively short interval of time, it was likely to be buried in a library, with an infinitesimal chance of subsequent rediscovery."[83] A similar affinity among travel, novelty and transgression is expressed by Thomas à Kempis in his *Imitation of Christ*, when he warns that journeys to marvel at the deeds of the saints, to satisfy curiosity or seek the "novelties of things not yet seen" may be inimical to salvation.[84] St. Augustine characterizes the pursuit of learning and science, and curiosity about the world it expresses, as "lust of the eyes."[85] Given the dangers of worldly curiosity, the ideal pilgrim "would have traveled . . .with his eyes upon the ground to shut out the glories of the world."[86] The *political* disruption latent in such mobility is perhaps best captured in the person of the vagabond, the perpetual wanderer who represents the danger of masterless men; as seventeenth-century Puritan William Perkins intones, such men "passe from place to place, being under no certaine Magistracie or Ministerie, nor joyning themselves to any set society in Church or Common-wealth, are plagues and banes of both, and are to be take as maine enemies of [the] ordinance of God . . ."[87]

To the extent that travel entails encounters with what is foreign, moreover, it has also been associated with corruption of several kinds in both Muslim and European thought. Despite the valorization of travel in Islam, for example, encounters with what is alien, that is, what is not Islamic, have repeatedly raised the fear that the purity of the Islamic message will be contaminated or debased.[88] Such anxieties include the opposition to the foreign provenance of Greek philosophy and rationalism in the work of al-Ghazali (d. 1111) and Ibn Taymiyya (d. 1328). They also include the more recent arguments of "conservative modernists"[89] such as Tariq al-Bishri about the threat to Islam from "that which is imported" [*al-wafid*], and the insistence of Islamic fundamentalists, such as Sayyid Qutb, that the rise of Western cultural, political and economic domination has occasioned a new *jahiliyya*, a modern age of ignorance in which the truths of Islam are either corrupted or occluded.

Just as Mill worries about the perceptual distortions latent in exposure to foreignness, there are untold others anxious about the ever present danger of "going native." Inasmuch as travel becomes implicated in imperialist ventures, however, there are also those, such as Denis Diderot, who argue that *both* the European traveler to 'uncivilized' worlds and those he encounters there are disfigured by the experience. European travel to the Americas or India signifies the transformation of civilized man to savage, a reversal, in Anthony Pagden's words, of the "journey that his ancestors once made from the state of nature to civil society."[90] Here travel to other cultures is also a kind of time travel, a temporal journey back to an earlier stage of human development—a trope characteristic of much of European social contract theory in which the state of nature is said to still exist among "savage peoples" defined by innocence or barbarism, or both. Such excursions, Diderot goes on to write, "reared a new generation of savage nomads . . .Those men who visit so many countries that they end up belonging to none . . ."[91] Far from being men to admire, for Diderot, there is "no state more immoral than that of the continual traveler": taking his home for granted, the European traveler is driven by a "potentially destructive restlessness," seeking not only to see but also possess what he sees. The traveler is thus "always, potentially, a colonist," those he encounters always, potentially, the colonized.[92]

I have argued that theorizing is inherently comparative, for it presupposes literal or imaginative contrasts with purportedly alien lands, peoples and practices. I have also suggested that the implications for one's 'political home' of the critical distance such contrasts make possible are unpredictable, even contradictory. The preceding panoply of shared fears about travel across both culture and history is perhaps the clearest testimony to its transformative power; here exposures to the unfamiliar become a "form of dystopic transgression,"[93] provoking a riot of fantasy about the grave dangers for and of those who travel, those traveled to and those left behind. The intensity of the fears bespeaks a worry shared by Plato's Athenian, namely that knowledge and experience from afar may result either in the destruction or perfection of a soul or city, and that no particular outcome can be guaranteed in advance.

## *VI. TRAVEL AS TRANSLATION*

Inasmuch as the explicit link between travel and the pursuit of knowledge is itself mobile, transcending cultural and historical boundaries to evoke resonances and anxieties across language and time, travel is, in anthropologist

James Clifford's words, an invaluable term of translation.[94] Not only is travel a term of translation, reports of such travels are also *acts* of translation, practices, as François Hartog shows, of both "seeing and making seen" and, I would add, of hearing and making heard.[95] Importantly, however, those who are seeing and hearing, and *what* it is that is seen and heard, are in constant flux. This is in part because the categories of contrast are not fixed or stable; each new encounter discloses different vectors of comparison for the traveler. For example, Ibn Battuta, the fourteenth-century North African who traveled throughout the Middle East, the Asian steppes, India, China and sub-Saharan Africa for almost 30 years, classifies the unfamiliar by way of gradations of distance from the features of his 'home' in the Maghreb (here Morocco in particular, but Northwest Africa more generally), yet the categories of contrast shift, enlarge and constrict as his itinerary brings him into proximity with various frontiers, geographic, religious, linguistic, cultural and racial. Thus the audience for whom he translates his observations are alternately Maghrebis, Malikis (adherents of a particular school of Islamic law), Sunnis, Arabs, people with white skin, scholars of his class or, in his encounters with Jews, Christians and Hindus among others, simply 'Muslims' (they are, however, always male).

The fluidity of what is translated, by whom, and for whom is also due to the fact that travelers are not only receptacles of knowledge but agents of its dissemination. As James Redfield points out, Greeks carried a certain moralism with them, and traveled as much to teach as to learn; thus in the *Histories*, Herodotus writes of a Solon who is at once a traveler and purveyor of wisdom to those who seek it.[96] Similarly, Ibn Battuta both gathers and conveys knowledge to curious Sultans in far-flung places. There is, moreover, a certain indeterminacy to such practices of translation over time: the status and content of the knowledge gleaned from such encounters changes with each new generation of readers. The act of translation is thus double: the traveler "sees and makes seen" for those in his or her own world, but to audiences in a variety of cultural and historical locations, the travels may disclose different kinds of knowledge. The very claim that tales of "wonders and marvels" are translating practices that constitute a non-positivistic source of knowledge rather than a mere repository of fantasy is a case in point.

Among others, Edward Said has exposed the inequalities of power implicated in the imposition of Western language, concerns and categories on the rest of the world, and emphasized in particular the distortion of the "Orient" such power has produced. Here, however, travel is a term of translation precisely because its association with the pursuit of knowledge arises from within the cultural tradition commonly designated as 'Islamic' as well as within that which is called 'Western.' Taking my cue from the Islamic emphasis on *talab al-'ilm* attends to the danger of imposing Western preoccupations and takes up what I regard as a central challenge of "comparative political theory." Perhaps best defined as an approach to and argument for the comparative study of Western and non-Western political thought, comparative political theory presumes first, that political theory is not the purview of any particular culture or historical era and second, disparate cultures are not morally and cognitively incommensurable even if there are serious moral and political disagreements at stake.[97] As I have argued elsewhere, however, this possibility is not premised upon the existence of universal and perennial questions that arise by virtue of being human.[98] The universality of such questions—let alone a common human nature—cannot be assumed, and therefore the extent to which one does or does not share certain dilemmas with others by virtue of being human is an inquiry central to the project of comparative political theory itself. A cross-cultural investigation into the connections between travel and the search for knowledge is just such an inquiry, for it operates against a background of assumptions that overlap sufficiently to make comparisons possible without presupposing a particular outcome.

Importantly, the operations of representational power against which Said warns are discernible not only between cultures but within them. All comparisons entail acts of translation—of seeing and making seen, hearing and making heard—which are at once invaluable to "make sense of an otherness which would otherwise remain altogether opaque" and suspect for the cultural grammar they inevitably impose.[99] This is because representation through translation at least initially organizes the unfamiliar by way of linguistic strategies and devices derived from the world of the translator, techniques by which what is foreign is charted, decoded and domesticated for an audience at a cultural or historical remove. Thus, it is dramatically evident in efforts to translate something called Christianity for Hindus, but it is also evident in less obviously loaded practices of translation across time, for example, twenty-first century Christian efforts to translate Jesus's teachings within a radically altered context,[100] or the use of analogical thinking by intellectual historians to bridge the "otherness of the past."[101]

These examples illustrate that the ideological impulse Said emphasizes does not exhaust what is going on in translation. As Catherine Gimelli Martin argues persuasively, while translation "presumes the hegemony of self over other," it does so dialogically in the quite specific sense that it is "polysemic and multivocal rather than monological or unidirectional."[102] A model of translation that implies approximation rather than correspondence means that "[i]nterpretative 'facts' must be represented as acts, partial recognitions, which are never either fully translatable or fully comprehensible."[103] Good translation, as Walter Benjamin notes, is not a matter of reproducing meaning but rather of locating echoes:

> The task of the translator consists in finding that intended effect upon the language into which he is translating which produces in it the echo of the original . . .Unlike a work of literature, translation does not find itself in the center of the language forest but on the outside facing the wooded ridge; it calls into it without entering, aiming at that single spot where the echo is able to give, in its own language, the reverberation of the work in the alien one.[104]

Translation can be bad translation (mistranslation) but if it is understood as a process of approximation, the criteria by which 'better' translations are distinguished emphasize opacity and translucence rather than coherence and transparency. As opposed to the presumption that the translator floats, *tabula rasa*, above a linear process culminating in the faithful and complete reproduction of the original in a new language, here the translator is understood to be dialogically implicated[105] in a jagged and perpetually unfinished endeavor constrained by power inequalities and social institutions, characterized as much by moments of incomprehension as illumination, and where the translator, translated and language of translation are transformed in the process.[106] Thus, the practices travel occasions entail the search for those echoes and reverberations across spatial or temporal difference that make some measure of understanding possible. Like the inevitable lament that there is always "something lost in translation," however, it also entails the acknowledgment that distortion, far from an occasional feature of bad translation or a characteristic of only historically specific inequalities of power, inheres in but does not exclusively define the endeavor itself. Instead of presuming that there is a fully accessible universality (psychological, moral or otherwise) lurking just beneath 'surface' differences, better translations register rather than efface the untranslatable: translators "can help preserve the linguistic and cultural difference of the foreign text by producing translations which are strange and estranging, which mark the limits of dominant values in the target-language culture and hinder those values from enacting an imperialistic domestication of a cultural other."[107]

My understanding of the connection among travel, theory and vision grounds the acquisition of knowledge in those concrete, inescapable yet inevitably flawed practices of translation that are part of the realm of ordinary rather than extraordinary experience. If travel is both a term and a practice of translation, and translation entails the "paradoxical duality of blindness and insight" which is, in turn, the "precondition of all knowledge,"[108] there is a simultaneous embrace of and resistance to what is radically unfamiliar built into both the metaphor and the practice, a simultaneous opening and closing. Those moments in which prejudices (in Gadamer's sense) congeal are thus not necessarily a matter of bad faith or malicious intent but are part and parcel of an inevitably recurring yet intermittent myopia captured by Socrates' insistence that "he will carry part of his native city with him wherever he goes."[109] This way of rendering the link between mobility and knowledge, then, does not rest on an ideal of disembodied objectivity but rather derives from the multiplication of vision—and the recognitions and misrecognitions it inevitably entails—made possible by a condition of simultaneous rootedness and estrangement. As such, it is part of a broader reconsideration of knowledge and vision effected by various feminist, social and cultural theorists who emphasize, for example, the mutual implication of the visual and linguistic "turn,"[110] and develop a non-imperialist conception of travel that substitutes the association of travel/connectedness/understanding for travel/detachment/domination.[111]

Such reconsiderations suggest that, far from privileging a disembodied "gaze," travel as both a metaphor and practice makes possible knowledges that are necessarily partial and contingent yet constitutive of both self-understanding and understanding of others. Rather than coding travel as 'scientific and heroic," a symptom and symbol of certain kinds of gender, racial and cultural privilege, then, the preceding arguments about travel, theory and translation pluralize the locations, genres and agents that occasion or engage in the practice of theorizing.[112] Let me conclude with a brief account of just one area of inquiry these arguments bring into view.

Within the last 20 years, there has been a virtual explosion of scholarship on Western travels to the non-West, and travel writing by Europeans in particular has come to be regarded as a window onto the production of knowledge and, more particularly, onto the mutually constitutive images of colonizer and colonized. These efforts are vital interventions into the operations of power, particularly in a colonial and postcolonial world in which such operations both establish distinctions between "center and periphery" and constitute their relationship hierarchically. Yet paradoxically, attempts to deconstruct these mechanisms of domination have tended to reproduce this structure and organization. From hermeneutically informed ethnography that aims at the "comprehension of the self by the detour of the comprehension of the other" to investigations into the way colonial European travel writing "*produced* 'the rest of the world' for European readerships at particular points in Europe's expansionist trajectory," the West is continually reconstituted as the epicenter.[113] Seeking to displace hubristic self-images of the West as the beacon that "shows to the less developed the image of its own future," these analyses re-establish the West as a beacon, only now it is not a promise but a warning against a presumption of cultural superiority wedded to overwhelming political and economic power.[114]

What would it mean to invert the questions that reproduce the West as the epicenter of the world? Instead of asking, for example, how does Western travel writing produce the colonized other, what features of travel, translation and theory might be disclosed by shifting the theoretical perspective entirely?[115] The genre of Arabic literature known as the *rihla*, a book recounting travels, particularly those undertaken in pursuit of knowledge (*talab al-'ilm*), is an opportunity to explore just these questions.[116] This is not because all Arab or Muslim travel is theory, or because all accounts of travel in pursuit of knowledge are by definition reflective or even interesting.[117] Rather, as theory is inherently comparative, and as comparisons entail acts of translation that simultaneously make sense of and distort the unfamiliar, the *rihla* is an occasion to map complex connections among travel, theory and knowledge rarely developed outside of the confines of Euroamerican political thought. Such analyses may well disclose significant differences occluded by the tendency to view the rest of the world through a Euroamerican lens. For example, many scholars of cross-cultural encounters tend to focus upon other cultures' engagement with the West. Yet much of Muslim travel throughout the centuries has been *within* (as well as beyond) the *Dar al-Islam*, loosely linked territory which, in its heyday, constituted a trans-hemispheric Afro-Eurasian civilization in almost continuous intercommunication by way of an extraordinary fluidity of people and knowledge across political, cultural and linguistic boundaries.[118] Juxtapositions of Muslim and European travels thus do not disclose a neat symmetry: in the precolonial period, for example, the preoccupation of Europeans with the "Muslim East" is not mirrored by a Muslim preoccupation with Europeans (although in more recent history, the reverse has tended to be true). If interest in Europe is the index of philosophical and intellectual curiosity, this can be taken as evidence of Muslim insularity. Yet this misses entirely the opportunity the *rihla* provides to see the ways in which critical reflection as well as narrowness of vision is borne of encounters with multiple Others, where otherness is defined not just against the West but also by differences—regional, racial, ethnic, linguistic, sexual and otherwise—somewhat closer to home. Indeed, these journeys suggest that the very nature and locale of 'home' often emerges out of, and is transformed by, such voyages abroad.

But by the same token, the *rihla* may disclose common patterns where perhaps only difference was expected. Far from representing two incommensurable civilizations, one insular, the other characterized by boundless curiosity, those from the 'East' and 'West' have long compared and understood themselves in terms of a shifting panoply of others. Indeed, whether the subject is Montesquieu's Persians or Ibn Battuta's Sudanese, such 'journeys,' whether explicitly fictional or ostensibly factual, often serve less as reliable geographical or anthropological documents of actual places and peoples than as windows onto the dialectical process of acquiring knowledge about others and about one's own cultural and political world. Thus these juxtapositions disclose common mechanisms of translation and mistranslation, transcultural and transhistorical patterns by which both Muslim and European travelers seek and produce knowledge about others as well as themselves. More particularly, they make visible the ways in which such knowledge is often constituted through a set of nested polarities—us and them, self and other, male and female—endemic to comparative inquiry yet also characterized by a dialectical process where the terms of comparison and reference are constantly shifting.

Such commonalities at once complicate Lewis's somewhat essentialist contrast between Christendom and Islam and challenge Habermas's presumption that there is an inevitable and exclusive relationship between Western rationalism and critical reflection. At the same time, it suggests that despite the legacy of colonialist and imperialist enterprises, the West does not have a monopoly on what María Lugones and Elizabeth Spelman have called "imperialist theorizing," the kind of theorizing that happens when "I observe myself and others like me culturally and in other ways and use that account to give an account of you. In doing this, I remake you in my own image."[119] Representational power is an inescapable feature of translation—the women, Shi'ites and Chinese of Ibn Battuta's *rihla* no more speak for themselves than did Herodotus's non-Greeks—yet techniques of representation may also be said to constitute the very conditions of intelligibility across difference; they make it possible to locate reverberations between what is unfamiliar and familiar. Using travel as a term of translation, then, makes visible the extent to which the desire for new knowledge, the capacity for critical distance, the attainment of political wisdom about others and oneself, and the will to remake another in one's own image is not the purview of any particular era or cultural constellation.

### NOTES

*I am grateful to Shahrough Akhavi, Lawrie Balfour, Carol Dougherty, Pratap Mehta, J. Donald Moon, James Petterson, Marilyn Sides and Keith Topper for their comments on earlier drafts of this chapter.*

1. Edward Westermarck, *Wit and Wisdom in Morocco: A Study of Native Proverbs* (London: George Routledge & Sons, Ltd., 1930), 136, 351.

2. Here I borrow from James Clifford's "Traveling Cultures," in *Cultural Studies*, Lawrence Grossberg, Cary Nelson, and Paula A. Treichler, eds. (New York: Routledge, 1992), 110.

3. Despite the frequency with which "the West" is invoked by peoples all over the world, and the very real allegiances and enmities it may evoke among them, terms such as West and non-West carve up the world in ways that obscure their mutual historical indebtedness and the cross-pollination of the present. All subsequent references should be read as problematic, although I will omit the quotation marks.

4. Mill, *The History of British India*, 3$^{rd}$ edition (London: Baldwin, Cradock and Joy, 1826), xii.

5. The Epic of Gilgamesh, trans. N.K. Sandars (New York: Penguin Books, 1972), 61.

6. Homer's *Odyssey*, trans. Carol Dougherty, *The Raft of Odysseus: The Ethnographic Imagination of Homer's Odyssey* (Oxford: Oxford University Press, 2001), 4.

7. Eric J. Leed, *The Mind of the Traveler: From Gilgamesh to Global Tourism* (U.S.: HarperCollins, 1991), 5-6.

8. Herodotus, *Histories*, trans. George Rawlinson (New York: Alfred A. Knopf, 1997), 1.30; Clarence P. Bill, "Notes on the Greek Θεωρός and Θεωρία," *Transactions and Proceedings of the American Philological Association* 33 (1991), 196-97.

9. Bill, 196-97.

10. Trans. James Ker, in "Solon's Theôria and the End of the City," *Classical Antiquity* 19(2), October 2000: 314.

11. *The Laws*, trans. A.E. Taylor in *Plato: The Collected Dialogues*, Edith Hamilton and Huntington Cairns, eds. (Princeton: Princeton University Press, 1987), 13$^{th}$ ed.

12. Ian Rutherford, "Theoric Crisis: The Dangers of Pilgrimage in Greek Religion and Society," *Studi e materiali di storia delle religioni* 61 (1995), 283.

13. Ibid., 282.

14. Ker, "Solon's Theôria and the End of the City," 309-10, 326-27.

15. The extent to which *The Republic* can be regarded as a kind of journey—both literal and epistemological— and thus that such solitary reflection may be contingent on, rather than inimical to "travel" broadly understood, is beyond my focus here.

16. Dougherty, *The Raft of Odysseus*, 6.

17. James Redfield, "Herodotus the Tourist," *Classical Philology* 80 (1985), 98.

18. Bacon, *New Atlantis and the Great Instauration,* Jerry Weinberger, ed. (Arlington Heights, IL: Harlan Davidson, Inc., 1989), 81; *The Persian Letters* (New York: Bobbs-Merrill, Co., 1964), trans. George R. Healy, 9; Nietzsche, *Human All-Too-Human*, trans. Paul V. Cohn (New York: The MacMillan Co, 1924), 117-18.

19. This intellectual tradition is not, of course, coextensive with actual practice, for while theory is embedded in practice, these terms and categories can never fully capture of the varieties of actual instances and motivations of European travelers.

20. Said, *The World, the Text and the Critic* (Cambridge, MA: Harvard University Press, 1983), 8.

21. *The Prince and Discourses*, trans. Luigi Ricci (New York: Random House, 1950), 4.

22. Thucydides, *The Peloponnesian War*, V: 26, I:22.

23. Tocqueville, *Democracy in America* (New York: Anchor Books, 1969), trans. George Lawrence, "Author's Preface to the 12$^{th}$ Edition"; Vol. I, conclusion, 408.

24. Al-Afghani left Iran voluntarily and over the years travelled to India, France, Russia and England, as well as to Afghanistan, Turkey and Egypt, countries from which he was ignominiously expelled for his political and intellectual activities.

25. Khomeini and the Egyptian Sayyid Qutb, two of the most influential twentieth-century Islamist thinkers, are perfect illustrations of what I will argue is the double-edged nature of travel, that is, the extent to which exposures to the unfamiliar can occasion 'closings' as well as 'openings': Khomeini is well-known for his invectives against 'Westoxification' and Qutb's experience of exile in post-War America only intensified his dislike of foreign influence on Islam. Qutb, of course, did not associate his sojourn with a narrowing of vision; he thought he was seeing clearly for the first time. Among the many other prominent contemporary Muslims who have traveled are Tariq al-Bishri, Amin Huwaydi, Muhsin Kadivar, (Ayat Allah) Mihdi Ha'iri Yazdi, Rachid Ghannouchi, 'Abd al-Karim Soroush, Muhammad Khatami and Hasan al-Turabi.

26. Abdul R. JanMohamed, "Worldliness-Without-World, Homelessness-as-Home: Toward a Definition of the Specular Border Intellectual," in *Edward Said: A Critical Reader*, Michael Sprinker, ed. (Cambridge, MA: Blackwell Publishers, 1992), 96-120.

27. Said, "The Mind of Winter: Reflections on Life in Exile" *Harper's*, Vol. 269 (September 1984), 49; "Edward Said: The Voice of a Palestinian Exile," *Third Text*, 3/4 (Spring/Summer 1998), 48.

28. Said, "The Mind of Winter," 55, emphasis in the original.

29. Walzer, *Interpretation and Social Criticism* (Cambridge, MA: Harvard University Press, 1987), 36-37.

30. Janet Wolff, "On the Road Again: Metaphors of Travel in Cultural Criticism," *Cultural Studies* 7, (1993), 228.

31. Mary Louise Pratt, *Imperial Eyes: Travel Writing and Transculturation* (London and New York: Routledge, 1992), 6. Here I stretch Pratt's meaning of "contact zones."

32. The literature here is extensive; some examples include Pratt, *Imperial Eyes*; Clifford, "Traveling Cultures"; Benedict Anderson, "Exodus," *Critical Inquiry* 20 (2), Winter 1994: 314-27; Lawrence Grossberg, "Wandering Audiences, Nomadic Critics," *Bringing it All Back Home* (Durham, NC: Duke University Press, 1997), 305-19; Gilles Deleuze, "Nomad Thought," in *The New Nietzsche: Contemporary Styles of Interpretation*, David B. Allison, ed. (NY: Dell Publishing Co., 1977), 142-47.

33. See, for example, Paul Gilroy's *The Black Atlantic: Modernity and Double Consciousness* (New York: Verso, 1993) and James Clifford, "Diasporas," *Cultural Anthropology* 9 (3): 302-38;

34. Fred Dallmayr, *Alternative Visions: Paths in the Global Village* (New York: Rowman & Littlefield, 1998).

35. Wolff, "On the Road Again," 224-39. See also Sara Mills, *Discourses of Difference: An Analysis of Women's Travel Writing and Colonialism* (New York: Routledge, 1991), Caren Kaplan, *Questions of Travel: Postmodern Discourses of Displacement* (Durham, NC: Duke University Press, 1996), and Pratt, *Imperial Eyes*.

36. Clifford, "Traveling Cultures," 105. Although Clifford, along with Said, have been criticized for failing to acknowledge fully how travel is itself a gendered category.

37. See, for example, Nancy Tapper, "*Ziyarat*: Gender, Movement and Exchange in a Turkish Community," in *Muslim Travellers: Pilgramage, Migration, and the Religious Imagination,* Date F. Eickelman and James Piscabori, eds. (Berkeley: University of California Press, 1990) 236-55.

38. Patrick Holland and Graham Huggan, *Tourists with Typewriters: Critical Reflections on Contemporary Travel Writing* (Ann Arbor, MI: University of Michigan Press, 2002), 111.

39. Wolff, "On the Road Again," 234, emphasis in the original.

40. Stephen Melville, "Division of the Gaze, or, Remarks on the Color and Tenor of Contemporary 'Theory'," in *Vision in Context*, 103. Martin Jay surveys both the privileging

and denigration of vision in Western thought in his *Downcast Eyes: The Denigration of Vision in Twentieth-Century French Thought* (Berkeley: University of California Press, 1994).

41. See for example, Michel Foucault, *Discipline and Punish*, Laura Mulvey, "Visual Pleasure and Narrative Cinema," in *Visual and Other Pleasures* (Bloomington: Indiana University Press, 1989) and Norman Bryson, *Vision and Painting: The Logic of the Gaze* (New Haven: Yale University Press, 1983) .

42. Pierre Loti, *Japan: Madame Chrysanthemum*, trans. Laura Ensor (London: KPI, 1985), 13. For a discussion about the feminization of Japan in travel literature, see *Tourists with Typewriters*, 81-90.

43. "Remarks on Legitimation," *Philosophy and Social Criticism* 24 (2/3), 1998, 162.

44. Mehta, "Cosmopolitanism and the Circle of Reason," *Political Theory* 28(5), October 2000, 681, emphasis in the original.

45. Samuel Huntington, "The Clash of Civilizations?" *Foreign Affairs* 72 (Summer, 1993): 22-49 and *The Clash of Civilizations and the Remaking of World Order* (New York: Simon & Schuster, 1996). The phrase is from Kishore Mahbubani, "The West and the Rest," *The National Interest* (Summer 1992): 3-13.

46. Lewis, *The Muslim Discovery of Europe* (New York: W.W. Norton & Company, 1982), 80.

47. Ibid., 280.

48. Ibid., 301.

49. Ibid., 87.

50. Ibid., 75.

51. Helms, *Ulysses Sail: An Ethnographic Odyssey of Power, Knowledge, and Geographical Distance* (Princeton: Princeton University Press, 1988), see Chapters 1 and 3 in particular.

52. Scholars have suggested a greater awareness of the diversity of languages and cultures within the category of "European" than Lewis suggests. *Images of the Other: Europe and the Muslim World before 1700*, David Blanks, ed. *Cairo Papers in Social Science*, Vol. 19, Monograph 2 (Egypt: American University in Cairo Press, 1996), see especially E.M. Sartain's chapter, "Medieval Muslim-European Relations: Islamic Juristic Theory and Chancery Practice," 81-95.

53. Cicero, *De Legibus [The Laws]*, trans. Clinton Walker Keyes (London: William Heinemann, 1928), I. I. 5, 301.

54. Importantly, Lewis does not attribute any inherent superiority to Europeans. Yet he notes that while Europe had "shared the general lack of curiosity concerning strange peoples," the combined impact of the discovery of the New World, the Renaissance and the Reformation produced a spirit of "intellectual curiosity and scientific inquiry" in direct contrast to the Muslim world. *The Muslim Discovery of Europe*, 300-01.

55. See, for eample, Thomas A. McCarthy, *The Critical Theory of Jürgen Habermas* (Cambridge, MA: MIT Press, 1991), 302.

56. *Muslim Travellers* and *Golden Roads: Migration, Pilgrimage and Travel in Mediaeval and Modern Islam*, Ian Richard Netton, ed. (United Kingdom: Curzon Press, 1993). Indeed, Eickelman and Piscatori invoke the frequent argument that "Muslims share more explicit doctrinal tenets enjoining movement than do the followers of other major religious traditions," but also note that "such phenomena need not be seen as unique to the Muslim world in order for their significance to be affirmed," xvii, 5.

57. Rosenthal, "The Stranger in Medieval Islam," *Arabica* 44 (1997), 54; *The Glorious Qur'an*, trans. Mohammed Marmaduke Pickthall (NY: Tahrike Tarsile Qur'an, Inc., 2000). See also suras 2:156, 50:43; 42:53.

58. "The Stranger in Medieval Islam," 42, 54, 58. See, for example, Yusuf Ibish, "Ibn 'Arabi's Theory of Journeying," in *Traditional Modes of Contemplation and Action*, Y. Ibish and P.L. Wilson, eds. (Tehran, Iran: Imperial Iranian Academy of Philosophy, 1977), 441-49.

59. *Al-Qur'an*, trans. Ahmed Ali (Princeton: Princeton University Press, 1984). The verb used in all eight verses is *sāra* / سار ).

60. Al-Suyuti, *Jami'al-ahadith lil-Jami'al-saghir wa-zawa'idihi wa-al-Jami'al-Kabir* (Dimashq: Matba'at, M.H. al-Kutubi, 1979-81), vol. 1, 3207, 3208, 618.

61. Muhammad al-Tirmidhi, *Sunan al-Tirmidhi wa-huwa al-Jami'al-Sahih* (al-Medina al-Munawwara: al-Maktaba al-Salafiyya, 1965), Vol. 4, 2:2785, 137; 2: 2786, 138, my translation.

62. Muhammad Ibn Yazid al-Qazwini Ibn Majah, *Sunan* (Cairo: 'Aisa al-Babi al-Halabi, 1972), Vol. I, hadith no. 223, 81, my translation.

63. Franz Rosenthal, *Knowledge Triumphant: The Concept of Knowledge in Medieval Islam* (Leiden: E.J. Brill, 1970), 28-32. Indeed, Rosenthal argues that "there is no other concept that has been operative as a determinant of Muslim civilization in all its aspects to the same text as *'ilm*," which is "something of supreme value for Muslim being." 2.

64. This is the reading offered in the *Encyclopedia of Islam*, CD-ROM Edition v. 1.0 (Leiden, The Netherlands: Koninklijke Brill NV, 1999), "*'ilm.*"

65. *Knowledge Triumphant*, 10.

66. Lenker, "The Importance of the Rihla for the Islamization of Spain," PhD. Dissertation, the University of Pennsylvania, 1982, 195, 194, 189, 224.

67. See for example, "Pilgrimages as Social Processes," in Victor Turner's *Dramas, Fields, and Metaphors: Symbolic Action in Human Society* (Ithaca: Cornell University Press, 1974); Simon Coleman and John Elsner, *Pilgrimage Past and Present in the World Religions* (Cambridge, MA: Harvard University Press, 1995); Juan Eduardo Campo, "The Mecca Pilgrimage in the Formation of Islam in Modern Egypt," in *Sacred Places and Profane Spaces: Essay in the Geographics of Judaism, Christianity and Islam*, Jamie S. Scott and Paul Simpson-Housley, eds. (NY: Greenwood Press, 1991); Noel Q. King, "Egeria, Fa Hsien and Ibn Battuta: Search for Identity through Pilgrimage?" *Identity Issues and World Religions* (Australia: Wakefield Press, 1986), 42-46; Rutherford, "Theoric Crisis," and "*Theoria and Darśan*: Pilgrimage and Vision in Greece and India," *Classical Quarterly* 50 (1), 2000, 133-46.

68. See Rutherford, "Theoric Crisis" and "*Theoria and Darśan.*"

69. J. Peter Euben, "Creatures of a Day: Thought and Action in Thucydides," in *Political Theory and Praxis*, Terence Ball, ed. (Minneapolis, MN: University of Minnesota Press, 1977), 33-35. The association of theory with the divine is even closer in the figure of Apollo who, because he "travels great distances to see his people, he is called a *theorios* and *thearios.*" Euben, 241, n. 17.

70. P. Euben, "Creatures of a Day," 35; Sam Gellens, "The Search for Knowledge in Medieval Muslim Societies: A Comparative Approach," in Eickelman and Piscatori, eds., *Muslim Travellers*, 53.

71. Eickelman and Piscatori, *Muslim Travellers*, xii.

72. Rosenthal, "The Stranger in Medieval Islam," 41.

73. As Eickelman and Piscatori argue, "historical 'Islam' does not neatly coincide with doctrinal 'Islam,' and . . .the practice and significance of Islamic faith in any given historical setting cannot readily be predicted from first principles of dogma or belief." This is especially so in Islam, "whose adherents assert that Islamic directives are universal

and clear and yet whose manifestations in thought and practice are so varied and indeterminate." *Muslim Travellers*, 18.

74. Charles Beckingham, "In Search of Ibn Battuta," *Royal Society for Asian Affairs* 8
(1977), 267

75. Gellens, "The Search for Knowledge in Medieval Muslim Societies," 51.

76. This is not an argument for Muslim exceptionalism; pilgrimage is part of many religions, including but not limited to the "people of the book," or Jews and Christians.

77. Colin Thubron, "Both Seer and Seen," *The Times Literary Supplement*, July 30, 1999.
Even this aspect of travel is gendered: women and men who travel face different kinds
of risks. See Mary Morris, *Maiden Voyages: Writings of Women Travelers* (New York:
Vintage, 1993).

78. Helms, *Ulysses Sail*, 17.

79. Herodotus, *Histories*, I: 52-54, 90-92. As James Ker points out, from Thucydides to
Plato, the "political function of *theôria*, as in conceptions of theory now, was not
always viewed as positive." "Solon's *Theôria* and the End of the City," 304-5.

80. *Information for Pilgrims Unto the Holy Land*, E. Gordon Duff, ed. (London: Lawrence
& Bullen, 1893), attributed to John Moreson and originally printed ca. 1498. See Donald R. Howard, *Writers and Pilgrims: Medieval Pilgrimage Narratives and their Pos-
terity* (Berkeley: University of California Press, 1980), 20-22.

81. Rosenthal, "The Stranger in Medieval Islam," 42-49; Al-Gahiz, *Hanin*, 8, Harun
*Rasa'il*, ed., II, 385, quoted in Rosenthal, 48.

82. This is somewhat at odds with Eric Leed's emphasis on the distinction between ancient
travel as "an explication of human fate and necessity" and modern travel as an "expression of freedom and an escape from necessity and purpose." *The Mind of the Traveler*,
p.7. While evocative, this distinction also makes less sense if, as I contend, travel in
search of knowledge is a consistent feature of both "ancient" and "modern" journeys.

83. Franz Rosenthal, "The Technique and Approach of Muslim Scholarship," *Analecta
Orientalia* 24 (1947), 57.

84. *Imitation of Christ*, Ernest Rhys, ed. (London: J.M. Dent & Sons Ltd., 1910), Part IV,
chapter 1, 233-34

85. *The Confessions of St. Augustine*, trans. Rex Warner (New York: New American
Library, 1963), Book X, ch. xxxv. Augustine's characterization of curiosity as a kind of
vice is echoed by later Christian thinkers increasingly worried about the temptations of
pilgrimages motivated by curiosity. See Christian K. Zacher, *Curiosity and Pilgrimage: The Literature of Discovery in Fourteenth-Century England* (Baltimore: Johns
Hopkins University Press, 1976).

86. Howard, *Writers and Pilgrims*, 24.

87. *The Workes of that Famous and Worthy Minister of Christ, In the Universitie of Cambridge, M.W. Perkins* (London: John Haviland, 1631), III, 539.

88. This tendency coexists with several others, however, most notably the Sufi exhortation
to become "fugitives, so as to avoid contamination by the worldly concerns of the
homebound." "The Stranger in Medieval Islam," 54.

89. Shahrough Akhavi, "Sunni Modernist Theories of Social Contract in Contemporary
Egypt," *International Journal of Middle East Studies* 35 (2003), 31.

90. Pagden, "The Effacement of Difference: Colonialism and the Origins of Nationalism in
Diderot and Herder," in Gyan Prakash, ed. *After Colonialism: Imperial Histories and
Postcolonial Displacements* (Princeton: Princeton University Press, 1995), 134.

91. Diderot, in *Histoire philosophique et politique des etablissemens et du commerce des
Européens dans les deux Indes* (Geneva, 1781), 10, 297 (XIX, 1), in Pagden, "The
Effacement of Difference," 134.

92. Diderot in Pagden, "The Effacement of Difference," 133, and Pagden, 132, 133.

93. *Tourists with Typewriters*, 70.

94. Clifford, "Traveling Cultures," 110.

95. Hartog, *The Mirror of Herodotus: The Representation of the Other in the Writing of History*, trans. Janet Lloyd (Berkeley: University of California Press, 1988).

96. Redfield, "Herodotus the Tourist," 102.

97. The "comparative" here does not preclude, and indeed requires, attending to the radically different historical contexts in which such work takes place and which, as Arjun Appadurai points out, today requires attending to the question: if comparative work "relies on the clear separation of the entities to be compared, before serious comparison can begin . . .[h]ow are we to compare fractally shaped cultural forms which are also polythetically overlapping in their coverage of terrestrial space?" "Disjuncture and Difference in the Global Cultural Economy," *Public Culture* 2 (2), 1990, 20. On comparative political theory see, for example, Roxanne L. Euben, *Enemy in the Mirror: Islamic Fundamentalism and the Limits of Modern Rationalism* (Princeton: Princeton University Press, 1999); Stephen Salkever and Michael Nylan, "Comparative Political Philosophy and Liberal Education: 'Looking for Friends in History'," *Political Science and Politics* 26 (June 1994): 238-47; Anthony Parel and Ronald C. Keith, eds. *Comparative Political Philosophy: Studies Under the Upas Tree* (New Delhi: Sage Publications, 1992); and *Border Crossings: Toward a Comparative Political Theory*, Fred R. Dallmayr, ed. (Lanham, MD: Lexington Books, 1999).

98. See Chapter one in R. Euben, *Enemy in the Mirror.*

99. Hartog, 214.

100. I am grateful to Pratap Mehta for these examples.

101. Margaret Leslie, "In Defense of Anachronism," *Political Studies* 18(4), 1970, 435.

102. Martin, "Orientalism and the Ethnographer: Said, Herodotus, and the Discourse of Alterity," *Criticism* 32(4), Fall 1990, 521.

103. Martin, 527.

104. Benjamin, "The Task of the Translator," *Illuminations*, Hannah Arendt, ed. (New York: Schocken Books, 1988), 76.

105. Benjamin, of course, does not here enter the wood, but he effectively displaces the "valorization of transparency" which, in other models of translation, have tended to efface the preconditions and effects of translating practices, Lawrence Venuti, ed., *Rethinking Translation: Discourse, Subjectivity, Ideology,* (New York: Routledge, 1992), 4-5. The extensive debates occasioned by Benjamin's "Task of the Translator" and the literature on the uses of Benjamin's essay in the work of Jacques Derrida and Paul de Man are beyond my focus here.

106. See, for example, Dipesh Chakrabarty, *Provincializing Europe: Postcolonial Thought and Historical Difference* (Princeton: Princeton University Press, 2000); Tejaswini Niranjana, *Siting Translation: History, Post-Structuralism, and the Colonial Context* (Berkeley: University of California Press, 1992); Gayatri Chakravorty Spivak, "Politics of Translation," *Outside in the Teaching Machine* (New York: Routledge, 1993); Ritva Leppihalme, *Culture Bumps: An Empirical Approach to the Translation of Allusions* (Philadelphia: Multilingual Matters, Ltd., 1997).

107. Venuti, 13. Understood in this way, translation can not only reveal how "language was . . .the companion of empire," but also how "vernacularization" could deflect the exercise of colonial power. Vincente L Rafael, *Contracting Colonialism: Translation and Christian Conversion in Tagalog Society under Early Spanish Rule* (Ithaca, NY: Cornell University Press, 1988), 21, 23.

108. Martin, 523.

109. J. Peter Euben, "Philosophy and Politics in Plato's *Crito,*" *Political Theory* 6 (2), May 1978, 165.

110. Martin Jay, "Vision in Context: Reflections and Refractions," in *Vision in Context.*

111. Isabelle R. Gunning, "Arrogant Perception, World-Travelling and Multicultural Feminism: The Case of Female Genital Surgeries," *Columbia Human Rights Law Review* 23 (1991-92): 189-248; María Lugones, "Playfulness, 'World'-Travelling, and Loving Perception," in *Making Face, Making Soul: Haciendo Caras,* Gloria Anzaldúa, ed. (San Francisco: Aunt Lute Foundation Books, 1990), 390-402.

112. This argument takes seriously the insistence of feminist theorists, critical race theorists and theorists of postcoloniality, among others, who have stressed the importance of recognizing theory in a variety of settings, practiced by a variety of people, in a variety of genres. See, for example, bell hooks, *Talking Back: thinking feminist, thinking black* (Boston, MA: South End Press, 1989), 36-37.

113. Paul Rabinow, *Reflections on Fieldwork in Morocco* (Berkeley: University of California Press, 1977), 5, quoting from Paul Ricoeur, *The Conflict of Interpretations* (Evanston, IL: Northwestern University Press, 1974), 17; Pratt, *Imperial Eyes,* 5, emphasis in the original.

114. Marx, *Capital* (New York: The Modern Library, 1936), 12-13.

115. This question is not an attempt to simply invert the 'center-periphery' polarity, but rather contribute to a more textured history of our present "complex, overlapping, disjunctive order."Appadurai, 6.

116. I use the term *rihla* in the general sense of a "book of travels," and in particular those "books of travels" motivated by, among other things, *talab al'ilm,* which I employ in the quite general sense of "pursuit of knowledge."

117. Nor need such travel accounts embrace the dialogic model of understanding presupposed by my emphasis on translation; Qutb's sojourn in America in the 1950s, for example, contributed to an increasingly anti-hermeneutic fundamentalism.

118. Marshall Hodgson, "Hemispheric Inter-regional History as an Approach to World History," *Journal of World History* 1 (1954): 715-23, and *The Venture of Islam,* 3 vols. See also William H. McNeill, *The Rise of the West: A History of the Human Community* (Chicago: Chicago University Press, 1963) and Philip D. Curtin, *Cross-Cultural Trade in World History* (Cambridge, England: Cambridge University Press, 1984).

119. Lugones and Spelman, "Have We Got a Theory for You!: Feminist Theory, Cultural Imperialism and the Demand for 'the Woman's Voice,'" *Women's Studies International Forum* 6 (6), 577.

# 8    POLITICAL THEORY, POLITICAL
SCIENCE, AND POLITICS

*RUTH W. GRANT*

**F**orty years ago, Isaiah Berlin published an essay in which he argued that political theory would never become a science because of the character of the questions with which it is concerned. Normative questions are among those "that remain obstinately philosophical." And what is "characteristic of specifically philosophical questions is that they do not . . . satisfy conditions required by an independent science, the principal among which is that the path to their solution must be implicit in their very formulation."[1] According to Berlin, both formal and empirical sciences satisfy these conditions, whereas political theory does not. During the past forty years, political theory has grown considerably faster within political science departments than within philosophy departments in the United States, and today 81 percent of professional political theorists find themselves housed in departments of political science.[2] Far from indicating that Berlin had it wrong, this accident of academic history merely sharpens the issue that he so cogently explicated. Political theory as a field remains "obstinately philosophical."

On a practical level, of course, this is a source of considerable frustration for political scientists and political theorists alike. To political scientists, the perpetual disagreements among political theorists and the repeated reconsiderations of the same issues and texts are indications that political theorists lack meaningful standards for assessing what constitutes good research. And worse, they lack standards because they have no idea what it would mean for research to progress in their field. Political theorists, on their part, find their work evaluated by people who believe that research must have a "cutting edge" and that its aim is to produce new knowledge, beliefs that they often do not share.[3] The practical problem is that political theorists do humanistic research in a social science discipline. This is a contestable claim of course.

One might argue, contra Berlin, that the proper distinction is not between philosophy and science but between humanistic sciences and natural sciences, or interpretive sciences and experimental ones.[4] Or, political theory might be distinguished from inquiries in the humanities in important respects because politics is its particular subject matter. But, for the sake of argument at the very least, let us embrace the premise of those critics of political theory whose fundamental claim is that because political theory is not a science, it does not belong in a discipline devoted to the systematic, scientific understanding of political phenomena. In the eyes of its critics, research in political theory resembles humanities research far more closely than it does scientific research.

The practical problem this presents might be adequately solved through institutional reorganization, making everyone considerably more comfortable, but the theoretical problems that it raises certainly cannot be resolved in this way. Moreover, the discomfort can be productive, confronting us with two important questions. What is humanities research? And must the study of *politics* include research of this kind? The first question is a serious one for the humanities in general, since major universities increasingly conceptualize research as if the hard sciences provided an appropriate model for research altogether and increasingly speak of research in the language of commerce. A typical depiction of the research enterprise of a university might speak of the investment in research resulting in research products in the form of new knowledge, preferably of a kind that has useful applications.[5] Researchers in the humanities find it difficult to recognize their activity in descriptions of this kind. The second question is particularly pressing for both political theorists and political scientists. Can we know what is worth knowing about politics through scientific research methods alone? In addressing this question, let us suppose that Isaiah Berlin was right that political theory will never be a science and that it should not aspire to become scientific. In that case, the question can be rephrased: Is research in political theory worth doing, or can politics be adequately understood without it?

What follows is an attempt to illuminate these two issues: the character of humanities research and its importance for the study of politics. The discussion is neither complete nor particularly original.[6] It aims to articulate some of the common presuppositions, generally unspoken, that guide the ways in which research in political theory is done. And it aims to frame the theoretical tasks that must be addressed if we are to understand our own activity. Let us begin with the charges leveled at research in the humanities by those who aspire to be scientists, that is, that there are no accepted standards for judging interpretive research and that such research tells us nothing new. Humanities research neither adds to our store of knowledge nor increases our understanding of the world, since its claims cannot be either validated or falsified. At their worst, the interpretive and historical methods of the humanities give rise to a kind of secular "religion" in which members of competing interpretive "sects" generate partisan commentaries on the "sacred" texts of the "canon."

I see three possible responses to this sort of characterization. The first is to accept it in certain crucial respects. There is no need to defend humanities research seriously because the essential mission of the humanities is not research but education. Study in the humanities provides a kind of educational experience—inspirational, revelatory, and transformative—that resembles religious experience. An education of this kind comes about only through the study of and confrontation with the greatest products of the human imagination. Andrew Delbanco puts the case provocatively and well with respect to literature, arguing that historically "literary studies, in fact, have their roots in religion" and that the transformative power of a literary education

> has little to do with the positivist idea of education to which the modern research university is chiefly devoted—learning 'how to extend, even by minute accretions, the realm of knowledge.' This corporate notion of knowledge as a growing sum of discoveries no longer in need of rediscovery once they are recorded, and transmittable to those whose ambition it is to add to them, is a great achievement of our civilization. But except in a very limited sense, it is not the kind of knowledge that is at stake in a literary education.[7]

An education in the humanities is not so much about acquiring knowledge of this kind as it is about acquiring humility in the face of your own ignorance, perspective when confronted with your own particularity, and the capacity for judgment in the light of a universe of possibilities that you had never before imagined. This education is the crucial thing; humanities research is not at the core of the enterprise.[8] Or perhaps more accurately still, there is no deep division between the two. Unlike in the sciences, the activity of teaching and the activity of research in the humanities are almost identical. Our language reflects this reality by distinguishing between the "researcher" in the sciences and the "scholar" in the humanities.[9] What humanists do in the classroom resembles what they do in their studies; in both settings, they engage in the interpretation of texts and the examination of concepts, their origins, and their consequences. Teaching and writing alike aim to educate.

The second possibility, which is not mutually exclusive of the first, is to argue that the "hard" sciences and the social sciences are "softer" than they seem. Scientists certainly discover new facts, but the great advances in science are frequently advances of interpretation that allow us to explain more coherently a set of facts that are already known. Science is a creative enterprise.[10] Moreover, in science, as in the humanities, arguments are often as much about which facts are important as they are about truth claims. Standards for judging scientific research include coherence, comprehensiveness, and elegance, just as in the humanities. And even mathematics must confront the reality of uncertainty, irrationality, and indeterminacy. Gödel's proof can serve as an example. Kurt Gödel showed that it is impossible to deduce the principles of even elementary arithmetic from a finite set of axioms or to establish the logical consistency of many deductive systems.[11] Uncertainty is inevitable even in the formal sciences. The world simply may not be tractable to human intelligence in a manner that will allow us to have confidence in our knowledge of its workings. Research in the sciences is more like humanities research than its practitioners are willing to admit.

Both of these lines of argument have something to be said for them, but they are not sufficient to the task. Humanities research requires a defense on its own terms. The third possibility, then, is to acknowledge the distinctiveness of humanities research, articulate its particular characteristics, and defend them as integrally related to the aims and the limits of humanistic inquiry. Why "the aims *and* the limits"? Because the questions that humanists aim to clarify are questions about which human understanding cannot be certain and complete. Often, those questions are identified as questions of value, normative questions.[12] But this characterization is misleading to the extent that it implies that humanities research is concerned with values *instead of* with facts. Certainly, political theory has never divorced itself from knowledge of empirical reality and argumentation on the basis of historical evidence. Aristotle's discussion of regime types in the *Politics* should suffice as a typical illustration. Moreover, scientific research cannot escape normative considerations, if only because truth itself is a value.[13] Most important though, the identification of the humanities with normative questions and of the sciences with factual questions is generally tied to the association of the humanities with uncertain, subjective speculation and of the sciences with known probabilities, falsifiable theories, and the progress of knowledge. The implication that knowledge of matters of value is impossible, whereas knowledge is available in factual investigations, is itself highly problematic.

Instead of conceptualizing the humanities as concerned with value, whereas the sciences are concerned with facts, I would suggest provisionally that the former seeks to explain meaning and significance, whereas the latter seeks to explain mechanisms of cause and effect.[14] These are all terms that describe kinds of relations. The phrase "cause and effect" defines a relation. The "meaning" of an action or a statement changes radically depending on its context, which is to say, depending on its relation to other actions, statements, and so on. The concept of "significance" is also inherently relational. Something is significant only in comparison to some other thing that is less so. Actually, the term "significance" includes both "meaning" and "importance": the significance of a thing involves both what it means and why it matters. These are the two primary questions for humanities research.

And that is why its methods are interpretive and historical. There is nothing arbitrary about the methodological approach. You cannot discover either what something means or why it matters without both interpretation and historical understanding. The characteristic uncertainty, disagreement, and lack of closure found in the discourse of the humanities are not arbitrary either. These characteristics reflect both historical and epistemological realities. Meaning and significance refer to relations that vary through time, and questions of meaning and significance are thus deeply historical. It should come as no surprise that they are questions that must be revisited in every age. The question of the meaning of a particular text or of any work of the imagination is always accompanied by the questions, "What does it mean for us?" and "Why should we care?" It makes no sense to seek a definitive and permanent answer to questions of this sort. In fact, instead of providing a new understanding that supersedes all previous ones and moves the progress of knowledge forward, some of the most important humanities research is devoted to projects of recovery. Historical research reminds us not to forget by keeping alive in the present the submerged possibilities of the human experience of the past. It forces us to ask whether where we stand today truly represents progress.

While the open-endedness of humanities research is grounded in its historical character, its uncertainties and the disagreements that follow from them are consequences of our epistemological situation. Different sorts of things are knowable in different ways and with correspondingly varying degrees of certainty. This is a reality that is revealed in ordinary language. The number of words that differentiate among the kinds of knowing is impressive: knowledge, understanding, wisdom, judgment, opinion, belief, know-how, conviction, recognition, memory, and so on. And of course, such a list could be generated in any language. Within the philosophical tradition of Western civilization, these distinctions have been central from the beginning. Plato made much of distinctions between *episteme, techne,* and *doxa*; Aquinas distinguished *scientia* from *opinio*; Kant differentiated pure speculative reason, pure practical reason, and judgment. The human mind apprehends the world in a variety of ways. There are some things that we may want to know that cannot be known with anything remotely like mathematical certainty, for example. Nonetheless, those things can be understood in some sense; reasonable judgments about them are possible. I would suggest that, whereas the sciences are primarily concerned with knowledge of cause and effect, the humanities are primarily concerned with understanding of meaning and judgment of significance.

Judgment is peculiarly married to uncertainty. If we knew, we would not need to judge. Judgment is required because the world always remains opaque to us in important respects. Both demonstrative reason and empirical evidence have their limits. Judgment is the faculty at work in any situation where reasonable people might disagree. And the premise of every truly political situation, particularly in democratic politics, is that reasonable people can disagree.[15] Certainly in political theory, the central issues are often those in which people differ over a judgment of what matters most.[16] Is it more important to seek the best political possibility or to guard against the worst political disaster? Plato describes the best regime; Locke looks for "fences" against the worst.[17] Is the important thing about totalitarianism its rationalism and scientism or its romanticism and nationalism? This is one central question that has divided liberals from their critics since the Second World War.[18] In considering complex problems, determining the relative significance of various elements is highly consequential, and it requires the exercise of judgment. These examples are drawn from political theory, but the claim can be sustained that they illustrate a characteristic of the humanities in general. The primary concerns of humanities research are matters of judgment.[19]

Part of the reason that humanities research is currently in need of defense is that we seem to have lost our bearings with respect to matters of judgment. This is particularly so with respect to moral judgment. Often, the problem of moral judgment is framed as if there were only two mutually exclusive alternatives, neither of which is satisfactory: abstract, universal moral values that can be known or culturally specific moral values that can be understood, and even appreciated in some sense, but not evaluated. Framing the problem in this way leaves many people torn since each alternative is problematic in its own way. On one hand, to embrace moral values on the grounds of abstract, universal principles implies in the minds of many that dogmatic certitude and arrogant uniformity must be embraced as well. On the other hand, to embrace cultural specificity seems to render moral convictions so particular that the only ground for their justification is that they are "ours." Any possibility of defense or critique in conversation with others is undermined.[20] In either case, then, whether moral values are universally true or culturally specific, it would seem that there is no room for judgment among competing moral claims and hence no room for legitimate moral controversy.

But exactly the opposite is the case. Moral judgment cannot be avoided whichever of the two alternatives is true and neither can disagreement. If there are universal moral truths that we can know with certainty, at the very least we must judge among them when they come in conflict (are the demands of loyalty greater than the demands of justice in this case?) and we must judge how best to apply these principles in practice (what does justice require of us in this particular situation?). If there are no universals but only specific cultural practices, we are no less obliged to judge, since no culture is univocal; practices are continually contested and change over time. At the very least, we must determine which of the voices within our own culture ought to guide our judgment in any given situation, and this is so no matter how homogeneous the culture appears to be.[21] (Even within a single church, there will be debate over the proper stance for that church with respect to homosexuality or abortion, for example.). Moreover, we exercise prudential judgment at the outset in determining what sort of a problem we face in any given case, and this determination often has enormous implications for how the moral issues are framed. (Was the war in Bosnia more like WWI, WWII, or the Vietnam War?).[22]

Judgment is inescapable, yet we act as if it is not even possible. The problem recalls the conflicts between dogmatism and skepticism in the seventeenth century. Like the opposition between universal absolutes and cultural relativism, the earlier dichotomy obscured the importance of judgment. John Locke, in responding to the earlier controversy between dogmatism and skepticism had the following to say to those who put an undue emphasis on the certainty of knowledge:

> 'Tis of great use to the Sailor to know the length of his Line, though he cannot with it fathom all the depths of the Ocean. 'Tis well he knows that it is long enough to reach the bottom, at such Places, as are necessary to direct his Voyage, and caution him against running upon Shoals, that may ruin him.[23]

And,

> Man would be at a great loss, if he had nothing to direct him, but what has the Certainty of true Knowledge. . . . He that will not eat, till he has Demonstration that it will nourish him; he that will not stir, till he infallibly knows the Business he goes about will succeed, will have little else to do, but sit still and perish.[24]

There are limits to the extent and the certainty of what human beings can know. Nonetheless, we are able to make reasonable judgments about how to proceed in life. By the eighteenth century, there was a great deal of interest in judgment, moral as well as aesthetic. The improvement of judgment is both the aim and the subject of many of Jane Austen's novels as well as the aim of a moral education according to Adam Smith. To judge from the perspective of the impartial spectator is to judge well, which is the essential requirement of an ethical life. Fortunately, judgment can be educated. This is so in aesthetics as well as in ethics. To become a good critic requires certain basic knowledge, practice, opportunities for comparison, and so on.[25]

Today, if something is a matter of taste, it is often taken to be a matter of individual preference, as if there were no such thing as educated taste. Worse, matters of moral judgment are treated too often as if they too were merely matters of taste. Different people like different sorts of movies. Does it follow that it is impossible to be a good movie critic? Different people profess different moral values or apply similar moral principles differently. Does it follow that there are no grounds for moral judgment? For centuries, philosophers have noted the fact of moral disagreement without drawing the epistemological conclusion that moral judgment is impossible. It is a mistake to infer from the lack of consensus on questions of moral, aesthetic, or political judgment that there are no grounds for judgment or that all judgments are equally arbitrary.[26] On a subject on which reasonable people can disagree, some arguments still will be more plausible, persuasive, or convincing than others. And if people are open to persuasion on the subject, a degree of agreement may be achieved.[27] But, in these matters, one rarely finds the sort of evidence or argument that is simply incontestable, compelling, or self-evident, and consequently, one rarely finds universal agreement. In a formal mathematical demonstration, for example, if the axiomatic premises are accepted, the conclusion will follow in a manner that commands agreement from any reasonable person. In this situation, agreement attests to the validity of truth claims. But agreement and disagreement do not carry the same implications when judgment is at issue, and here, we should not expect to find the same kind of consensus that is compelled by formal demonstration. If we fail to recognize this, we will mistakenly infer from the lack of moral consensus that nothing can be understood about moral matters that can inform sound judgments. Seeking agreement as the grounds for confidence in our moral opinions and not finding it, we abdicate judgment.[28] As a practical matter, of course, we cannot do without it. Judge we must, and so, we judge badly and without reflection. Believing judgment to be without rational foundation and believing questions concerning judgment to be beyond the scope of legitimate inquiry, the gap between intellectual activity and the practice of living grows.

The fact of disagreement does not imply that nothing can be known, only that everything cannot be. Between ignorance and knowledge, in the realm of judgment, is where the humanities reside. Understanding meaning and significance in the effort to educate judgment is its task. And judgment can be better or worse. There may be no definitive interpretation, but some interpretations are surely more plausible than others. Good research in the humanities requires the identification of a significant problem, informed judgment, critical acumen, and so forth. When humanities research is evaluated, a judgment is made as to the quality of the judgments it contains. Whereas the sciences seek to increase our knowledge of cause and effect in a cumulative, linear fashion, the humanities seek to improve our judgment by deepening our understanding of the meaning and significance of its objects of study. In the former case, acquiring new knowledge is a primary goal. In the latter case, emphasis is placed on understanding why it is that old questions remain questions for us. In the former case, progress is conceived in terms of quantitative increase and forward motion. In the latter case, progress is measured by increasing depth, clarity, and comprehensiveness.[29] It is simply not the case that there are no standards in humanities research, but the standards are appropriately different from those in the sciences. Why would we want to impose the same standards on two such different undertakings? "For a well-schooled man is one who searches for that degree of precision in each kind of study which the nature of the subject at hand admits."[30]

The open-endedness, uncertainties, and disagreements of humanities research flow from the very same source as its more positive characteristics. Because its aim is understanding of meaning and judgment of significance, its methods are interpretive and historical. And because it employs these methods, humanities research is simultaneously conservative, critical, and constructive. The best humanities research returns to old material in response to new circumstances when those circumstances cannot be adequately understood within the dominant conceptual regime in order to construct a creative and credible response to them. It is conservative in the obvious and rather literal sense that it depends on the conservation of the past, of the records of human action, thought, and imagination. Humanities research is also part of a discourse that has a past and so depends as well on the conservation of that discursive tradition. It is conservative in a less obvious sense as well. To study the products of human thought and imagination through history and across cultures produces an appreciation of the immensity of human achievement but also a recognition of the limits of human understanding and human capabilities. It becomes apparent that there is nothing new under the sun, and this is an insight that tempers the impulse toward scientific utopianism. That same impulse is tempered as well by knowledge of the significance of the particularities of time and place. Confidence in our knowledge and our capabilities is required to fuel projects of social and political engineering, and the humanities tend to undermine that confidence. At their best, they cultivate a healthy skepticism. Knowledge, particularly historical knowledge, can be humbling as well as empowering.

Always joined to this conservative tendency, and in tension with it, is a critical impulse, equally strong. The same familiarity with the variety of human experience fosters both. Humanistic inquiry provides the perspective required for critical judgment. By exploring alternatives, unexamined conceptual premises of contemporary culture can be subjected to scrutiny. One must step beyond one's own cave to see it as a cave, whether escape from a troglodyte existence is possible for human beings or whether spelunking through the multiplicity of human cave dwellings is the best that we can do. In either case, the object is to find some critical purchase on our situation. And our situation is constantly changing. Research agendas are shaped by those changing realities because research is motivated by critique of existing conceptual frames as insufficient to explain contemporary situations. The agenda in political theory in America, for example, centered more on law and institutions fifty years ago, whereas now its center is culture and identity; and surely this has as much to do with political history as with intellectual history. The point is that the two are inseparable. I have said that the interpretive questions, "What does this mean for us?" and "Why should we care?" are inherently historical questions. They are also inherently critical ones.

Critique suggests projects for improvement, and so humanities research is constructive as well. We are in the business of altering meanings as well as of understanding them. Humanities research uses resources from the past to open possibilities, construct alternatives, or generate new insights. This is a creative enterprise, but not an arbitrary one. What is offered as new and original must be at the least a credible improvement over current understandings, explaining a wider range of phenomena, reconfiguring a conceptual opposition that had produced an impasse, overcoming or accounting for logical contradictions in earlier work, and so forth. But no new formulation will last forever either. The process of reconceptualization is ongoing, again, because of the nature of investigation into the meaning and significance of phenomena. Addressing questions of significance through historically informed interpretation produces inconclusive, contentious, conservative, critical, and constructive results. These are the distinctive features of humanities research.

Why is it necessary to study *political* phenomena in this way? One might argue that questions of meaning and significance ought to be brought to bear in the investigation of art, literature, and music as expressions of human consciousness, but political life, where the subject of investigation is behavior, lends itself to altogether different questions. The distinction between the humanities and the social sciences ought to be governed roughly by the ancient distinction between "speech," broadly understood, and "deed." When studying the latter, our concern ought to be restricted to identifying causal mechanisms and general laws that improve our power to predict (and direct) human action. For a variety of reasons, this is a mistake.

First, in choosing how to act and deciding what to do, people always understand themselves to be acting for a reason. Generally speaking, people (and nations) need to believe that they have a coherent answer to the question, "Why did you do that?" The answer, beginning with the word "because," is itself a judgment of the meaning and significance of the various factors under consideration in the situation. To the extent that conscious rationales are themselves causal factors, any attempt at explanation that excludes them from consideration distorts the political phenomena it seeks to explain. An account of politics that cannot explain the self-understanding of political actors is radically incomplete.[31] A full account requires consideration of how judgments are made, how they influence events, and how they should be assessed. There is no human "deed" without "speech." To approach the study of politics humanistically has the advantage that the language of political inquiry remains close to the language of political action.

Second, political behavior is a manifestation of human freedom and, as such, it is an expression of human purposes and intentions. People make choices that could have been made differently. There is thus a limit to what general causal laws can explain. This is another way of saying that political life cannot be purged of contingency or of particularity. For the same reason, the practice of politics is an art, not a technique. You cannot teach people to be expert politicians by presenting them with a rulebook.[32] Politics is learned through accumulated practical experience in particular circumstances. The lessons of experience are applied at least as much through a process of reasoning by analogy as they are through deductive logic, and analogy proceeds through judgment of the relative significance of features of similar, but never identical, situations.[33] To understand the choices of political actors and to anticipate their probable consequences requires attention to particularity and contingency. The brief for political theory as a humanistic approach to the study of politics is also a brief for the historical study of politics altogether.

Third, as I said earlier, politics, and particularly democratic politics, presupposes that reasonable people will disagree. Knowledge alone is not sufficient to settle political disagreements. Competing claims of political partisans may each represent a partial truth.[34] The terms of the debate may set the limits to the alternatives considered by the partisans. Or, the contest itself may reflect a conflict between competing goods that is irreconcilable in principle.[35] Humanistic inquiry addresses these dimensions of political life in a way that scientific inquiry cannot. Political theory as a discipline develops diagnostic tools to identify and to understand what sort of political disagree-

ment is involved in any given situation, and theorists sometimes construct
new alternatives that alter the nature of the conflict.

At bottom, political theory is an extension of a natural, daily activity. In
this it resembles ethics. Every human being engages in some form of ethical
reflection as a condition of action. This is one respect in which judgment is
unavoidable. Ethics as an academic discipline is an extension of, not a departure from, that daily activity. Similarly, every political actor operates within a
conceptual regime as well as within an institutional one. No one in political
life can afford to ignore legitimating conceptions, constraints on acceptable
public speech, or considerations of how actions are likely to be interpreted. It
is simply impossible, when considering what should be done, to ask only
"What will happen next?" and not "How should I understand what has happened?" "What difference does it make?" and "What should be my goal?"
Political theory extends these sorts of inquiries, exploring existing conceptual regimes, their value, their origins, and their transformations. In ordinary
times, these are inquiries that form the background of the daily texture of politics. Crises bring them to the fore when events reveal the problematic character of accepted answers to them. If politics itself includes political theory, the
study of politics must include political theory.

But there are those who challenge this conclusion. They recognize the
ubiquity of talk about the meaning and significance of political phenomena
but deny the significance of such talk. They question in particular whether
norms matter in political life. If behavior can be explained by underlying
interests, norms and talk about them are merely epiphenomenal.[36] Speech
happens, they suggest, but only deeds matter, and the former has no appreciable effect on the latter. This position rests, of course, on a prior determination
of what it means for something to "matter" in politics and in the study of politics, a determination that must itself be grounded theoretically. How do we
know that knowledge matters only if it helps to predict behavior? Is that the
only way in which knowledge or understanding can be important? Why are
causal mechanisms the most important thing to study if the subject is politics? That we can have scientific knowledge of causation, but not of other
aspects of politics, is utterly insufficient as grounds for determining their relative importance in political life. It is perfectly possible that what is most
accessible to scientific understanding is least politically important and vice
versa. If deeds or behavior are all that we allow ourselves to see, or if we limit
our inquiries to questions of outcomes and effects, it becomes quite difficult,
for example, to account for the distinction between a government organization and the mafia, or representing the electorate and pandering to it, or court-
ship and sexual harassment, and so on. To grasp these sorts of distinctions

requires addressing questions of meaning and purpose and forming judgments about them. Behavior is not the only thing that matters.

The ubiquity of political speech ought to be sufficient evidence that it matters too in some important sense. Speech in fact seems to matter in a variety of
ways in political life. For example, I doubt that political legitimacy can be
fully understood without taking political rhetoric into account. One of the
things that legal systems do is determine what counts as a legitimate reason in
settling different sorts of controversies, and so on. Hobbes had a point when
he included eloquence in his list of the forms of power.[37] Moreover, it was
Hobbes who wrote, "The actions of men proceed from their *opinions*; and in
the well-governing of opinions, consisteth the well-governing of men's
actions, in order to their peace and concord."[38] Most contemporary political
scientists would expect to find the word "interests," or perhaps "passions,"
where "opinions" appears in the original. But Hobbes's position is clear;
opinions are primary causes of behavior.

Even if we suppose that interests are the sole or sufficient cause of political behavior and even if behavior is all that matters, interests themselves are
subject to interpretation and judgment. Opinions affect not only what we
understand our interests to be but also whether we believe that interests ought
to motivate our action or whether we believe that interested motivations must
be hidden from view and disguised by hypocritical rhetoric. Last, if
reputational or status interests matter in motivating behavior, considerations
of meaning and significance, norms and opinions, are even more determina-
tive than they are if interests are understood to be purely material. In short, a
good causal explanation of behavior cannot exclude the questions of interpretation and meaning that drive political theory.

Evidently, either I must revisit my initial "provisional" claim that science
deals with cause and effect relations while the humanities deal with relations
of meaning and significance or I must revisit the claim that the distinction
between the humanities and the sciences is the same as that between political
theory and political science. When politics is the subject of investigation, the
division between the questions governing scientific and humanistic inquiry
seems to mark a permeable line—causal relations cannot be adequately
explained without consideration of meaning. But the reverse is also true. The
significance of something may well include its causal impact. Political theory as an enterprise assumes that interpretations, conceptual regimes, judgments of significance, and ideas of all kinds are themselves both causes and
effects. Ideas have significant consequences. If we did not believe that, we
would not study them. Thus, our inquiries must also include consideration of
the origin and impact of ideas. It behooves political theorists to attend to the
causal force of ideas in the way in which causal relations in general can best

be understood. We can learn from the scientists here as well as from the intellectual historians.[39] Whether the question is primarily one of causation or primarily one of significance, complete understanding of political life requires a synthesis of what can be learned from both scientific and humanistic approaches.

In other words, the study of politics needs both to seek general laws to explain the causes of political behavior and to develop interpretations of the meaning and significance of political events and conceptual regimes to inform evaluative judgments of them. Political studies has both scientific and humanistic aims. These are distinct but complementary enterprises; the "permeability" does not efface the distinction. But at the same time, the analysis indicates that political scientists would do better to admit the degree to which the study of human political behavior ought to be a "soft" science. I recur here to the second of the three possibilities that I canvassed at the outset. Interpretation must play some role in the scientific study of politics so long as "deeds" cannot be isolated from "speech."

What does this analysis indicate for the tasks of political theory? Two very different temptations draw political theorists on account of their cohabitation with political scientists within the same departments. The first is the temptation to turn their attention to contemporary public policy debates, to measure their work by the standard of its ability to contribute directly to the scientific enterprise of their colleagues, to formalize their theoretical claims, and to produce empirical demonstrations of their validity. The second temptation is to simply withdraw from a difficult relationship and to pursue political theory without regard for the activities of political scientists. Of course, it is not always a bad thing to succumb to temptation, but these particular temptations ought to be resisted. Political theorists need to engage political scientists without trying to become scientists. We need to maintain our differences, along with the friction that those differences often entail, to be useful to one another.

The distinctive contribution that political theory can make to the study of politics depends on its continued devotion to the humanistic questions as they arise in political life. And that, in turn, depends on its continued attachment to its historical and philosophic dimensions. The argument that I have developed here leads toward renewed engagement with philosophic questions: questions of metaphysics, epistemology, and hermeneutics. How do we understand freedom and causation? What can we know? How can we judge in the absence of certain knowledge? The argument leads also to continued concern with historical matters. We need to understand better the historical path that brought us to where we are today in our political conceptions, and we need to know how the recovery of alternatives embedded in the historical past might help us to judge and to interpret our current circumstances. In other words, we should continue to do what we do best: conceptual conservation, critique, and construction in the service both of deeper and more comprehensive understandings of political phenomena and of improved political judgment.

We need not be concerned that if we do this, our research will be removed from the practice of politics in the contemporary world. On the contrary. I have argued above that the questions, "What does it mean?" and "What really matters here?" are questions that are constantly present in the conduct of political life. And I have argued that what drives the agenda in political theory at any given time are the issues that are presented to us by our own historical moment. It is certainly incumbent on the political theorist to articulate the bearing of a historical interpretation on those contemporary issues, and generally speaking, that is not difficult to do. It is also incumbent on political theorists to ground our work in the knowledge of politics generated by political science research. We can only mislead ourselves if we ground political theory on false intuitions or theorize only within the framework of a self-referential narrative of the history of theorizing. It is not always easy to articulate the complementarity between the political theorist's humanistic approach to questions of meaning and significance and the political scientist's scientific approach to the question of causation, but it is not an impossible task, and it is essential if we are to remain engaged despite our differences.

Political theory and political science both belong in a discipline whose purpose is to improve our understanding of politics. In some respects, trying to explain political events is like trying to explain the flow of a river or a cycle of hurricanes. In other respects, it is like trying to explain the performance of a symphony or any other conscious collective human activity. There is more than one kind of question to bring to the study of politics, and the nature of the question ought to govern the method of investigation. We need to be able to ask about all kinds of relations: cause and effect, meaning, significance, and the relations among these. And we need to determine with some clarity what sort of knowledge is available to us with respect to each of them.

The biggest mistake is to conclude that we cannot ask the question unless we can guarantee knowledge of the answer. Many of the most important questions for the study of politics are not the sort for which "the path to their solution [is] implicit in their very formulation."[40] To delegitimate and abandon inquiry into these questions is to behave like the skeptic who, despairing at the limits of human understanding, "would not use his Legs . . . because he had no Wings to fly."[41] If we ignore the humanist's questions when studying politics, we will see only a small part of the political phenomena, and even that part we will see badly. To alter the metaphor, rejecting what can be learned from research in political theory because of its messy uncertainties and disagreements, is treating a problem of blurred vision by putting out one eye. The result will be that we will see like a cyclops, with no depth of field.

## NOTES

*I would like to thank Douglas Casson, Peter Euben, Michael Gillespie, Stephen Grant, Robert Keohane, Donald Moon, and Stephen White for comments that led to substantial improvements in this essay.*

1. Sir Isaiah Berlin, "Does Political Theory Still Exist?" in *Concepts and Categories: Philosophical Essays*, ed. Henry Hardy (London: Hogarth, 1978), 147.
2. In 1973, 11.2 percent of members of the American Political Science Association identified themselves as political theorists. In 1999, the figure had grown to 18.9 percent. In 1976-77, 5.3 percent of those listed in the Directory of American Philosophers identified themselves as political philosophers. In 1998-99, the figure was 6 percent. I am grateful to Alisa Kessel for compiling this data.
3. Of course, the questions of what counts as progress in science and of how scientific progress comes about are controversial questions as well. See Ian Hacking, *The Social Construction of What?* (Cambridge, MA: Harvard University Press, 1999), chap. 3, especially pp. 68-80; Imre Lakatos, "Falsification and the Methodology of Scientific Research Programmes," in *Criticism and the Growth of Knowledge*, ed. Imre Lakatos and Alan Musgrave (Cambridge, UK: Cambridge University Press, 1970), 91-196.
4. For the development of these distinctions, see Donald Moon, "The Logic of Political Inquiry: A Synthesis of Opposed Perspectives," in *Political Science: Scope and Theory*, ed. Fred I. Greenstein and Nelson W. Polsby (Reading, MA: Addison-Wesley, 1975), chap. 2; Clifford Geertz, *The Interpretation of Cultures* (New York: Basic Books, 1973), chap. 1. See also notes 6 and 29.
5. "University research is a long-term investment in the future . . . research creates the building blocks of future products and processes. . . . Along with creating new knowledge . . . [the] fusion of education and cutting-edge research has been a unique feature of the U.S. research university system," "University Research—Understanding Its Role," (Association of American Universities, May 2001); "The national investment in fundamental new knowledge is key to ensuring continued technological payoff," "America's Research Universities: Institutions in Service to the Nation," (Association of American Universities, white paper, January 2001).
6. For very interesting discussions of similar issues, see Donald Moon, "The Logic of Political Inquiry"; Michael Oakeshott, "Rationalism in Politics," in *Rationalism in Politics and Other Essays* (Indianapolis, IN: Liberty Fund Press, 1991), 5-42; Charles Taylor, "Interpretation and the Sciences of Man," in *Understanding and Social Inquiry*, ed. Fred R. Dallmayr and Thomas A. McCarthy (Notre Dame, IN: University of Notre Dame Press, 1977), 101-31; Sheldon S. Wolin, "Paradigms and Political Theories," in *Paradigms and Revolutions*, ed. Gary Gutting (Notre Dame, IN: University of Notre Dame Press, 1980), 160-94.
7. Andrew Delbanco, "The Decline and Fall of Literature," *The New York Review of Books*, November 4, 1999, 32-38 at 34. Delbanco is quoting Daniel Coit Gilman here, the first president of Johns Hopkins University.

8. Within political science, this view tends to support the idea that students need background in political theory, especially a familiarity with the likes of Machiavelli, Hobbes, and Locke, but that new dissertation work on these thinkers is not a serious priority.

9. A "researcher" is one who investigates, inquires, or searches for something. A "scholar" is a learner. "Scholar" originally simply meant any sort of "student," and later also came to mean a person who has learned what is taught in the universities.

10. This is why Michael Oakeshott is careful to distinguish true science from the technical rationalism he criticizes ("Rationalism in Politics," 13, 34-35). Thomas Kuhn distinguishes "normal science" from scientific revolutions that "transformed the scientific imagination." Thomas Kuhn, *The Structure of Scientific Revolutions* (Chicago: University of Chicago Press, 1962), 6. See also Michael Polanyi, *Science, Faith and Society* (London: Oxford University Press, 1946). Polanyi stresses the element of "guesswork" or "intuition" in scientific work, "mental processes which go beyond the application of any definite rules" (p. 29).

11. See Ernest Nagel and James R. Newman, *Gödel's Proof* (New York: New York University Press, 1958).

12. Berlin takes this approach. Because political theory deals with questions of the "human," it is necessarily evaluative. Human action always takes place within a general outlook framed by moral, aesthetic, and political conceptions "shot through with evaluation." Berlin, "Does Political Theory Still Exist?" 157.

13. See, for example, Hilary Putnam, *Reason, Truth and History* (Cambridge, UK: Cambridge University Press, 1981), chap. 6.

14. "A proposition might be said to be scientific only if it aims at expressing a causal connection." Lakatos, "Falsification and the Methodology," 102.

15. See notes 34 and 35 and accompanying text. Permanent dilemmas and irreconcilable conflicts of value also give rise to reasonable disagreements that call for judgment.

16. Berlin argues that political theory presupposes a pluralism of values and thus always generates disagreement with respect to both ends and means. This is why political theory does not fare well under totalitarian regimes. Berlin, "Does Political Theory Still Exist?" 149-54.

17. John Locke, *Two Treatises of Government*, ed. Peter Laslett (Cambridge, UK: Cambridge University Press, 1988), Second Treatise, paras. 57, 93, 226.

18. For important voices in this discussion, see Peter Gay, *The Enlightenment: An Interpretation* (New York: Knopf, 1966); idem, "The Living Enlightenment," in *The Tanner Lectures on Human Values* (Salt Lake City: University of Utah Press, 1998), 19; Max Horkheimer and Theodor W. Adorno, *Dialectic of Enlightenment* (New York: Continuum, 1991); Jacob Talmon, *Political Messianism: The Romantic Phase* (New York: Praeger, 1960).

19. There are many sorts of judgment, some of which figure in scientific inquiry as well. But judgment does not play the same role as it does in the humanities, particularly evaluative judgment, which is my primary concern here.

20. As Stanley Fish argued in a recent op-ed, an appeal to cultural specificity is not a claim that no moral stance can be taken. He claimed that while there are no independent abstract standards to which we can appeal to reach moral consensus, we can appeal to our own lived cultural practices (*The New York Times*, October 15, 2001). But, of course, the latter also give us no hope of persuading others on moral issues, or even engaging them in discussion. Fish also commented favorably here on the Reuters news agency decision discussed in note 28.

21. See Michael Walzer, *Interpretation and Social Criticism* (Cambridge, MA: Harvard University Press, 1987).

22. See John H. Holland, Keith H. Holyoak, and Richard E. Nisbet, *Induction: Processes of Inference, Learning and Discovery* (Cambridge, MA: MIT Press, reprint edition 1989), chap. 10. The authors discuss the impact of analogies on problem solving, including some fascinating experimental results.

23. John Locke, *An Essay Concerning Human Understanding*, ed. Peter H. Nidditch (Oxford, UK: Clarendon, 1975) bk. I, chap. 1, para. 6.

24. Ibid., bk. IV, chap. 14, para. 1.

25. See David Hume, "Of the Standard of Taste," in *Selected Essays* (Oxford, UK: Oxford University Press, 1996), 133-53.

26. It is also a mistake to infer from agreement on a moral, political, or aesthetic judgment that it is a valid judgment. Agreement may indicate nothing more than shared prejudice.

27. Of course, people are not always open to persuasion. Partiality sustains disagreements when the contested issues involve interests and identities. When the implications of an argument are highly consequential for the parties involved, the more plausible argument is not necessarily the more persuasive one.

28. Reuters news agency did just this recently when it decided not to use the word "terrorist" because people disagree as to who is a "terrorist" and who is a "freedom fighter." The disagreement should not have discouraged them from thinking the problem through. Reuters was confusing terms that refer to means and terms that refer to ends in a manner that makes as little sense as wondering whether we can distinguish between "torturers" and "patriots." Some freedom fighters are also terrorists; some are not (e.g., Gandhi). Some terrorists employ terror in the name of tyrannical theocracies, others in the name of freedom. Some patriots are also torturers, some are not, and so on. The moral judgment to be made here is when, if ever, terror (or torture) is justified.

29. Clifford Geertz, discussing cultural anthropology, distinguishes "experimental science in search of a law" from "interpretive [science] in search of meaning" in much the same way that I distinguish research in the sciences from research in the humanities. Interpretive sciences, according to Geertz, resemble literature, are "inherently inconclusive," intrinsically incomplete, build on previous work by "plunging more deeply into the same things" rather than by incremental additions, are diagnostic rather than predictive, and measure progress "less by a perfection of consensus than by a refinement of debate." Clifford Geertz, *The Interpretation of Cultures*, especially pp. 5, 9, 23, 26, 29.

30. Aristotle, *Nicomachean Ethics*, trans. Martin Ostwald (New York: Macmillan, 1962), I.3.23. In introducing his study of ethics, Aristotle comments that precision is not possible with regard to "problems of what is noble and just, which politics examines."

31. For an examination of the importance of considering political self-understandings in one historical case, see John H. Aldrich and Ruth W. Grant, "The Antifederalists, the First Congress, and the First Parties," *Journal of Politics* 55, no. 2 (1993): 295-326.

32. Politics requires both "technical" and "practical" knowledge. Oakeshott, "Rationalism in Politics," 7-17.

33. Holland, Holyoak, and Nisbet, *Induction*.

34. Aristotle is famous for this observation. *Politics*, III.9, V,1.

35. For a compelling argument that societies cannot escape moral antinomies (where "A is unjust but not-A is unjust also"), see Thomas A. Spragens Jr., "The Antinomies of Social Justice," *The Review of Politics*, 55, no. 2 (1993): 193-216 at 205.

36. James Fearon puts the question directly, "Why discuss things?" and finds that there are some good reasons for discussion. James Fearon, "Deliberation as Discussion," in

*Deliberative Democracy*, ed. Jon Elster (Cambridge, UK: Cambridge University Press, 1998). For attempts to explore how theories emphasizing "deeds" or "interests" might be brought in contact with theories emphasizing "speech" or "norms," see James Fearon and Alexander Wendt, "Rationalism vs. Constructivism: A Skeptical View," in *Handbook of International Relations*, ed. Walter Carlsnaes, Thomas Risse, and Beth Simmons (London: Sage, 2002), chap. 3; James Johnson, "Is Talk Really Cheap? Prompting Conversation between Critical Theory and Rational Choice," *American Political Science Review*, 87, no. 1 (1993): 74-86.

37. Thomas Hobbes, *Leviathan*, ed. Michael Oakeshott (New York: Collier, 1962), chap. 10, p. 73.

38. Ibid., chap. 18, p. 137, emphasis added. In a very important sense, *Leviathan* is a book on civic education (see chaps. 30, 46).

39. See for example, Judith Goldstein and Robert O. Keohane, eds., *Ideas and Foreign Policy: Beliefs, Institutions, and Political Change* (Ithaca, NY: Cornell University Press, 1993), 3, which opens, "As social scientists we are interested in using empirical evidence to evaluate the hypothesis that ideas are often important determinants of government policy."

40. Berlin, "Does Political Theory Still Exist?"

41. Locke, *Essay*, bk. I, chap. 1, para. 5.

# 9     PROBLEMS, METHODS, AND THEORIES: WHAT'S WRONG WITH POLITICAL SCIENCE AND WHAT TO DO ABOUT IT

*IAN SHAPIRO*

Our mandate is to engage in navel-gazing about the condition of political theory. I confess that I find myself uncomfortable with this charge because I think political theorists have become altogether too narcissistic over the past half-century. Increasingly, they have come to see themselves as engaged in a specialized activity distinct from the rest of political science—either a bounded subdiscipline within it or an alternative to it. Political theorists are scarcely unusual in this regard; advancing specialization has been a hallmark of most academic disciplines in recent decades. When warranted, it facilitates the accumulation of knowledge in ways that would not otherwise be achieved. In many physical, biomedical, and informational sciences, the benefits are visible in expanding bodies of knowledge that were scarcely conceivable a generation ago. Specialization has also proceeded apace in the human sciences, seen in the proliferation of dedicated journals, professional organizations and suborganizations, and esoteric discourses notable for their high entry costs to the uninitiated. Here tangible advances in knowledge are less easily identified, however. In political science, even when the new subfields fly interdisciplinary banners (as with the new political economy in much American and comparative politics, the turn to social theory in international relations, or to approaches from moral philosophy in theorizing about justice), those who have not paid the entry costs would be hard-pressed to understand—let alone evaluate—the alleged contributions of the new specialized fields.

The specialization that has divided political philosophy from the rest of political science has been aided and abetted by the separation of normative from empirical political theory, with political philosophers declaring a monopoly over the former while abandoning the enterprise of "positive" political theory to other political scientists. This seems to me to have been bad for both ventures. It has produced normative theory that is no longer informed, in the ways that the great theorists of the tradition took it for granted that political theory should be informed, by the state of empirical

193

knowledge of politics. A result is that normative theorists spend too much time commenting on one another, as if they were themselves the appropriate objects of study. This separation has also fed the tendency for empirical political theory to become banal and method driven—detached from the great questions of the day and focused instead on what seems methodologically most tractable. Both types of theory have evolved close to the point where they are of scant interest to anyone other than their practitioners. This might bump up citation indexes and bamboozle tenure committees in the desired ways, but it scarcely does much for the advancement of knowledge about what is or ought to be the case in politics.

My discomfort extends to commenting at length on this state of affairs, which replicates the disorder under discussion even more than Descartes's *cogito* established his existence. Rather, my plan here is to illustrate what I take to be one of the central challenges for political theorists: serving as roving ombudsmen for the truth and the right by stepping back from political science as practiced to see what is wrong with what is currently being done and say something about how it might be improved. Holding the discipline's feet to the fire might be an appropriate slogan. Let me hasten to add that I have no interest in declaring that this is the only important task for political theorists or indeed that it is the most important task, only that it is *an* indispensable task. If political theorists do not do it, then it seems to me to be unlikely that it will be done at all.

Donald Green and I have previously criticized contemporary political science for being too method driven and not sufficiently problem driven.[1] In various ways, many have responded that our critique fails to take full account of how inevitably theory laden empirical research is. Here I agree with many of these basic claims, but I argue that they do not weaken the contention that empirical research and explanatory theories should be problem driven. Rather, they suggest that one central task for political theorists should be to identify, criticize, and suggest plausible alternatives to the theoretical assumptions, interpretations of political conditions, and above all the specifications of problems that underlie prevailing empirical accounts and research programs and to do it in ways that can spark novel and promising problem-driven research agendas.

My procedure will be to develop and extend our arguments for problem-driven over method-driven approaches to the study of politics. Green and I made the case for starting with a problem in the world, next coming to grips with previous attempts that have been made to study it, and then defining the research task by reference to the value added. We argued that method-driven research leads to self-serving construction of problems, misuse of data in various ways, and related pathologies summed up in the old adage that if the only tool you have is a hammer, everything around you starts to look like a nail. Examples include collective action problems such as free riding that appear mysteriously to have been "solved" when perhaps it never occurred to anyone to free ride to begin with in many circumstances, or the concoction of elaborate explanations for why people "irrationally" vote, when perhaps it never occurred to most of them to think by reference to the individual costs and benefits of the voting act. The nub of our argument was that more attention to the problem and less to vindicating some pet approach would be less likely to send people on esoteric goose chases that contribute little to the advancement of knowledge.

What we dubbed "method-driven" work in fact conflated theory-driven and method-driven work. These can be quite different things, though in the literature they often morph into one another as when rational choice is said to be an "approach" rather than a theory. From the point of view elaborated here, the critical fact is that neither is problem driven, where this is understood to require specification of the problem under study in ways that are not mere artifacts of the theories and methods that are deployed to study it. Theory-drivenness and method-drivenness undermine problem-driven scholarship in different ways that are attended to below, necessitating different responses. This is not to say that problem selection is, or should be, uninfluenced by theories and methods, but I will contend that there are more ways than one of bringing theory to bear on the selection of problems and that some are better than others.

Some resisted our earlier argument on the grounds that refinement of theoretical models and methodological tools is a good gamble in the advancement of science as part of a division of labor. It is sometimes noted, for instance, that when John Nash came up with his equilibrium concept (an equilibrium from which no one has an incentive to defect), he could not think of an application, yet it has since become widely used in political science.[2] We registered skepticism at this approach in our book, partly because the ratio of success to failure is so low, and partly because our instinct is that better models are likely to be developed in applied contexts, in closer proximity to the data.

I do not want to rehearse those arguments here. Rather, my goal is to take up some weaknesses in our previous discussion of the contrast between problem-drivenness and method- and theory-drivenness and explore their implications for the study of politics. Our original formulation was open to two related objections: that the distinction we were attempting to draw is a distinction without a difference and that there is no theory-independent way of characterizing problems. These are important objections, necessitating more elaborate responses than Green and I offered. My response to them in parts I and II leads to a discussion, in part III, of the reality that there are always multiple true descriptions of any given piece of social reality, where I argue against the reductionist impulse always to select one type of description as apt. This leaves us with the difficulty of selecting among potential competing descriptions of what is to be accounted for in politics, taken up in part IV. There I explore the notion that the capacity to generate successful predictions is the appropriate criterion. In some circumstances this is the right answer, but it runs the risk of atrophying into a kind of method-drivenness that traps researchers into forlorn attempts to refine predictive instruments. Moreover, insisting on the capacity to generate predictions as the criterion for problem-selection risks predisposing the political science enterprise to the study of trivial, if tractable, problems. In light of prediction's limitations, I turn, in part V, to other ways in which the aptness of competing accounts can be assessed. There I argue that political theorists have an important role to play in scrutinizing accepted accounts of political reality: exhibiting their presuppositions, both empirical and normative, and posing alternatives. Just because observation is inescapably theory laden, this is bound to be an ongoing task. Political theorists have a particular responsibility to take it on when accepted depictions of political reality are both faulty and widely influential outside the academy.

## I. A DISTINCTION WITHOUT A DIFFERENCE?

The claim that the distinction between problem- and theory-driven research is a distinction without a difference turns on the observation that even the kind of work that Green and I characterized as theory driven in fact posits a problem to study. This can be seen by reflecting on some manifestly theory-driven accounts.

Consider, for instance, a paper sent to me for review by the *American Political Science Review* on the probability of successful negotiated transitions to democracy in South Africa and elsewhere. It contended, inter alia, that as the relative size of the dispossessed majority grows, the probability of a settlement decreases for the following reason: members of the dispossessed majority, as individual utility maximizers, confront a choice between working and fomenting revolution. Each one realizes that, as their numbers grow, the individual returns from revolution will decline, assuming that the expropriated proceeds of revolution will be equally divided among the expropriators. Accordingly, as their relative numbers grow, they will be more likely to devote their energy to work than to fomenting revolution, and, because the wealthy minority realizes this, its members will be less inclined to negotiate a settlement as their numbers diminish since the threat of revolution is receding.

One only has to describe the model for its absurdity to be plain. Even if one thought dwindling minorities are likely to become increasingly recalcitrant, it is hard to imagine anyone coming up with this reasoning as part of the explanation. In any event, the model seems so obtuse with respect to what drives the dispossessed to revolt and fails so obviously to take manifestly relevant factors into account (such as the changing likelihood of revolutionary success as the relative numbers change), that it is impossible to take seriously. In all likelihood, it is a model that was designed for some other purpose, and this person is trying to adapt it to the study of democratic transitions. One can concede that even such manifestly theory-driven work posits problems yet nonetheless insist that such specification is contrived. It is an artifact of the theoretical model in question.

Or consider the neo-Malthusian theory put forward by Charles Murray to the effect that poor women have children in response to the perverse incentives created by Aid to Families with Dependent Children and related benefits.[3] Critics such as Katz pointed out that on this theory, it is difficult to account for the steady increase in the numbers of children born into poverty since the early 1970s, when the real value of such benefits has been stagnant or declining.[4] Murray's response (in support of which he cited no evidence) has only to be stated for its absurdity to be plain: "In the late 1970s, social scientists knew that the real value of the welfare benefit was declining, but the young woman in the street probably did not."[5] This is clearly self-serving for the neo-Malthusian account, even if in a palpably implausible way. Again, the point to stress here is not that no problem is specified; Murray is interested in explaining why poor women have children. But the fact that he holds on to his construction of it as an attempt by poor women to maximize their income from the government even in the face of confounding evidence suggests that he is more interested in vindicating his theory than in understanding the problem.

Notice that this is not an objection to modeling. To see this, compare these examples to John Roemer's account of the relative dearth of redistributive policies advocated by either political party in a two-party democracy with substantial ex-ante inequality.[6] He develops a model that shows that if voters' preferences are arrayed along more than one dimension—such as "values" as well as "distributive" dimensions—then the median voter will not necessarily vote for downward redistribution as he would if there were only a single distributive dimension. His model seems to me worth taking seriously (leaving aside for present purposes how well it might do in systematic empirical testing) because the characterization of the problem that motivates it is not forced as in the earlier examples. Trying to develop the kind of model he proposes to account for it seems therefore to be worthwhile.[7]

In light of these examples, we can say that the objection that theory-driven research in fact posits problems is telling in a trivial sense only. If the problems posited are idiosyncratic artifacts of the researcher's theoretical priors, then they will seem tendentious, if not downright misleading, to everyone except those who are wedded to her priors. Put differently, if a phenomenon is characterized as it is so as to vindicate a particular theory rather than to illuminate a problem that is specified independently of the theory, then it is unlikely that the specification will gain much purchase on what is actually going on in the world. Rather, it will appear to be what it is: a strained and unconvincing specification driven by the impulse to vindicate a particular theoretical outlook. It makes better sense to start with the problem, perhaps asking what the conditions are that make transitions to democracy more or less likely, or what influences the fertility rates of poor women. Next see what previous attempts to account for the phenomenon have turned up and only then look to the possibility of whether a different theory will do better. To be sure, one's perception of what problems should be studied might be influenced by prevailing theories, as when the theory of evolution leads generations of researchers to study different forms of speciation. But the theory should not blind the researcher to the independent existence of the phenomenon under study. When that happens, appropriate theoretical influence has atrophied into theory-drivenness.

## II. ALL OBSERVATION IS THEORY LADEN?

It might be objected that the preceding discussion fails to come to grips with the reality that there is no theory-independent way to specify a problem. This claim is sometimes summed up with the epithet that "all observation is theory laden." Even when problems are thought to be specified independently of the theories that are deployed to account for them, in fact they always make implicit reference to some theory. From this perspective, the objection would be reformulated as the claim that the contrast between problem-driven and theory-driven research assumes there is some pretheoretical way of demarcating the problem. But we have known since the later Wittgenstein, J. L. Austin, and Thomas Kuhn that there is not. After all, in the example just mentioned, Roemer's specification of problem is an artifact of the median voter theorem and a number of assumptions about voter preferences. The relative dearth of redistributive policies is in tension with that specification, and it is this tension that seems to call for an explanation. Such considerations buttress the insistence that there simply is no pretheoretical account of "the facts" to be given.

A possible response at this juncture would be to grant that all description is theory laden but retort that some descriptions are more theory laden than others. Going back to my initial examples of democratic transitions and welfare mothers, we might say that tendentious or contrived theory-laden descriptions fail on their own terms: one does not need to challenge the theory that leads to them to challenge them. Indeed, the only point of referring to the theory at all is to explain how anyone might come to believe them. The failure stems from the fact that, taken on its own terms, the depiction of the problem does not compute. We have no good reason to suppose that revolutionaries will become less militant as their relative numbers increase or that poor women have increasing numbers of babies to get decreasingly valuable welfare checks. Convincing as this might be as response to the examples given, it does not quite come to grips with what is at stake for social research in the claim that all description is theory laden.

Consider theory-laden descriptions of institutions and practices that are problematic even though they do not fail on their own terms, such as Kathleen Bawn's claim that an ideology is a blueprint around which a group maintains a coalition[8] or Russell Hardin's claim that constitutions exist to solve coordination problems.[9] Here the difficulty is that, although it is arguable that ideologies and constitutions serve the designated purposes, they serve many other purposes as well. Moreover, it is far from clear that any serious investigation of how particular ideologies and constitutions came to be created or are subsequently sustained would reveal that the theorist's stipulated purpose has much to do with either. They are "just so" stories, debatably plausible conjectures about the creation and or operation of these phenomena.[10]

The difficulty here is not that Bawn's and Hardin's are functional explanations. Difficult as functional explanations are to test empirically, they may sometimes be true. Rather, the worry is that these descriptions might be of the following form: trees exist for dogs to pee on. Even when a sufficient account is not manifestly at odds with the facts, there is no reason to suppose that it will ever get us closer to reality unless it is put up against other plausible conjectures in such a way that there can be decisive adjudication among them. Otherwise we have "Well, in that case what are lamp posts for?" Ideologies may be blueprints for maintaining coalitions, but they also give meaning and purpose to people's lives, mobilize masses, reduce information costs, contribute to social solidarity, and facilitate the demonization of "out-groups"— to name some common candidates. Constitutions might help solve coordination problems, but they are also often charters to protect minority rights, legitimating statements of collective purpose, instruments to distinguish the rules of the game from the conflicts of the day, compromise agreements to end or avoid civil wars, and so on. Nor are these characterizations necessarily competing: ideologies and constitutions might well perform several such functions simultaneously. Selecting any one over others implies a theoretical commitment. This is one thing people may have in mind when asserting that all observation is theory laden.

One can concede the point without abandoning the problem-driven/theory-driven distinction, however. The theory-driven scholar commits to a sufficient account of a phenomenon, developing a "just so" story that might seem convincing to partisans of her theoretical priors. Others will see no more reason to believe it than a host of other "just so" stories that might have been developed, vindicating different theoretical priors. By contrast, the problem-driven scholar asks, "Why are constitutions enacted?" or "Why do they survive?" and "Why do ideologies develop?" or "Why do people adhere to them?" She then looks to previous theories that have been put forward to account for these phenomena, tries to see how they are lacking, and whether some alternative might do better. She need not deny that embracing one account rather than another implies different theoretical commitments, and she may even hope that one theoretical outcome will prevail. But she recognizes that she should be more concerned to discover which explanation works best than to vindicate any priors she may happen to have. As with the distinction-without-a-difference objection, then, this version of the theory-ladenness objection turns out on inspection at best to be trivially true.

## III. MULTIPLE TRUE DESCRIPTIONS AND APTNESS

There is a subtler sense in which observation is theory laden, untouched by the preceding discussion though implicit in it. The claim that all observation is theory laden scratches the surface of a larger set of issues having to do with the reality that all phenomena admit of multiple true descriptions. Consider possible descriptions of a woman who says "I do" in a conventional marriage ceremony. She could be

- expressing authentic love,
- doing (failing to do) what her father has told her to do,
- playing her expected part in a social ritual,
- unconsciously reproducing the patriarchal family,
- landing the richest husband that she can, or
- maximizing the chances of reproducing her genes.

Each description is theory laden in the sense that it leads to the search for a different type of explanation. This can be seen if in each case we ask the question *why?* and see what type of explanation is called forth.

- *Why does she love him?* predisposes us to look for an explanation in terms of her personal biography.
- *Why does she obey (disobey) her father?* predisposes us to look for a psychological explanation.
- *Why does she play her part in the social ritual?* predisposes us to look for an anthropological explanation.
- *Why does she unconsciously reproduce patriarchy?* predisposes us to look for an explanation in terms of ideology and power relations.
- *Why does she do as well as she can in the marriage market?* predisposes us to look for an interest-based rational choice explanation.
- *Why does she maximize the odds of reproducing her genes?* predisposes us to look for a socio-biological explanation.

The claim that all description is theory laden illustrated here is a claim that there is no "raw" description of "the facts" or "the data." There are always multiple possible true descriptions of a given action or phenomenon, and the challenge is to decide which is most apt.

From this perspective, theory-driven work is part of a reductionist program. It dictates always opting for the description that calls for the explanation that flows from the preferred model or theory. So the narrative historian who believes every event to be unique will reach for personal biography, the psychological reductionist will turn to the psychological determinants of her choice, the anthropologist will see the constitutive role of the social ritual as the relevant description, the feminist will focus on the action as reproducing patriarchy, the rational choice theorist will reach for the explanation in terms of maximizing success in the marriage market, and for the socio-biologist it will be evolutionary selection at the level of gene reproduction.

Why do this? Why plump for any reductionist program that is invariably going to load the dice in favor of one type of description? I hesitate to say "level" here, since that prejudges the question I want to highlight: whether some descriptions are invariably more basic than others. Perhaps one is, but to presume this to be the case is to make the theory-driven move. Why do it?

The common answer rests, I think, on the belief that it is necessary for the program of social science. In many minds this enterprise is concerned with the search for general explanations. How is one going to come up with general explanations if one cannot characterize the classes of phenomena one studies in similar terms? This view misunderstands the enterprise of science, provoking three responses: one skeptical, one ontological, and one occupational.

The skeptical response is that whether there are general explanations for classes of phenomena is a question for social-scientific inquiry, not one to be prejudged before conducting that inquiry. At stake here is a variant of the debate between deductivists and inductivists. The deductivist starts from the preferred theory or model and then opts for the type of description that will vindicate the general claims implied by the model, whereas the inductivist begins by trying to account for particular phenomena or classes of phenomena and then sees under what conditions, if any, such accounts might apply more generally. This enterprise might often be theory influenced for the reasons discussed in parts I and II, but it is less likely to be theory driven than the pure deductivist's one because the inductivist is not determined to arrive at any particular theoretical destination. The inductivist pursues general accounts, but she regards it as an open question whether they are out there waiting to be discovered.

The ontological response is that although science is in the second instance concerned with developing general knowledge claims, it must in the first instance be concerned with developing valid knowledge claims. It seems to be an endemic obsession of political scientists to believe that there must be general explanations of all political phenomena, indeed to subsume them into a single theoretical program. Theory-drivenness kicks in when the pursuit of generality comes at the expense of the pursuit of empirical validity. "Positive" theorists sometimes assert that it is an appropriate division of labor for them to pursue generality while others worry about validity. This leads to the various pathologies Green and I wrote about, but the one we did not mention that I emphasize here is that it invites tendentious characterizations of the phenomena under study because the selection of one description rather than another is driven by the impulse to vindicate a particular theoretical outlook.

The occupational response is that political scientists are pushed in the direction of theory-driven work as a result of their perceived need to differentiate themselves from others, such as journalists, who also write about political phenomena for a living, but without the job security and prestige of the professoriate. This aspiration to do better than journalists is laudable, but it should be unpacked in a Lakatosian fashion. When tackling a problem, we should come to grips with the previous attempts to study it, by journalists as well as scholars in all disciplines who have studied it, and then try to come up with an account that explains what was known before—and then some. Too often the aspiration to do better than journalists is cashed out as manufacturing esoteric discourses with high entry costs for outsiders. All the better if they involve inside-the-cranium exercises that never require one to leave one's computer screen.

## IV. PREDICTION AS A SORTING CRITERION?

A possible response to what has been said thus far is that prediction should be the arbiter. Perhaps my skepticism is misplaced, and some reductionist program is right. If so, it will lead to correct predictions, whereas those operating with explanations that focus on other types of description will fail. Theory driven or not, the predictive account should triumph as the one that shows that interest maximization, or gene preservation, or the oppression of women, or the domination of the father figure, and so on is "really going on." On this instrumentalist view, we would say, with Friedman, "deploy whatever theory-laden description you like, but lay it on the line and see how it does in predicting outcomes." If you can predict from your preferred cut, you win.[11]

This instrumental response is adequate up to a point. Part of what is wrong with many theory-driven enterprises, after all, is that their predictions can never be decisively falsified. From Bentham through Marx, Freud, functionalism, and much modern rational choice theory, too often the difficulty is that the theory is articulated in such a capacious manner that some version of it is consistent with every conceivable outcome. In effect, the theory predicts everything, so that it can never be shown to be false. This is why people say that a theory that predicts everything explains nothing. If a theory can never be put to a decisive predictive test, there seems little reason to take it seriously.

Theories of everything to one side, venturing down this path raises the difficulty that prediction is a tough test that is seldom met in political science. This difficulty calls to mind the job applicant who said on an interview that he would begin a course on comparative political institutions with a summary of the field's well-tested empirical findings but then had nothing to say when asked what he would teach for the remaining twelve weeks of the semester. Requiring the capacity to predict is in many cases a matter of requiring more than can be delivered, so that if political science is held to this standard, there would have to be a proliferation of exceedingly short courses. Does this reality suggest that we should give up on prediction as our sorting criterion?

Some, such as MacIntyre, have objected to prediction as inherently unattainable in the study of human affairs due to the existence of free will.[12] Such claims are not convincing, however. Whether or not human beings have free will is an empirical question. Even if we do, probabilistic generalizations might still be developed about the conditions under which we are more likely to behave in one way rather than another. To be sure, this assumes that people are likely to behave in similar ways in similar circumstances, which may or may not be true, but the possibility of its being true does not depend on denying the existence of free will. To say that someone will probably make choice

$x$ in circumstance $q$ does not mean that they cannot choose not-$x$ in that circumstance or, that, if do they choose not-$x$, it was not nonetheless more likely ex-ante that they would have chosen $x$. In any event, most successful science does not proceed by making point predictions. It predicts patterns of outcomes. There will always be outliers and error terms; the best theory minimizes them vis-à-vis the going alternatives.

A more general version of this objection is to insist that prediction is unlikely to be possible in politics because of the decisive role played by contingent events in most political outcomes. This, too, seems overstated unless one assumes in advance—with the narrative historian—that everything is contingent. A more epistemologically open approach is to assume that some things are contingent, others not, and try to develop predictive generalizations about the latter. For instance, Courtney Jung and I developed a theory of the conditions that make negotiated settlements to civil wars possible involving such factors as whether government reformers and opposition moderates can combine to marginalize reactionaries and revolutionary militants on their flanks. We also developed a theory of the conditions that are more and less likely to make reformers and moderates conclude that trying to do this is better for them than the going alternatives.[13] Assuming we are right, contingent triggers will nonetheless be critical in whether such agreements are successfully concluded, as can be seen by reflecting on how things might have developed differently in South Africa and the Middle East had F. W. DeKlerk been assassinated in 1992 or had Yitzhak Rabin not been assassinated in 1995. The decisive role of contingent events rules out ex-ante prediction of success, but the theory might correctly predict failure—as when a moderate IRA leader such as Jerry Adams emerges but the other necessary pieces are not in place, or if Yassir Arafat is offered a deal by Ehud Barak at a time when he is too weak to outflank Hamas and Islamic Jihad. Successful prediction of failure over a range of such cases would suggest that we have indeed taken the right descriptive cut at the problem.[14]

There are other types of circumstance in which capacity to predict will support one descriptive cut at a problem over others. For instance Przeworski et al. have shown that although level of economic development does not predict the installation of democracy, there is a strong relationship between level of per capita income and the survival of democratic regimes. Democracies appear never to die in wealthy countries, whereas poor democracies are fragile, exceedingly so when per capita incomes fall below $2,000 (in 1975 dollars). When per capita incomes fall below this threshold, democracies have a one in ten chance of collapsing within a year. Between per capita incomes of $2,001 and $5,000, this ratio falls to one in sixteen. Above $6,055 annual per capita income, democracies, once established, appear to last indefinitely.

Moreover, poor democracies are more likely to survive when governments succeed in generating development and avoiding economic crises.[15] If Przeworski et al. are right, as it seems presently that they are, then level of economic development is more important than institutional arrangements, cultural beliefs, presence or absence of a certain religion, or other variables for predicting democratic stability. For this problem, the political economist's cut seems to be the right sorting criterion.[16]

These examples suggest that prediction can sometimes help, but we should nonetheless be wary of making it the criterion for problem selection in political science. For one thing, this can divert us away from the study of important political phenomena where knowledge can advance even though prediction turns out not to be possible. For instance, generations of scholars have theorized about the conditions that give rise to democracy (as distinct from the conditions that make it more or less likely to survive once instituted, just discussed). Alexis de Tocqueville alleged it to be the product of egalitarian mores.[17] For Seymour Martin Lipset, it was a byproduct of modernization.[18] Barrington Moore identified the emergence of a bourgeoisie as critical, while Rueschemeyer, Stephens, and Stephens held the presence of an organized working class to be decisive.[19] We now know that there is no single path to democracy and therefore no generalization to be had about which conditions give rise to democratic transitions. Democracy can result from decades of gradual evolution (Britain and the United States), imitation (India), cascades (much of Eastern Europe in 1989), collapses (Russia after 1991), imposition from above (Spain and Brazil), revolutions (Portugal and Argentina), negotiated settlements (Bolivia, Nicaragua, and South Africa), or external imposition (Japan and West Germany).[20]

In retrospect, this is not surprising. Once someone invents a toaster, there is no good reason to suppose that others must go through the same invention processes. Perhaps some will, but some may copy it, some may buy it, some may receive it as a gift, and so on. Perhaps there is no cut at this problem that yields a serviceable generalization and, as a result, no possibility of successful prediction. Political scientists tend to think they must have general theories of everything, as we have seen, but looking for a general theory of what gives rise to democracy may be like looking for a general theory of holes.[21] Yet we would surely be making an error if our inability to predict in this area inclined us not to study it. It would prevent our discovering a great deal about democracy that is important to know, not least that there is no general theory of what gives rise to it to be had. Such knowledge would also be important for evaluating claims by defenders of authoritarianism who contend that democracy cannot be instituted in their countries because they have not gone through the requisite path-dependent evolution.

Reflecting on this example raises the possibility I want to consider next: making a fetish of prediction can undermine problem-driven research via wag-the-dog scenarios in which we elect to study phenomena because they seem to admit the possibility of prediction rather than because we have independent reasons for thinking it worthwhile to study them. This is what I mean by method-drivenness, as distinct from theory-drivenness. It gains impetus from a number of sources, perhaps the most important being the lack of uncontroversial data concerning many political phenomena. Predictions about whether or not constitutional courts protect civil rights run into disagreements over which rights are to count and how to measure their protection. Predictions about the incidence of war run into objections about how to measure and count the relevant conflicts. In principle, it sounds right to say "let's test the model against the data." In reality, there are few uncontroversial data sets in political science.

A related difficulty is that it is usually impossible to disentangle the complex interacting causal processes that operate in the actual world. We will always find political economists on both sides of the question whether cutting taxes leads to increases or decreases in government revenue, and predictive tests will not settle their disagreements. Isolating the effects of tax cuts from the other changing factors that influence government revenues is just too difficult to do in ways that are likely to convince a skeptic. Likewise, political economists have been arguing at least since Bentham's time over whether trickle-down policies benefit the poor more than do government transfers, and it seems unlikely that the key variables will ever be isolated in ways that can settle this question decisively.

An understandable response to this is to suggest that we should tackle questions where good data is readily available. But taking this tack courts the danger of self-defeating method-drivenness, because there is no reason to suppose that the phenomena about which uncontroversial data are available are those about which valid generalizations are possible. My point here is not one about curve fitting—running regression after regression on the same data set until one finds the mix of explanatory variables that passes most closely through all the points to be explained. Leaving the well-known difficulties with this kind of data mining to one side, my worry is that working with uncontroversial data because of the ease of getting it can lead to endless quests for a holy grail that may be nowhere to be found.

The difficulty here is related to my earlier discussion of contingency, to wit, that many phenomena political scientists try to generalize about may exhibit secular changes that will always defy their explanatory theories. For instance, trying to predict election outcomes from various mixes of macro political and economic variables has been a growth industry in political science for more than a generation. But perhaps the factors that caused people to vote as they did in the 1950s differ from those forty or fifty years later. After all, this is not an activity with much of a track record of success in political science. We saw this dramatically in the 2000 election in which all of the standard models predicted a decisive Gore victory.[22] Despite endless post hoc tinkering with the models after elections in which they fare poorly, this is not an enterprise that appears to be advancing. They will never get it right if my conjecture about secular change is correct.

It might be replied that if that is really so, either they will come up with historically nuanced models that do a better job or universities and funding agencies will pull the plug on them. But this ignores an occupational factor that might be dubbed the Morton Thiokol phenomenon. When the Challenger blew up in 1986, there was much blame to go around, but it became clear that Morton Thiokol, manufacturer of the faulty O-ring seals, shouldered a huge part of the responsibility. A naïve observer might have thought that this would mean the end of their contract with NASA, but, of course, this was not so. The combination of high entry costs to others, the dependence of the space program on Morton Thiokol, and their access to those who control resources mean that they continue to make O-ring seals for the space shuttle. Likewise with those who work on general models of election forecasting. Established scholars with an investment in the activity have the protections of tenure and legitimacy, as well as privileged access to those who control research resources. Moreover, high methodological entry costs are likely to self-select new generations of researchers who are predisposed to believe that the grail is there to be found. Even if their space shuttles will never fly, it is far from clear that they will ever have the incentive to stop building them.

To this it might be objected that it is not as if others are building successful shuttles in this area. Perhaps so, but this observation misses my point here: that the main impetus for the exercise appears to be the ready availability of data, which sustains a coterie of scholars who are likely to continue to try to generalize on the basis of it until the end of time. Unless one provides an account, that, like the others on offer, purports to retrodict past elections and predict the next one, one cannot aspire to be a player in this game at which everyone is failing. If there is no such account to be found, however, then perhaps some other game should be played. For instance, we might learn more about why people vote in the ways that they do by asking them. Proceeding instead with the macro models risks becoming a matter of endlessly refining the predictive instrument as an end in itself—even in the face of continual failure and the absence of an argument about why we should expect it to be successful. Discovering where generalization is possible is a taxing empirical task. Perhaps it should proceed on the basis of trial and error, perhaps on the basis of theoretical argument, perhaps some combination. What should *not* drive it, however, is the ready availability of data and technique.

A more promising response to the difficulties of bad data and of disentangling complex causal process in the "open systems" of the actual world is to do experimental work where parameters can be controlled and key variables more easily isolated.[23] There is some history of this in political science and political psychology, but the main problem has been that of external validity. Even when subjects are randomly selected and control groups are included in the experiments (which often is not done), it is far from clear that results produced under lab conditions will replicate themselves outside the lab.

To deal with these problems, Donald Green and Alan Gerber have revived the practice of field experiments, in which subjects can be randomized, experimental controls can be introduced, and questions about external validity disappear.[24] Prediction can operate once more, and when it is successful there are good reasons for supposing that the researcher has taken the right cut at the problem. In some ways this is an exciting development. It yields decisive answers to questions such as which forms of mobilizing voters are most effective in increasing turnout, or what the best ways are for partisans to get their grassroots supporters to the polls without also mobilizing their opponents.

Granting that this is an enterprise that leads to increments in knowledge, I want nonetheless to suggest that it carries risks of falling into a kind of method-drivenness that threatens to diminish the field-experiment research program unless they are confronted. The potential difficulties arise from the fact that field experiments are limited to studying comparatively small questions in well-defined settings, where it is possible to intervene in ways that allow for experimental controls. Usually this means designing or piggybacking on interventions in the world such as get-out-the-vote efforts or attempts at partisan mobilization. Green and Gerber have shown that such efforts can be adapted to incorporate field experiments.

To be sure, the relative smallness of questions is to some extent in the eye of the beholder. But consider a list of phenomena that political scientists have sought to study, and those drawn to political science often want to understand, that are not likely to lend themselves to field experiments:

- the effects of regime type on the economy, and vice versa;
- the determinants of peace, war, and revolution;
- the causes and consequences of the trend toward creating independent central banks;
- the causes and consequences of the growth in transnational political and economic institutions;

- the relative merits of alternative policies for achieving racial integration, such as mandatory bussing, magnet schools, and voluntary desegregation plans;
- the importance of constitutional courts in protecting civil liberties, property rights, and limiting the power of legislatures;
- the effects of other institutional arrangements, such as parliamentarism versus presidentialism, unicameralism versus bicameralism, federalism versus centralism on such things as the distribution of income and wealth, the effectiveness of macroeconomic policies, and the types of social policies that are enacted; and
- the dynamics of political negotiations to institute democracy.

I could go on, but you get the point.

This is not to denigrate field experiments. One of the worst features of methodological disagreement in political science is the propensity of protagonists to compare the inadequacies of one method with the adequacies of a second and then declare the first to be wanting.[25] Since all methods have limitations and none should be expected to be serviceable for all purposes, this is little more than a shell game. If a method can do some things well that are worth doing, that is a sufficient justification for investing some research resources in it. With methods, as with people, if you focus only on their limitations you will always be disappointed.

Field experiments lend themselves to the study of behavioral variation in settings where the institutional context is relatively fixed and where the stakes are comparatively low so that the kinds of interventions required do not violate accepted ethical criteria for experimentation on human subjects. They do not obviously lend themselves to the study of life-or-death and other high-stakes politics, war and civil war, institutional variation, the macropolitical economy, or the determinants of regime stability and change. This still leaves a great deal to study that is worth studying, and creative use of the method might render it deployable in a wider array of areas than I have noted here. But it must be conceded that it also leaves out a great deal that draws people to political science, so that if susceptibility to study via field experiment becomes the criterion for problem selection, then it risks degenerating into method-drivenness.

This is an important caution. I would conjecture that part of the disaffection with 1960s behaviorism in the study of American politics that spawned the model mania of the 1990s was that the behaviorists became so mindlessly preoccupied with demonstrating propositions of the order "Catholics in Detroit vote Democrat."[26] As a result, the mainstream of political science that they came to define seemed to others to be both utterly devoid of theoretical ambition as well as detached from consequential questions of politics, frankly boring. To paraphrase Kant, theoretical ambition without empirical research may well be vacuous, but empirical research without theoretical ambition will be blind.


## V. UNDERVALUING CRITICAL REAPPRAISAL OF WHAT IS TO BE EXPLAINED

The emphasis on prediction can lead to method-drivenness in another way: it can lead us to undervalue critical reappraisals of accepted descriptions of reality. To see why this is so, one must realize that much commentary on politics, both lay and professional, takes depictions of political reality for granted that closer critical scrutiny would reveal as problematic. Particularly, though not only, when prediction is not going to supply the sorting device to get us the right cut, political theorists have an important role to play in exhibiting what is at stake in taking one cut rather than another and in proposing alternatives. Consider some examples.

For more than a generation in debates about American exceptionalism, the United States was contrasted with Europe as a world of relative social and legal equality deriving from the lack of a feudal past. This began with de Tocqueville, but it has been endlessly repeated and became conventional wisdom, if not a mantra, when restated by Louis Hartz in *The Liberal Tradition in America*. But as Rogers Smith showed decisively in *Civic Ideals*, it is highly misleading as a descriptive matter.[27] Throughout American history, the law has recognized explicit hierarchies based on race and gender whose effects are still very much with us. Smith's book advances no well-specified predictive model, let alone tests one, but it displaces a highly influential orthodoxy that has long been taken for granted in debates about pluralism and cross-cutting cleavages, the absence of socialism in America, arguments about the so-called end of ideology, and the ideological neutrality of the liberal tradition.[28] Important causal questions are to be asked and answered about these matters, but my point here is that what was thought to stand in need of explanation was so misspecified that the right causal questions were not even on the table.

Likewise with the debate about the determinants of industrial policy in capitalist democracies. In the 1970s, it occurred to students of this subject to focus less on politicians' voting records and campaign statements and look at who actually writes the legislation. This led to the discovery that significant chunks of it were actually written by organized business and organized labor with government (usually in the form of the relevant minister or ministry) in a mediating role. The reality was more of a "liberal corporatist" one, and less of a pluralist one, than most commentators who had not focused on this had realized.[29] The questions that then motivated the next generation of research became as follows: Under what conditions do we get liberal corporatism, and what are its effects on industrial relations and industrial policy? As with the Tocqueville-Hartz orthodoxy, the causal questions had to be reframed because of the ascendancy of a different depiction of the reality.[30]

In one respect, the Tocqueville-Hartz and pluralist accounts debunked by Smith and the liberal corporatists are more like those of democratic transitions and the fertility rates of welfare mothers discussed in part I than the multiple descriptions problem discussed in part III. The difficulty is not how to choose one rather than another true description but rather that the Tocqueville-Hartz and pluralist descriptions fail on their own terms. By focusing so myopically on the absence of feudalism and the activities of politicians, their proponents ignored other sources of social hierarchy and decision making that are undeniably relevant once they have been called to attention. The main difference is that the democratic transition and welfare mother examples are not as widely accepted as the Tocqueville-Hartz and pluralist orthodoxies were before the debunkers came along. This should serve as a salutary reminder that orthodox views can be highly misleading and that an important ongoing task for political theorists is to subject them to critical scrutiny. This involves exhibiting their presuppositions, assessing their plausibility, and proposing alternatives when they are found wanting. This is particularly important when the defective account is widely accepted outside the academy. If political science has a role to play in social betterment, it must surely include debunking myths and misunderstandings that shape political practice.[31]

Notice that descriptions are theory laden not only in calling for a particular empirical story but often also in implying a normative theory that may or may not be evident unless this is made explicit. Compare the following two descriptions:

- The Westphalian system is based on the norm of national sovereignty.
- The Westphalian system is based on the norm of global apartheid.

Both are arguably accurate descriptions, but, depending which of the two we adopt, we will be prompted to ask exceedingly different questions about justification as well as causation. Consider another instance:

- When substantial majorities in both parties support legislation, we have bipartisan agreement.
- When substantial majorities in both parties support legislation, we have collusion in restraint of democracy.

The first draws on a view of democracy in which deliberation and agreement are assumed to be unproblematic, even desirable goals in a democracy. The second, antitrust-framed, formulation calls to mind Mill's emphasis on the centrality of argument and contestation and the Schumpeterian impulse to think of well-functioning democracy as requiring competition for power.[32]

Both *global apartheid* and *collusion in restraint of democracy* here are instances of problematizing redescriptions. Just as Smith's depiction of American public law called the Tocqueville-Hartz consensus into question, and the liberal corporatist description of industrial legislation called then-conventional assumptions about pluralist decision making into question, so do these. But they do it not so much by questioning the veracity of the accepted descriptions as by throwing their undernoticed benign normative assumptions into sharp relief. Describing the Westphalian system as based on a norm of global apartheid, or political agreement among the major players in a democracy as collusion in restraint of democracy, shifts the focus to underattended features of reality, placing different empirical and justificatory questions on the table.

But are they the right questions?

To answer this by saying that one needs a theory of politics would be to turn once more to theory-drivenness. I want to suggest a more complex answer, one that sustains problematizing redescription as a problem-driven enterprise. It is a two-step venture that starts when one shows that the accepted way of characterizing a piece of political reality fails to capture an important feature of what stands in need of explanation or justification. One then offers a recharacterization that speaks to the inadequacies in the prior account.

When convincingly done, prior adherents to the old view will be unable to ignore it and remain credible. This is vital because it will, of course, be true that the problematizing redescription is itself usually a theory-influenced, if not a theory-laden, endeavor. But if the problematizing redescription assumes a theory that seems convincing only to partisans of her priors, or is validated only by reference to evidence that is projected from her alternative theory, then it will be judged tendentious by the rest of the scholarly community for the reasons I set out in parts I and II of this essay. It is important, therefore, to devote considerable effort to making the case that will persuade a skeptic of the superiority of the proffered redescription over the accepted one. One of the significant failings of many of the rational choice theories Green and I discussed is that their proponents failed to do this. They offered problematizing redescriptions that were sometimes arrestingly radical, but their failure to take the second step made them unconvincing to all except those who agreed with them in advance.

## VI. CONCLUDING COMMENTS

The recent emphases in political science on modeling for its own sake and on decisive predictive tests both give short shrift to the value of problematizing redescription in the study of politics. It is intrinsically worthwhile to unmask an accepted depiction as inadequate and to make a convincing case for an alternative as more apt. Just because observation is inescapably theory laden for the reasons explored in this essay, political theorists have an ongoing role to play in exhibiting what is at stake in accepted depictions of reality and reinterpreting what is known so as to put new problems onto the research agenda. This is important for scientific reasons when accepted descriptions are both faulty and influential in the conduct of social science. It is important for political reasons when the faulty understandings shape politics outside the academy.

If the problems thus placed on the agenda are difficult to study by means of theories and methods that are currently in vogue, an additional task arises that is no less important: to keep them there and challenge the ingenuity of scholars who are sufficiently open-minded to devise creative ways of grappling with them. It is important for political theorists to throw their weight against the powerful forces that entice scholars to embroider fashionable theories and massage methods in which they are professionally invested while failing to illuminate the world of politics. They should remind each generation of scholars that unless problems are identified in ways that are both theoretically illuminating and convincingly intelligible to outsiders, nothing that they say about them is likely to persuade anyone who stands in need of persuasion. Perhaps they will enjoy professional success of a sort, but at the price of trivializing their discipline and what one hopes is their vocation.

## NOTES

*Helpful comments have been received from Robert Dahl, Donald Green, Ariela Gross, Clarissa Hayward, Courtney Jung, John Kane, Ed Lindblom, Donald Moon, Adolph Reed Jr., Rogers Smith, Peter Swenson, Nomi Stolzenberg, and Stephen White. The research assistance of Jeffrey Mueller is gratefully acknowledged.*

1. See Donald Green and Ian Shapiro, *Pathologies of Rational Choice Theory: A Critique of Applications in Political Science* (New Haven, CT: Yale University Press, 1994); idem, "Pathologies Revisited: Reflections on Our Critics," in *The Rational Choice Controversy: Economic Models of Politics Reconsidered*, ed. Jeffrey Friedman (New Haven, CT: Yale University Press, 1996), 235-76.

2. John Nash, "The Bargaining Problem," *Econometrica* 18 (1950): 155-62. For explication, see John Harsanyi, "Advances in Understanding Rational Behavior," in *Rational Choice*, ed. Jon Elster (New York: New York University Press, 1986), 92-94.

3. See Charles Murray, *Losing Ground: American Social Policy, 1950-1980* (New York: Basic Books, 1984).

4. Michael B. Katz, *The Undeserving Poor: From the War on Poverty to the War on Welfare* (New York: Pantheon, 1989), 151-56.

5. Charles Murray, "Does Welfare Bring More Babies?" *The Public Interest*, spring 1994, 25.

6. John Roemer, "Does Democracy Engender Justice?" in *Democracy's Value*, ed. Ian Shapiro and Casiano Hacker-Cordón (Cambridge, UK: Cambridge University Press, 1999), 56-68.

7. It should be noted, however, that the median voter theorem is eminently debatable empirically. For discussion, see Green and Shapiro, *Pathologies*, 146-78.

8. Kathleen Bawn, "Constructing 'Us': "Ideology, Coalition Politics and False Consciousness," *American Journal of Political Science* 43, no. 2 (1999): 303-34.

9. Russell Hardin, *Liberalism, Constitutionalism, and Democracy* (Oxford, UK: Oxford University Press, 2000), 35, 86-88, 106, 114, 144, 285.

10. I leave aside, for present purposes, how convincing the debatable conjectures are. Consider the great difficulties Republican candidates face in forging winning coalitions in American politics that keep both social and libertarian conservatives on board. If one were to set out to define a blueprint to put together a winning coalition, trying to fashion it out of these conflicting elements scarcely seems like a logical place to start. Likewise with constitutions viewed as coordinating devices, the many veto points in the American constitutional system could just as arguably be said to be obstacles to coordination. See George Tsebelis, *Veto Players: How Political Institutions Work* (Princeton, NJ: Princeton University Press, 2002). This might not seem problematic if one takes the view, as Hardin does, that the central purpose of the U.S. Constitution is to facilitate commerce. On such a view, institutional sclerosis might arguably be an advantage, limiting government's capacity to interfere with the economy. The difficulty with going that route is that we then have a theory for all seasons: constitutions lacking multiple veto points facilitate political coordination, while those containing them facilitate coordination in realms that might otherwise be interfered with by politicians. Certainly nothing in Hardin's argument accounts for why some constitutions facilitate more coordination of a particular kind than do others.

11. Milton Friedman, "The Methodology of Positive Economics," in *Essays in Positive Economics* (Oxford, UK: Oxford University Press, 1953).

12. Alasdair MacIntyre, *After Virtue* (Notre Dame, IN: University of Notre Dame Press, 1984), 88-108.

13. See Courtney Jung and Ian Shapiro, "South Africa's Negotiated Transition: Democracy, Opposition, and the New Constitutional Order," *Politics and Society* 23 (1995): 269-308.

14. What is necessary in the context of one problem may, of course, be contingent in another. When we postulate that it was necessary that Arafat be strong enough to marginalize the radicals on his flank if he were to make an agreement with Barak, we do not mean to deny that his relative strength in this regard was dependent on many contingent factors. For further discussion, see Courtney Jung, Ellen Lust-Okar, and Ian Shapiro, "Problems and Prospects for Democratic Transitions: South Africa as a Model for the Middle East and Northern Ireland?" (mimeo, Yale University, 2002). In some ultimate—if uninter-

esting—sense, everything social scientists study is contingent on factors such as that the possibility of life on Earth not be destroyed due to a collision with a giant meteor. To be intelligible, the search for lawlike generalizations must be couched in "if . . . then" statements that make reference, however implicitly, to the problem under study.

15. Adam Przeworski, Michael Alvarez, Jose Cheibub, and Fernando Limongi, *Democracy and Development: Political Institutions and Well-Being in the World, 1950-1990* (Cambridge, UK: Cambridge University Press, 2000), 106-17.

16. For Przeworski et al.'s discussion of other explanatory variables, see ibid., 122-37.

17. Alexis de Tocqueville, *Democracy in America*, ed. J. P. Mayer, trans. George Lawrence (New York: Harper Perennial, 1966).

18. Seymour Martin Lipset, "Some Social Requisites of Democracy: Economic Development and Political Legitimacy," *American Political Science Review* 53 (1959): 69-105.

19. Barrington Moore, *The Social Origins of Dictatorship and Democracy: Lord and Peasant in the Making of the Modern World* (Boston: Beacon, 1966), 413-32; Dietrich Rueschemeyer, Evelyne Huber Stephens, and John D. Stephens, *Capitalist Development and Democracy* (Oxford, UK: Polity, 1992).

20. See Adam Przeworski, *Democracy and the Market* (Cambridge, UK: Cambridge University Press, 1991), ix-xii, 1-9, 51-99; Przeworski et al., *Democracy and Development*, 78-106; Samuel P. Huntington, *The Third Wave: Democratization in the Late Twentieth Century* (Norman: University of Oklahoma Press, 1991), 3-18; Ian Shapiro, *Democracy's Place* (Ithaca, NY: Cornell University Press, 1996), 79-108.

21. Perhaps one could develop such a theory but only of an exceedingly general kind such as "holes are created when something takes material content out of something else." This would not be of much help in understanding or predicting anything worth knowing about holes.

22. See the various postmortem papers in the March 2001 issue of *PS: Political Science and Politics*, vol. 34, no. 1, pp. 9-58.

23. For discussion of the difficulties with prediction in open systems, see Roy Bhaskar, *A Realist Theory of Science* (Sussex, UK: Harvester Wheatsheaf, 1975), 63-142; idem, *The Possibility of Naturalism* (Sussex, UK: Harvester Wheatsheaf, 1979), 158-69.

24. Alan Gerber and Donald Green, "Do Phone Calls Increase Voter Turnout? A Field Experiment," *Public Opinion Quarterly* 65 (2001): 75-85; idem, "Reclaiming the Experimental Tradition in Political Science," in *Political Science: The State of the Discipline*, 3rd ed., ed. Ira Katznelson and Helen Milner (forthcoming).

25. For discussion of an analogous phenomenon that plagues normative debates in political theory, see Ian Shapiro, "Gross Concepts in Political Argument," *Political Theory* 17, no. 1 (1989): 51-76.

26. Charles Taylor, "Neutrality in Political Science," in *Philosophical Papers II: Philosophy and the Human Sciences*, ed. Charles Taylor (Cambridge, UK: Cambridge University Press, 1985), 90.

27. See Louis Hartz, *The Liberal Tradition in America* (New York: Harcourt Brace, 1955); Rogers Smith, *Civic Ideals: Changing Conceptions of Citizenship in US Law* (New Haven, CT: Yale University Press, 1995).

28. Indeed, Smith's argument turns out to be the tip of an iceberg in debunking misleading orthodoxy about American exceptionalism. Eric Foner has shown that its assumptions about Europe are no less questionable than its assumptions about the United States. See Eric Foner, "Why Is There No Socialism in the United States?" *History Workshop Journal* 17 (1984): 57-80.

29. Philippe Schmitter, "Still the Century of Corporatism?" *Review of Politics* 36, no. 1 (1974): 85-121; Leo Panitch, "The Development of Corporatism in Liberal Democracies," *Comparative Political Studies*, April 1977, 61-90.

30. It turns out that joint legislation writing is a small part of the story. What often matters more is ongoing tripartite consultation about public policy and mutual adjustment of legislation/macroeconomic policy and "private" but quasi-public policy (e.g., wage increases, or multiemployer pension and health plans). There is also the formalized inclusion of private interest representatives in the administration and implementation process where de facto legislation and common law-like adjudication takes place. The extent of their influence in the political process varies from country to country and even industry to industry, but the overall picture is a far cry from the standard pluralist account.

31. For a discussion of the dangers of convergent thinking, see Charles E. Lindblom, *Inquiry and Change: The Troubled Attempt to Understand and Shape Society* (New Haven, CT: Yale University Press, 1990), 118-32.

32. For a discussion of differences between these models, see Ian Shapiro, "The State of Democratic Theory," in *Political Science: The State of the Discipline*, 3rd ed., ed. Ira Katznelson and Helen Milner (forthcoming).

# INDEX